THE WISDOM *of*
the LOTUS SUTRA

THE WISDOM OF THE

LOTUS SUTRA

A DISCUSSION

VOLUME VI

EXAMINING CHAPTERS 23–28

FORMER AFFAIRS OF THE BODHISATTVA MEDICINE KING
THE BODHISATTVA WONDERFUL SOUND
THE UNIVERSAL GATEWAY OF THE BODHISATTVA PERCEIVER
OF THE WORLD'S SOUNDS · DHARANI · FORMER AFFAIRS
OF KING WONDERFUL ADORNMENT · ENCOURAGEMENTS OF
THE BODHISATTVA UNIVERSAL WORTHY

Daisaku Ikeda

Katsuji Saito • Takanori Endo • Haruo Suda

World Tribune
——Press——

Published by
World Tribune Press
606 Wilshire Blvd.
Santa Monica, CA 90401

© 2012, 2008, 2003 by the Soka Gakkai

ISBN 978-0-915678-74-7

Design by Gopa & Ted2, INC.
Cover image © Photodisc

10 9 8 7 6 5

Library of Congress Cataloging-in-Publication Data

The Wisdom of the Lotus Sutra : a discussion : /
    Daisaku Ikeda... [et al].
        p. cm.
        Includes index.
        ISBN: 0-915678-70-5 (v. 2 : alk.paper)
        1. Tripitaka. Sutrapitaka.
    Saddharmapundarikasutra — Criticism.
    interpretation, etc. I. Ikeda, Daisaku.

BQ2057.W57 2000
294.3'85—dc21
                                    00-011670

Table of Contents

Editor's Note

This book is a series of discussions among SGI President Daisaku Ikeda, Soka Gakkai Study Department Chief Katsuji Saito and vice chiefs Takanori Endo and Haruo Suda. It was first serialized in English starting with the April 1995 issue of *Seikyo Times* (now *Living Buddhism*).

The following abbreviations appear in some citations:

+ GZ, page number(s)—refers to the *Nichiren Daishonin Gosho zenshu*, the Japanese-language compilation of letters, treatises, essays and oral teachings of Nichiren Daishonin.

+ LSOC, page number(s)—refers to *The Lotus Sutra and Its Opening and Closing Sutras*, translated by Burton Watson (Tokyo: Soka Gakkai, 2009).

+ OTT, page number(s)—refers to *The Record of the Orally Transmitted Teachings*, translated by Burton Watson (Tokyo: Soka Gakkai, 2004).

+ WND, page number(s)—refers to *The Writings of Nichiren Daishonin*, vol. 1 (WND-1)(Tokyo: Soka Gakkai, 1999) and vol. 2 (WND-2)(Tokyo: Soka Gakkai, 2006).

PART I

*"Former Affairs of the Bodhisattva
Medicine King" Chapter*

1 True Health Can Be Found in the Bodhisattva Practice

This sutra can save all living beings. This sutra can cause all living beings to free themselves from suffering and anguish. This sutra can bring great benefits to all living beings and fulfill their desires, as a clear cool pond can satisfy all those who are thirsty. It is like . . . a child finding its mother, someone finding a ship in which to cross the water, a sick man finding a doctor, someone in darkness finding a lamp . . . Such is this Lotus Sutra. It can cause living beings to cast off all distress, all sickness and pain. It can unloose all the bonds of birth and death. (LSOC, 327–28)

This sutra provides good medicine for the ills of the people of Jambudvipa. If a person who has an illness is able to hear this sutra, then his illness will be wiped out and he will know neither aging nor death. (LSOC, 330)

Ikeda: What is the purpose of faith? It is to transform one's state of life.

There are those who, upon seeing a flower, can immediately compose a poem. The great Japanese haiku artist Matsuo Basho was one such person. At a juncture in his travels, he once wrote: "The wild violets—somehow strangely appealing on the mountain track."[1]

Others, though they may not go as far as composing a poem, are filled with joy at the sight of a beautiful flower.

We may see a single flower and think how lonely it appears. It may remind us of someone, causing us to wonder, "How is so-and-so doing? Is he or she in good health?" and inspire us to call that person. This is a reflection of the bodhisattva state of life.

There are also those, however, in whom the sight of a flower or the moon stirs no reaction at all. They must have hearts of stone!

When Beethoven composed his Symphony no. 6 (*Pastoral*), he was already fairly hard of hearing. But in his heart he could hear birds singing in the countryside and the murmur of a meandering brook. He could hear the joyous voices of country folk, the clamor of a fierce storm and smell of the freshness in the air that follows—all of this was in his heart. And through his music he communicated to humankind the great expanse of nature filling his heart. Such was his incredible state of life, even without the ability to hear or without knowledge of Buddhism.

It is impossible, therefore, that we who practice the Mystic Law cannot expand the universe of our heart. Mystic, or *myo*, means "to open." We practice faith in order to open the vast treasures in our hearts, to establish a state of life through which we can enjoy all that life brings.

Shakyamuni says, "Let us live most happily, free from disease in the midst of the diseased; let us remain free from disease in the midst of diseased people."[2] Being free of suffering means transforming earthly desires or illusions into enlightenment. It means changing them into joy and fulfillment; into a profound sense of happiness that transcends all suffering.

The passage continues, "Let us live most happily, free from restlessness in the midst of the restless; let us remain free from restlessness in the midst of restlessness."[3] Suffering is born of greed. Shakyamuni is encouraging us to strive joyfully to accumulate the treasures of the heart.

He also says, "Freedom from sickness is a holy gift; / Contentment is opulence. / [Indulgence] the finest friend, / And nirvana the finest bliss."[4]

This refers to the principle that the sufferings of birth and death are nirvana, and it is what Shakyamuni means when he talks about achieving an "immortal" state of life. He is talking about the world of Buddhahood.

Saito: It is said that, when Shakyamuni began preaching at the request of the god Brahma following his attainment of enlightenment, his first words were, "I have opened the gate of immortality!"

Suda: And when he first expounded the Law for others, he called out to the five practitioners: "Lend me your ears. I have attained immortality!"

Ikeda: He had awakened to the Law transcending the suffering of death, the Mystic Law. Nichiren Daishonin says, "*Myo* is the elixir of immortality" (GZ, 831).

Saito: The "Former Affairs of the Bodhisattva Medicine King" chapter contains these famous words: "This sutra provides good medicine for the ills of the people of Jambudvipa. If a person who has an illness is able to hear this sutra, then his illness will be wiped out and he will know neither aging nor death" (LSOC, 330). Eternal youth and immortality are the benefits of the Lotus Sutra.

Endo: In other words, the Lotus Sutra elucidates the immortal state to which Shakyamuni had awakened.

Ikeda: The Lotus Sutra is the true purpose of Shakyamuni's advent; it is the conclusion to his life of preaching.

Suda: To say that we "will know neither aging nor death" actually sounds impossible!

Ikeda: This of course does not mean that we won't grow old and die. If that were the case, then the already serious problem of overpopulation would be completely out of control!

What it means is that we will not experience suffering because of aging and death. True to Shakyamuni's words "Let us live with great joy," we can develop our lives to the extent that, as we overcome various hardships, we will live each day, each moment, savoring the joy of being alive. This is true health.

Suda: In a passage cited earlier, Shakyamuni says that "freedom from sickness is a holy gift." In other words, health is the supreme benefit.

Endo: And that "contentment is opulence"—satisfaction is the supreme treasure.

Ikeda: This is health in both body and mind. To be healthy in body and mind is to live vigorously, dedicated wholeheartedly to accomplishing one's mission in this existence. It means that, as long as we are alive, even should illness overtake us, we will continue chanting daimoku and telling others about the Mystic Law. It means living fully for our mission throughout eternity. To have such faith is to possess a state of life free from aging and death.

This is the teaching of "Bodhisattva Medicine King," the twenty-third chapter. Bodhisattva Medicine King demonstrates this with his own life. Let's examine this chapter.

BODHISATTVAS OF THE ESSENTIAL AND THEORETICAL TEACHINGS

Suda: The section of the Lotus Sutra where the ceremony of transmission takes place concludes with the prior "Entrustment" chapter. So in a sense it could be said that this previous chapter completes the Lotus Sutra.

But there are in fact six more chapters. These are the "Medicine King," "Bodhisattva Wonderful Sound," "Universal Gateway of the Bodhisattva Perceiver of the World's Sounds," "Dharani," "Former Affairs of King Wonderful Adornment" and "Encouragements of the Bodhisattva Universal Worthy" chapters. Why is this? The Daishonin compares the preaching in these last six chapters of the sutra to a post-harvest gleaning of the fields (see WND-1, 372–74).

Endo: "Gleaning" means collecting the fallen grain left by reapers. After harvesting a crop, people would pick up the grain that remained.

The ceremony for transferring responsibility to carry on the work of leading humankind to enlightenment after Shakyamuni's death concludes with the essential transmission to the Bodhisattvas of the Earth in the "Supernatural Powers of the Thus Come One" chapter and the general transmission to all bodhisattvas in the "Entrustment" chapter.

To ensure that the Law is transmitted, Shakyamuni then emphasizes the role of the bodhisattvas of the theoretical teachings and those from other worlds and entrusts them with propagating the Lotus Sutra. I think we could say that these six chapters provide added insurance, as it were.

Ikeda: Pervading these six chapters is Shakyamuni's spirit to show all people without exception the way to enlightenment and to accomplish the widespread propagation of the Mystic Law, no matter what difficulties that task might entail. In terms of format, they resemble an addendum; and in fact, research on the history of the Lotus Sutra's origins strongly suggests that these chapters were added to the text at a later date.

Saito: Certainly, each of these chapters stands largely on its own, like a series of independent sutras, and the connections between them are also very tenuous. The "Bodhisattva Wonderful

Sound" chapter is actually sometimes called the "Bodhisattva Wonderful Sound Sutra," and historically people have placed their faith in this text as an independent sutra.

Ikeda: Even so, these six chapters are not simply an addendum. In terms of the three assemblies in two places, the second assembly at Eagle Peak and the Ceremony in the Air take place in six chapters. This section elucidates the important role of bodhisattvas returning to society with the eternal Mystic Law that had been engraved deeply in their hearts.

Suda: This signifies moving from the world of Buddhahood, or the "effect" of enlightenment, to the nine worlds, or the "cause" of enlightenment.

Ikeda: The bodhisattvas, believing in and accepting Nam-myoho-renge-kyo contained in the depths of the "Life Span" chapter, show actual proof of the Mystic Law in their respective fields of endeavor. They each test and prove, and then propagate the Mystic Law. That is probably why the bodhisattvas appearing in these six chapters are extraordinarily varied in their appearances and activities.

Endo: Bodhisattvas Medicine King, Wonderful Sound, Perceiver of the World's Sounds, Brave Donor (who appears in the "Dharani" chapter), Medicine Superior (who appears in the "King Wonderful Adornment" chapter) and Universal Worthy are indeed each very different.

Ikeda: As you know, when light passes through a standard triangular prism, it breaks into the seven main colors of a spectrum. Light is the totality, and the seven colors are its constituent parts. Similarly, the bodhisattvas of the theoretical teaching who appear in the latter assembly at Eagle Peak, while each carrying in their heart the light of Buddhahood, richly exhibit the hues of their individual mission.

Saito: The term *theoretical* implies an image or reflection of the truth. The Great Teacher T'ien-t'ai of China compares *essential* of "essential teaching" to the actual moon in the sky, and *theoretical* to the moon reflected in the pond.

Endo: While there is only one moon in the sky, its reflections are countless given the number of ponds in existence.

Suda: The bodhisattvas of the essential teaching, or the Bodhisattvas of the Earth, are rather unassuming in comparison to those of the theoretical teaching; they are straightforward and unadorned.

From their names alone, we see that the four leaders of the Bodhisattvas of the Earth—Superior Practices, Boundless Practices, Pure Practices and Firmly Established Practices—are completely different from the bodhisattvas of the theoretical teaching.

Ikeda: That's right. They are on a different level. The names of the four bodhisattvas refer to functions of the Mystic Law itself, and they are compared to the moon in the sky. Their mission is simply the propagation of the Mystic Law. This is as the Daishonin indicates when he says, "The action carried out by the bodhisattvas of the essential teaching is [to propagate] Nam-myoho-renge-kyo" (OTT, 117).

Endo: The bodhisattvas of the theoretical teaching are bodhisattvas instructed by provisional Buddhas. In other words, they are Buddhas who do not reveal their true identity but assume transient identities to lead people to enlightenment. By contrast, the bodhisattvas of the essential teaching are the direct disciples of the true Buddha and are one with the true Buddha.

Ikeda: Yes. The two groups could not be more different.

Endo: The protagonists of widespread propagation after Shakya-muni's passing are none other than the bodhisattvas of the essential teaching, the Bodhisattvas of the Earth. The bodhi-sattvas of the theoretical teaching play a supporting or assisting role.

In these six final chapters, the function of these bodhisattvas to assist the Bodhisattvas of the Earth in accomplishing their mission is clarified. This, at least, is the surface meaning.

Suda: Throughout the world today there are many people who, while not practicing Buddhism themselves, agree with, support and praise the movement to spread the ideals of Buddhism. Perhaps they can be thought of as representing a function of the bodhisattvas of the theoretical teaching.

Ikeda: I think we could say that.

Of course, what we are talking about here are activities or functions that support kosen-rufu, and not a fixed identity.

ACTUAL PROOF THROUGH MULTIFACETED ACTIVITIES

Endo: On a deeper level, it seems that "bodhisattvas of the theoretical teaching" actually signifies activities carried out in a wide range of areas based on the world of Buddhahood, as in the prism metaphor mentioned earlier.

Saito: That makes it easy to understand.

Endo: For example, Bodhisattva Medicine King is active in the area of medicine, Bodhisattva Wonderful Sound in the area of music and other arts, and Bodhisattva Universal Wor-thy in the area of scholarship. Their activities reflect various functions of the bodhisattvas of the essential teaching. This refers to our respective roles in society as bodhisattvas of the essential teaching.

Ikeda: Yes, that is the conclusion. Through our SGI activities we are advancing the widespread propagation of the Mystic Law as bodhisattvas of the essential teaching. But we each have different jobs, roles and positions in society, in the family and in the community.

Based on faith, it is important that we fulfill our respective responsibilities in a way people can really appreciate. This itself is showing proof of faith and of the Mystic Law. Through observing SGI members in action, people can sense the sun that burns brightly in their hearts.

It's impossible that someone practicing Nichiren Buddhism correctly is living irresponsibly. Such a person is not a true practitioner of faith; in fact, he or she is degrading the Law.

As bodhisattvas of the essential teaching, we need to reveal in society and our daily lives the life force of Buddhahood we develop by practicing for ourselves and others. By continually doing so, we further deepen our faith and strengthen our true potential.

It is a two-way process. Through this cycle of practicing faith and taking action in society, we can realize boundless growth in our lives and limitlessly advance kosen-rufu. I think this is the practical standpoint of these six chapters, which make up the second assembly at Eagle Peak.

Suda: I understand more clearly the role of the bodhisattvas of the theoretical teaching. Until now I viewed them as something completely unrelated to us. Perhaps I even looked down on them.

Ikeda: Faith is what matters. A person who is active in society yet forgets about faith is neither a bodhisattva of the essential teaching nor of the theoretical teaching. Such people will inevitably succumb to the desire for fame and fortune representative of the worlds of hunger and animality. This is because, in forgetting about faith, they are concealing their life state of Buddhahood. Ultimately, they will fall into the world of hell. Actually, given the reality of the simultaneity of cause and effect, the moment we lose faith, we are in the world of hell.

Saito: I can really see why the bodhisattvas of the theoretical teaching are so varied in their appearance. The reason Wonderful Sound has thirty-four forms and Perceiver of the World's Sounds has thirty-three forms is so that they can assume a multitude of guises to help people become happy, to demonstrate the validity of the Mystic Law and to promote kosen-rufu.

Ikeda: They are splendid and free of all impediments. The SGI's path of promoting peace, culture and education based on Buddhism has its origin in the principle of this second assembly at Eagle Peak. We are advancing just as the Lotus Sutra teaches.

"I Must Repay My Debt to My Mentor!"

Suda: In a word, the "Bodhisattva Medicine King" chapter is a tale about Medicine King's efforts to repay his debt of gratitude to his mentor. A bodhisattva named Constellation King Flower asks Shakyamuni why Bodhisattva Medicine King engages in difficult and arduous practices in the saha world, adding that everyone wishes to understand this (see LSOC, 321).

Shakyamuni replies that in the past there was a Buddha named Sun Moon Pure Bright Virtue who expounded the Lotus Sutra to a bodhisattva named Gladly Seen by All Living Beings. The bodhisattva practiced the sutra single-mindedly for twelve thousand years. As a result, he attained the "samadhi in which one can manifest all physical forms" (LSOC, 322).

Endo: This is the state of life where one can freely display the forms of all living beings in the Ten Worlds. This is what is meant by thirty-four forms or thirty-three forms.

Suda: Realizing he could attain this state thanks to the Lotus Sutra and Sun Moon Pure Bright Virtue Buddha, the bodhisattva makes a vow to repay his debt, saying, "I must now make an offering to the Buddha Sun Moon Pure Bright Virtue and to the Lotus Sutra!" (LSOC, 322). Reasoning that the greatest offering would be his own life, he drinks various perfumes and fragrant oils, pours fragrant oil over his body and sets fire to himself, making an offering of the light given off by this flame. This flame burns continuously for a period of twelve hundred years, illuminating the entire world. All Buddhas praise this offering as the "foremost donation of all" and as a "true Dharma offering" (LSOC, 323).

Ikeda: The sincerity of his efforts to repay his debt of gratitude illuminates the world. We, too, have become happy thanks to the Gohonzon. And thanks to the SGI, which has taught us about the Gohonzon, we have learned the correct path in life.

If we cherish the spirit to repay this debt of gratitude in the depths of our hearts, then our good fortune will increase by leaps and bounds. No matter how much action people might seem to be taking outwardly, if they lack the spirit to repay their debt of gratitude, their arrogance will destroy their good fortune. Consequently, they will be unable to transform genuinely their state of life. A subtle difference in our spirit produces diametrically different results.

Even those who have high positions in the organization or are successful in society, if they forget to work to repay their debts of gratitude, then, even though others may not notice their decline, in their hearts they will become destitute.

Endo: The desire of Gladly Seen by All Living Beings to repay his debt of gratitude does not subside even after he has burned his body for twelve hundred years. After the flame burns out and his life comes to an end, he is born again in the land of Sun Moon Pure Bright Virtue Buddha and the household of the king Pure Virtue. He goes back to Sun Moon Pure Bright Virtue intending to make offerings to repay his debt of gratitude.

Ikeda: His spirit to repay his debt of gratitude transcends life and death. He is resolved that after his death he will come back again to be with his mentor and continue the struggle. Since he has attained the state of being in which he can manifest all physical forms, he can choose to be born exactly where he wishes. Those who dedicate themselves wholeheartedly to faith in the Mystic Law are completely free.

Saito: The Buddha then tells Gladly Seen by All Living Beings that he, the Buddha, is about to die, and he transfers the Law to this disciple who has again returned to his service. Not only that, he also entrusts him with all of his other disciples and all of his treasures.

Ikeda: He leaves everything to this disciple who is foremost in repaying his debt of gratitude.

Suda: Gladly Seen by All Living Beings builds eighty-four thousand stupas as offerings to house the remains of Sun Moon Pure Bright Virtue Buddha. But he is still not satisfied. So, standing before the eighty-four thousand stupas, he burns his arms as an offering of light.

And he continues doing this for seventy-two thousand years.

At this time, seeing his disciples saddened that he has lost his arms, Gladly Seen by All Living Beings declares: "I have cast away both my arms. [But] I am certain to attain the golden body of a Buddha. If this is true and not false, then may my two arms become as they were before!" (LSOC, 326). His arms are then restored, just as he said.

Ikeda: When we make offerings with utmost confidence, we are certain to receive even greater good fortune and benefit in return. An offering made reluctantly and with skepticism is not genuine. What is in one's heart is all-important.

Suda: After relating these events from the past, Shakyamuni explains that Bodhisattva Gladly Seen by All Living Beings was Bodhisattva Medicine King in a previous existence.

PRESIDENT MAKIGUCHI'S SELFLESSNESS AND BODHISATTVA MEDICINE KING

Ikeda: To give one's life for the sake of the Law is the ultimate act of repaying one's debt of gratitude.

The "Medicine King" chapter came to have a great deal of influence in later generations. In China and Japan, there were even some who literally burned their arms or their bodies to make an offering to the Buddha.

Today of course there is no need to go to such extremes. The fire referred to in this chapter is the fire of wisdom. When we burn the body of earthly desires with the fire of wisdom, the light of the world of Buddhahood shines forth. Supreme wisdom is faith; it is chanting daimoku. Also, in burning incense and candles as offerings to the Gohonzon, we are demonstrating faith that can illuminate the entire universe.

The "Medicine King" chapter essentially teaches the faith to dedicate one's life to the Law. I recall that my mentor, the second Soka Gakkai president Josei Toda, always used to describe Mr. Makiguchi's death in prison as the offering of Bodhisattva Medicine King. Mr. Toda said:

Why was a person of such exalted virtue made to die in prison? If he had not been a votary of the Lotus Sutra, he could never have had such a destiny.

He gave his life for the sake of the Lotus Sutra; he is a model of dedicating one's life to the Lotus Sutra by facing persecution. His death was the offering of Bodhisattva Medicine King. President Makiguchi is qualified to be praised by the words used in the sutra to describe Medicine King's offering of self-immolation, "Among all donations, this is the most highly prized" (LSOC, 323).

President Makiguchi, who continually cited the words of the Daishonin that for a person of wisdom to be praised by fools is a disgrace, was in the end hailed as a person of the foremost wisdom.

The "Bodhisattva Medicine King" chapter says: "After the bodhisattva Gladly Seen by All Living Beings had made this Dharma offering and his life had come to an end, he was reborn in the land of the Buddha Sun Moon Pure Bright Virtue, in the household of the king Pure Virtue. Sitting in cross-legged position, he was suddenly born by transformation" (LSOC, 323).

Nichiren Daishonin teaches that the Lotus Sutra is a mirror reflecting all phenomena. The Daishonin does not lie—he always speaks the truth. Therefore, believing in the Daishonin's words and looking into this clear mirror, I am firmly confident that Mr. Makiguchi will be reborn as a prince in a land where the Lotus Sutra has spread and into the home of a royal family of pure virtue. His happiness in his next life must be thousands, tens of thousands of times greater than our own.[5]

President Toda was always earnest when he spoke about Mr. Makiguchi. His heart was filled with memories of his mentor, praise and thoughts of him. When many years of hard struggle finally caught up with him, Mr. Toda would often remark: "I am lonely without President Makiguchi. I would like to return to my mentor's side."

Mr. Toda lived on so that he could devote himself completely to kosen-rufu. The two years he spent in prison during the war had seriously undermined his health. Once when he was weary with fatigue but deep in thought, he remarked to me as I gave him a back rub: "No matter how many centuries it might take, we absolutely have to accomplish kosen-rufu. Encountering persecution and criticism goes hand in hand with waging a revolution. No matter what happens, we must not be afraid. If we stake our lives on this, we will have nothing to fear."

He spoke these words as though his life depended on it. President Toda also made the offering of Bodhisattva Medicine King. Burning with the desire for kosen-rufu, he alone protected the flame of the True Law, causing it to shine brightly.

BODHISATTVAS OF THE EARTH
ENJOY PROTECTION

Saito: The "Medicine King" chapter contains the famous line that directly refers to kosen-rufu: "After I have passed into extinction, in the last five-hundred-year period you must spread it abroad widely throughout Jambudvipa and never allow it to be cut off, nor must you allow evil devils, the devils' people, heavenly beings, dragons, yakshas, or kumbhanda demons, or others to seize the advantage!" (LSOC, 330).

"Don't allow devils in!" it implores. This is the Buddha's will. We must not allow the flow of worldwide kosen-rufu to be obstructed. We must continue passing the teachings from mentor to disciple and from one generation to the next, illuminating our lives like a lighthouse for the sake of others with the spirit to practice even at the cost of our lives.

Endo: The bodhisattvas of the theoretical teaching also exert themselves in this fashion. Nichiren Daishonin says that T'ien-t'ai is the reincarnation of Bodhisattva Medicine King. Repeatedly he says things like, "Bodhisattva Medicine King is T'ien-t'ai, leader of the Middle Day of the Law" (GZ, 857). T'ien-t'ai steadfastly protected the flame of the True Law during the Middle Day.

Suda: The Great Teacher Dengyo of Japan, born two hundred years after T'ien-t'ai, is said to have been his reincarnation.

Endo: The Daishonin designates the Buddhism of T'ien-t'ai as a prelude to the widespread propagation of the Mystic Law called for in the depths of the Lotus Sutra. Until the arrival of the time for the widespread propagation by the bodhisattvas of the essential teaching, the bodhisattvas of the theoretical teaching protect the Lotus Sutra.

Also, we may speculate that in the Latter Day of the Law, it is their mission to venerate and support the Bodhisattvas of the Earth of the essential teaching who directly work for kosen-rufu.

Ikeda: Sometimes it is people who offer protection, and sometimes protection comes from forces we cannot see. Either way, the principle applies that "when the Buddha nature manifests itself from within, it will receive protection from without" (WND-1, 848). Because the Bodhisattvas of the Earth practice the Mystic Law in the depths of their lives and manifest the world of Buddhahood, they enjoy protection from external forces.

Everything depends on our faith. No matter how tumultuous the times, those who struggle to the end to open a path of hope for the sake of kosen-rufu will be protected by all Buddhas and heavenly deities.

In the "Medicine King" chapter, Shakyamuni describes the benefit of those who spread the Mystic Law, saying:

> The good fortune you gain thereby is immeasurable and boundless. It cannot be burned by fire or washed away by water. Your benefits are such that a thousand Buddhas speaking all together could never finish describing them. Now you have been able to destroy all devils and thieves, to annihilate the army of birth and death, and all others who bore you enmity or malice have likewise been wiped out.
>
> Good man, a hundred, a thousand Buddhas will employ their transcendental powers to join in guarding and protecting you. (LSOC, 329)

In other words, the good fortune and benefit of those who carry out the practice of propagation cannot be destroyed by the fires of suffering or washed away by the waves of misfortune. This passage also states that the benefit of such a person is so great that even a thousand Buddhas speaking all together could not fully describe it. The person has destroyed all devils, broken the forces of the sufferings of birth and death, and vanquished all enemies. And a thousand Buddhas will protect that person using their transcendental powers.

Buddhism is a win-or-lose struggle. It is a struggle between the Buddha and the devil. Therefore, we have to win. Only by realizing victory through faith can we become truly happy and accomplish kosen-rufu. "Triumphant One" is another name for the Buddha.

Medicine King Prepares the Groundwork for Kosen-rufu

Ikeda: The Buddha is also called the "King of Physicians" and the "Great King of Physicians." The Buddha is like a skilled doctor who cures the illness of the sufferings of birth and death. In that sense, the name Medicine King suggests a high-ranking bodhisattva whose state of life is close to that of the Buddha.

If we say that the Buddha is a physician, the Law is medicine, and the practitioners are nurses, then we can think of Medicine King—given that his name indicates he is the king of the medicine that cures suffering—as representing all bodhisattvas.

Saito: In the Lotus Sutra, Bodhisattva Medicine King indeed represents the bodhisattvas of the theoretical teaching. He appears as early as the "Introduction" chapter, and the preaching of the "Teacher of the Law" chapter is addressed to him.

Endo: The transmission section[6] of the first half or theoretical teaching of the Lotus Sutra begins with the "Teacher of the Law" chapter. The recipients of the preaching are initially voice-hearers, but from this chapter on they become bodhisattvas. And Medicine King is named from the very outset.

Saito: In the next chapter, "Emergence of the Treasure Tower," Shakyamuni calls on those in the assembly to spread the sutra after his passing; and in the "Encouraging Devotion" chapter the innumerable bodhisattvas vow to uphold the Mystic Law in an evil age. Medicine King is the central figure among these bodhisattvas. I think he could have been considered the principal player in the propagation of the Law after the Buddha's death.

Suda: But afterward the Bodhisattvas of the Earth appear, and it is established that they will be the main proponents of the propagation of the Mystic Law in the Latter Day of the Law.

Ikeda: So, what about Bodhisattva Medicine King? The answer seems to lie in the "Medicine King" chapter.

Saito: Yes. The bodhisattvas of the theoretical teaching, as represented by Medicine King, have the mission to prepare the groundwork for kosen-rufu until the bodhisattvas of the essential teaching appear and then to thoroughly protect and support them.

THE POWER OF THE "MEDICINE KING" IN OUR LIVES

Ikeda: Now that we understand the concept of Medicine King from the doctrinal standpoint of the Lotus Sutra, let's consider Bodhisattva Medicine King from the standpoint of the observation of the mind.

In its entirety, the Lotus Sutra is a ceremony that takes place in our heart. If we view the sutra as merely a text that is separate from ourselves, we will fail to understand its essence. As this idea suggests, Bodhisattva Medicine King in our own lives could be thought of as the function that cures physical and spiritual ills and restores good health. It originates from nowhere other than the Mystic Law and the world of Buddhahood. The great life force of Buddhahood that functions to cure life's sufferings is named "Medicine King." Therefore, when we chant daimoku to the Gohonzon, we activate Bodhisattva Medicine King in our own lives. President Toda said: "When you go to a doctor, even if he is incompetent, because Medicine King is functioning in your own life, the doctor naturally cannot help but provide a cure."[7]

This is not to say that we should not look for a good doctor. The point, rather, is that ultimately we have to cure ourselves. Above all, our own life force and natural healing powers are fundamental powers to cure illness. A physician merely assists that process.

Suda: This is what is meant by the saying, "A doctor stitches the wound, but the gods make it heal."

Endo: I have also heard: "The gods heal the illness, but the doctor takes the money!"

Saito: The underlying source of this healing power is the world of Buddhahood. Buddhahood is the great life force that "will know neither aging nor death" (LSOC, 330).

APPRECIATION AND CONFIDENCE ACTIVATE THE LIFE OF MEDICINE KING

Ikeda: President Toda had incredible confidence. In question-and-answer sessions there would frequently be inquiries concerning illness. Often he would reply: "You mustn't ask, 'Will I get better?' You will recover without fail as long as you continue practicing in earnest.

"If, on the other hand, you have doubts as to whether you will get better, then your prayers will not be answered.

"People's bodies are susceptible to such ailments as those of the stomach, including stomach cancer and lung disease. Because our bodies have the ability to become ill, they also possess the power to fix themselves. It's similar to how a person who has climbed a hill can also descend the hill. This is my own personal outlook, and I can say these things based on a correct philosophy of life."[8]

Saito: I understand that he would often reprimand people who would start out with a complaint, saying something like, "I'm not better yet even though I've been chanting for some time."

Ikeda: When he heard someone speak of illness, President Toda would empathize to such an extent that he would often dream about him or her that night.

That's why he would strictly correct the attitude in faith of those who craved only benefit while not practicing sincerely, or who would complain that they were not completely cured even though they had seen some improvement.

"It's not a matter of form," he would say. "We need to pour our lives into praying to the Gohonzon; we need to engrave the Gohonzon in our lives. When we chant daimoku with true determination as though offering up our very lives, we cannot fail to overcome any illness.

"It is completely brazen to think that you can cure an illness that even doctors at the best of hospitals cannot cure without giving yourself completely to the Gohonzon. The Buddha is not obligated to provide a cure! How many hundreds of people have you introduced to this Buddhism? How much have you helped your chapter flourish? You should reflect on this. If you turn over a new leaf and can truly dedicate yourself to kosen-rufu, staking your very life on it, then I can say with confidence that you will be cured without fail."[9]

He would also say: "If your condition improves even a little, you should feel appreciation from the depths of your heart. If, on the other hand, instead of feeling appreciation, you are disappointed because you have not improved more and treat the Gohonzon as though it owes you a debt—that will not do.

"If you take action, yet forget your debt of gratitude, then even those areas that have improved will get worse. You must practice faith with abundant gratitude, deeply appreciative of even the slightest improvement! If you have the attitude 'Please cure me quickly,' just making demands without really devoting yourself, then the Gohonzon will be deaf to your prayers."[10]

This is how President Toda taught the faith of repaying one's debt of gratitude that is exemplified by Bodhisattva Medicine King. When we base ourselves on this faith, the spirit of Bodhisattva Medicine King in our hearts springs into vigorous activity on our behalf. We need to pray with such determination as to cause all the cells in our bodies to renew themselves; we need to spur all sixty trillion of them into action.

Although as a youth I was told that I would only live to about the age of thirty, I have thoroughly exerted myself for kosen-rufu and have as a result extended my life. I lived the line in the "Life Span" chapter, "Let us live out our lives!" (LSOC, 269), and for this I feel immense appreciation. *Life span* has the meaning of longevity. Simply put, the "Life Span" chapter expounds the underlying life force needed to extend our lives and live to the fullest. From one standpoint, therefore, it could be said that Buddhism pursues the question of what constitutes true health.

Suda: Would you elaborate on this?

THE PRECEPTS ARE RULES OF HEALTH

Ikeda: Overcoming the four sufferings of birth, old age, sickness and death is not just a matter of theory. We mustn't move away from the issues of how we can lead healthy, fulfilling and long lives, and how we can die without suffering. Buddhism teaches the wisdom that enables us to do this.

The Hinayana teachings, for example, include the eight precepts that lay followers were supposed to observe on specific days. One of these stipulates that a practitioner should not eat food after the noon hour. These seem to be practices for prolonging one's life.

Saito: In other words, this is an admonition against overeating.

Ikeda: Other precepts also aim to control desires and harmonize the body and mind. Buddhist practice could be described as a health regimen for regulating the body and mind.

Endo: Precepts certainly do cover the key points for maintaining a pure life. And this is not limited to the Hinayana teachings. On the whole, by purifying ourselves through Buddhist practice, the original functions of our lives become more highly activated. For example, the practice established by T'ien-t'ai entails twenty-five preparatory exercises; one of these, "regulating the five matters," seems to be on one level concerned with maintaining good health as it prescribes proper regulation of eating, sleeping, posture, breathing and the mind.

Ikeda: Through regulating the body and mind, we establish a foundation for the practice of observing the mind; that is to say, for observing that one's own life is an entity of three thousand realms in a single moment of life. Good health is a necessary condition for awakening to the eternity of life. Only then can we perceive the universe in our own being. Thus, illness can throw the "venue" of one's life into disarray.

Therefore, we can think of the Hinayana and provisional Mahayana teachings as progressively seeking to create balance and harmony in life, with the Lotus Sutra finally revealing the great life force that is free of aging and death.

Health is a precious treasure. An acquaintance that had suffered from illness for many years once remarked, "Some people complain about being busy and exhausted, but I can only imagine how wonderful it would be to be busy and exhausted!"

It is to our advantage to accumulate as much good fortune and wisdom as we can while we are healthy. Buddhism is wisdom. Health is wisdom, too.

"Not begrudging one's life" does not mean pushing oneself unreasonably. We cannot continue if we run ourselves into the ground. Buddhism is reason; and unless we live wisely based on reason and in accord with the principle of faith manifesting itself in daily life, our efforts will produce only anti-value. Our organization could not then be called a society for value creation.

Based on reason, we need to maintain, develop and control our life force in accord with our age and circumstances. We have to become physicians of our own lives, Medicine Kings.

To think that no harm can come to us just because we are practicing or because we are leaders in the organization is arrogance.

In general, it could be said that the period of life through the forties is a time of training, and after the forties we enter a period of preservation. It is important, therefore, that we exercise wisdom and are careful not to overextend ourselves.

Suda: Getting enough sleep is probably the best way to prevent exhaustion.

Ikeda: That's right. Sleep is a kind of "minor death." It is an activity in which our body and mind temporarily merge with the sea of the universal life. Through this rest, our life force is recharged, and we gain power to take action the next day.

In the same way, death also helps us recharge our life force. For someone whose body is old and sick, to return to the sea of revitalization of the universal life and then be reborn with a body full of new vitality may be the best thing. So much, of course, depends on the individual's karma and condition of faith.

What can be said with certainty, however, is that a person who maintains the faith of Bodhisattva Medicine King will enjoy still more good fortune in the next existence and be reborn in exactly the circumstances desired.

Saito: In the sutra's account of the previous existences of Bodhisattva Medicine King, Bodhisattva Gladly Seen by All Living Beings is reborn in the house of a king.

Ikeda: The key point is which of the Ten Worlds our lives melt into at the moment of death. Those whose lives merge with the world of Buddhahood can be said to have attained eternal life regardless of their age at the time of death. These are people who have read the "Life Span" chapter with their lives and have developed the state of life described by the line "he will know neither aging nor death" (LSOC, 330).

On the other hand, even if people live to a ripe old age, if in the end they enter the three evil paths or the four evil paths, then their lives will ultimately have been in vain and fruitless. From the standpoint of the eternity of life, the difference between fifty years and seventy years hardly amounts to an instant.

Shakyamuni says, "Better than a hundred years not seeing one's own immortality is one single day of life if one sees one's own immortality."[11] Taking into account the concept of life over the three existences—past, present and future—everything depends on the extent to which we can establish the state of immortality—that is, the world of Buddhahood and faith—in our lives in this existence. I think we can say that this is the true measure of longevity.

Endo: That makes sense to me. For even if individuals should have a short life, as long as they have faith, they will be reborn immediately.

SPAIN'S FIRST YOUNG WOMEN'S LEADER

Ikeda: Spain's first young women's leader was Junko Kobayashi. She lived a fresh and vibrant youth and then died as though galloping ahead to the next life. But her golden achievements still shine brilliantly.

Ms. Kobayashi was born in Tokyo's Shibuya Ward in 1949. She joined the Soka Gakkai in 1966, three months after both her parents took faith. At that time she was sixteen and a freshman at Hibiya High School.

Cherishing the dream of contributing to worldwide kosen-rufu as a member of the high school division, Ms. Kobayashi applied herself to studying foreign languages. She was an outstanding student and set her sights on entering the prestigious University of Tokyo.

When she was twenty, she underwent an unexpected ordeal. Her mother died of cancer, and her father, as though following her, fell ill and also died shortly thereafter. In an instant,

Ms. Kobayashi found herself completely alone in the world. At that point, she was no longer in a position to think of pursuing her studies.

I met Ms. Kobayashi one year later. It was during a summer training course. After hearing her talk about the death of her parents, I told her: "For someone your age, the death of a parent is something that you would expect to experience twice in the future. So really all that has happened is that you have experienced this somewhat earlier than others. But because you have the Gohonzon, everything will be all right!"

She may have been hoping for words of consolation. But I wanted to talk to her candidly about the true essence of life, about the eternally unchanging entity of life. Death is inevitable; to avoid confronting this reality is not Buddhism.

The Daishonin goes so far as to declare incomplete the passage of the "Medicine King" chapter that says of the Lotus Sutra, "It can cause living beings to cast off all distress, all sickness and pain. It can unloose all the bonds of birth and death" (LSOC, 328).

Saito: The Daishonin suggests that the terms *cast off* and *unloose* go against the spirit of the Lotus Sutra's teaching of "earthly desires are enlightenment" and "the sufferings of birth and death are nirvana." Therefore, he says, "we should take the words 'cast off' in the sense of 'becoming enlightened concerning.' If we look with the eyes of wisdom as they are opened by the 'Life Span' chapter of the essential teaching, we will become enlightened to the truth that sickness, pain, and distress are, and have always been, an innate part of life" (OTT, 174). "Become enlightened to the truth" here means "to perceive clearly." He is imploring us to clearly recognize that life and death are innate sufferings, that they are part of the eternal cycle of birth and death.

Ikeda: That's right. Birth and death are aspects of change of the universal life. They are expressions of the life of the Buddha.

Therefore, to loathe birth and death is to loathe the life of the Buddha. Also, someone who is drowning in the sufferings of birth and death cannot be said to enjoy a state of freedom at one with the great life of the Buddha. We need to use the sufferings of life and death as nutrition to help us strengthen our faith. Only then do they become nirvana.

Even so, Junko, given her young age, must have been deeply pained by the loss of her parents. I frequently offered her encouragement. I fondly recall joining members of the Miyahara Group, a young women's training group to which she belonged, on a trip to a farm where we enjoyed watermelon and corn-on-the-cob.

In her job and in young women's activities, she produced striking results through her inherent cheerfulness and tenacity. Precisely ten years after she joined the Soka Gakkai, she finally realized the dream she had cherished since her high school days of studying abroad in Spain.

Two weeks after she arrived in Spain, when she had just completed chanting ten million daimoku, the first chapter of Spain was organized and she was appointed the leader of the newly formed young women's division in Spain.

Ms. Kobayashi struggled hard. In the pioneering days of the movement in Spain, she continuously chanted daimoku with the determination to imbue this land with daimoku. She would often travel ten hours by car to attend a discussion meeting. And when she returned from a meeting, she would stay up till dawn translating passages of the Daishonin's works or materials from the *Daibyakurenge*, the Soka Gakkai's monthly study journal.

She once said: "What I'm doing cannot be called trying work. My efforts turn to joy whenever I see one person stand up. Rather than it being an ordeal, having known only the solid Soka Gakkai in Japan, I am elated to experience the struggles of a pioneer."

After exerting herself selflessly in this way for two years, she was again beset by a major obstacle. She developed a node in her left knee. When she returned to Japan to have it examined, it turned out to be a malignant tumor. She was told that to save her life she would have to have her left leg amputated at the hip. In her state of shock at hearing this, she felt as though time had stopped.

At that moment, the image of her mother's face flashed before her eyes. She thought of her mother, who looked so lovely in her state of Buddhahood when she died that neighbors who saw her were very moved. Junko heard her say: "Don't you have the Gohonzon, Junko? I have prayed to the Gohonzon for everything for you, so you don't have anything at all to worry about."

That's right, she thought. *It was for just these circumstances that my mother gave her all in order to teach me about faith!*

She made up her mind to have surgery in Japan. While she was able to avoid having her leg amputated, she had to have a major operation that required fifty stitches to close. And her principal physician told her she would never walk again.

But she determined, "I will definitely walk again for the sake of my fellow members in Spain!" With that spirit, she fought the devil of illness.

Although her left leg was completely stiff, several weeks after surgery her big toe twitched, and the muscle around the knee that was removed in the operation began to grow back little by little. She worked hard at her regimen of physical therapy, and seven months after the operation, she walked out of the hospital. The doctors were astounded by her recovery.

It was a great struggle. Economically, too, she was driven right to the brink. Still, she continued to burn with passion for kosen-rufu. And she again stood up in Spain. This was in April 1979, the month that I announced my intention to step down as third Soka Gakkai president. She fought with the determination to win in her struggle and to prove that what I had been striving for was correct. I will never forget her spirit.

Due to physical infirmity and poor finances, she had to return to Japan. Whenever she heard of people doing *shakubuku* somewhere, she would fly there and relate her experience. If she heard about a member who was suffering, she would go to the person and offer encouragement.

She also exerted herself as a member of the translation group of the international division. She personally brought more than ten people to join the Soka Gakkai. She also encouraged a young girl who was suffering from a leg tumor similar to her own. The girl was deeply impressed and went on to attend Soka University.

Suda: Your account has reminded me once again that we must never practice faith halfheartedly.

"WHAT A LOVELY FACE!"

Ikeda: Junko continued working tirelessly with the determination: "I don't know when I will die, so I will continue to fight so that no matter when I go I will have no regrets."

I saw her again at the Kanagawa Culture Center (on December 14, 1980), where she sang "Prayer of the Moon" with other members of the translation group.

She died one year later (on June 26, 1982). The cancer had metastasized to her lungs. As a side effect of the medications she was taking, she became visibly emaciated. Even so, Junko continued chanting daimoku, praying for her fellow members in Japan and in Spain.

In the terminal stages of the illness, she continued chanting daimoku, though she could only manage a single syllable with each labored breath. It took her five years from the time she first went to Spain to realize her goal of a second ten million daimoku.

Even the nurses were moved by her ardent spirit, her passion to live. People who came to encourage her in the hospital left feeling like they were the ones who had been encouraged. She turned herself into a flame and shed light on others. After an eight-month battle in the hospital, she went on to her next existence. She was thirty-two at the time.

People who saw her countenance after she died were amazed. "She was incredibly beautiful," one person remarked. "I never saw Junko looking that beautiful when she was alive." One woman commented that Junko looked so lovely that she did not even need any make-up, and that she found herself even feeling envious. Someone else commented that her hands were soft and warm, and her face, serene.

With a gentle smile on her face, and her eyes and mouth partly opened, she was the very image of the description of Buddhahood found in the Daishonin's writings. Her funeral was attended by several hundred people from throughout the country, causing those in the neighborhood to wonder just who had died.

The Daishonin says that when people have attained Buddhahood, "they will be received into the hands of a thousand Buddhas, who will free them from all fear and keep them from falling into the evil paths of existence" (WND-1, 216). I think that having so many people mourn her death and chant daimoku for her repose is one manifestation of this. To the extent that we sincerely look after many others, we ourselves will be eternally protected over the three existences.

Moreover, Junko's friends were confident that she was truly happy. One commented: "Even though she had been orphaned and she died from illness, no one who knew Junko thought of her as someone to be pitied. Rather, they thought of her as an outstanding person, as someone who had won in every respect. Therefore, we're not the least saddened by her death. I think that Junko is probably already back in Spain. I think she was probably reborn there to continue the fight for kosen-rufu."

Saito: This is the meaning of the "Bodhisattva Medicine King" chapter. While we may speak of experiencing "neither aging nor death," this does not refer simply to the length of one's life.

A Mission Transcending Life and Death

Ikeda: Although Ms. Kobayashi's body was ailing, her heart shone bright as the sun. Her life itself was her health.

When I visited Spain the following year (in 1983), I praised her valiant efforts and awarded her the posthumous title of honorary European young women's leader.

What is health? In conclusion, it is the life of the bodhisattva. I think that true health is the spirit to continue struggling for the sake of others. To just eat health food, aiming to lead a peaceful and secure existence while thinking only about oneself—this is not the image of health.

Bodhisattva Medicine King, who symbolizes health, gave his life for his convictions. A life of struggle is a healthy life.

Dr. René Dubos, a world renowned physician whom I had the privilege of meeting, remarked, "While it may be comforting to imagine a life free of stresses and strains in a carefree world, this will remain an idle dream." He continued: "The earth is not a resting place. Man has elected to fight, not necessarily for himself, but for a process of emotional, intellectual, and ethical growth that goes on forever. To grow in the midst of dangers is the fate of the human race, because it is the law of the spirit."[12]

Turning stress and worries into life force—this is the principle of changing poison into medicine. We need to realize a state of life that allows us to live with great joy. Toward that end, struggle is required.

Buddhism urges us: "Over life and death, accomplish what you must accomplish!" With such a sense of mission, there is neither birth nor death. In the face of such commitment, even the pain of death turns into strength to advance.

The Daishonin teaches that the transmission section of the latter half of the sutra, or the essential teaching, explains the method of practicing the "Life Span" and "Expedient Means" chapters (see WND-1, 91–92). I think that the "Medicine King" chapter truly calls out: "Champions of kosen-rufu in the Latter Day of the Law! Make your life burn like Bodhisattva Medicine King!"

When many youth possessing such spirit appear, the SGI will truly become eternal. It will become a body that "will know neither aging nor death," sending out a healing light to all humankind over the eternal future.

NOTES

1. *From The Journey of 1684*, cited in Classical Japanese Prose: An Anthology, ed. Helen Craig McCullough (Stanford, CA: Stanford University Press, 1990), p. 520.

2. *The Dhammapada: Sayings of Buddha*, trans. Thomas Cleary (New York: Bantam Books,1994), p. 69.

3. Ibid., 70.

4. *The Tibetan Dhammapada Sayings of the Buddha: A translation of the Tibetan version of the Udanavarga*, trans. Gareth Sparham (London:Wisdom Publications, 1986), p. 130.

5. *Toda Josei zenshu* (Collected Writings of Josei Toda) (Tokyo: Seikyo Shimbunsha, 1981), vol. 1, pp. 319–20.

6. Transmission section: One of the three divisions of a sutra, together with preparation and revelation. The preparation section explains the reason a sutra is being expounded. The revelation section constitutes the main body of the teaching. And the transmission section is the concluding part where the benefit of the sutra is set forth and its transmission to future generations is urged.

7. *Toda Josei zenshu* (Tokyo: Seikyo Shimbunsha, 1986), vol. 6, p. 601.

8. Ibid., (Tokyo: Seikyo Shimbunsha, 1982), vol. 2, p. 375.

9. See *Toda Josei zenshu*, pp. 353–54.

10. See *Toda Josei zenshu*, pp. 365–66.

11. *Budda no shinri no kotoba, kankyo no kotoba* (The Buddha's Words of Truth and Inspiration), trans. Hajime Nakamura (Tokyo: Iwanami Bunko 1994), p. 26. See *The Dhammapada: Sayings of Buddha*, p. 41.

12. René Dubos, *Mirage of Health: Utopias, Progress, and Biological Change* (New York: Doubleday & Company, Inc., 1959), p. 230.

PART II
"The Bodhisattva Wonderful Sound" Chapter

2 Cultural Activities Based on the Mystic Law Are "Wonderful Sounds"

Ikeda: The Institute of Oriental Philosophy co-sponsored [on November 8, 1998] the exhibition "The Lotus Sutra and Its World: Buddhist Manuscripts of the Great Silk Road." It was the first public showing anywhere in the world of forty-seven extremely valuable handwritten copies and wood-block prints from the collection of the Russian Academy of Sciences' Institute of Oriental Study in St. Petersburg.

When I saw the exhibition, the texts seemed to radiate joy and light; smiling as though they were truly happy. There were Sanskrit texts [of the Lotus Sutra] dating back twelve or thirteen hundred years.

Saito: The highlight of the exhibition was a text known as the Petrovsky manuscript. Dating from the seventh or eighth century, it was excavated at Khotan in western China and named after the Russian consul general of Kashgal, a major link along the ancient trade route known as the Silk Road.

Ikeda: Dr. Margarita Vorobyova-Desyatovskaya of the St. Petersburg branch of the Russian Academy of Sciences' Institute of Oriental Studies related that the Petrovsky manuscript had been copied in Khotan in memory of the deceased relative of a person whose name appears at the end of the text. The manuscript overflows with prayers for "good circumstances in future existences" (LSOC, 136).

Words are words, but they are also something more. They are imbued with spirit, with feeling. Nichiren Daishonin says, "Words and writing are the medium by which the minds of all living beings are revealed" (WND-2, 18).

Suda: Words are physical phenomena that express spiritual phenomena invisible to the eye. Whether we can perceive this depends on the depth of our awareness.

Ikeda: That's all the more true in the case of the Lotus Sutra. The words of the Lotus Sutra are expressions that capture the rhythm of the great life force swirling and pulsing at the very marrow of the universe.

GRASPING THE HEART OF THE PEOPLE

Saito: Specialists in the field were excited at this opportunity to view, in person, items they could only see previously in photographs. Dr. Charles Le Blanc, former director of the Center of East Asian Studies at the University of Montreal, said that to view for the first time so many translations of the Lotus Sutra was memorable. And he remarked that a Buddhist scripture having been translated into so many languages attests to the power of Buddhism's appeal to many different peoples.

Ikeda: The ancient Lotus Sutra is known to have versions in seven different languages. The exhibition included texts in five of them.

Suda: These were Sanskrit, Old Uighur, Xixia (Tangut), Khotan Saka and Chinese.

Endo: Dr. Kychanov, a specialist in Saka literature, explained that the Lotus Sutra was the first Buddhist text to be translated into Saka, a language formulated in the eleventh century.

Ikeda: This shows how the Lotus Sutra has captured people's hearts. While there are of course several reasons for this, put simply, it is because the Lotus Sutra is so alive. It gives hope to all people without discrimination. It exudes the warmth and brightness of the sun.

Another reason is that it is written in such beautiful language. It is a work of art filled with the exquisiteness of a blossoming lotus flower emitting a lovely fragrance. It radiates joy that wins people's hearts. That is why people are naturally drawn to it.

BODHISATTVA WONDERFUL SOUND IS LARGER THAN THE EARTH

> *If the form of a voice-hearer is what is needed to bring salvation, [Bodhisattva Wonderful Sound] manifests himself in the form of a voice-hearer and proceeds to preach the Law. If the form of a pratyekabuddha will bring salvation, he manifests himself in the form of a pratyekabuddha and preaches the Law. If the form of a bodhisattva will bring salvation, he manifests a bodhisattva form and preaches the Law. If the form of a Buddha will bring salvation, he immediately manifests a Buddha form and preaches the Law. Thus he manifests himself in various different forms, depending upon what is appropriate for salvation. And if it is appropriate to enter extinction in order to bring salvation, he manifests himself as entering extinction.* (LSOC, 336–37)

Saito: The Lotus Sutra has an artistry capable of inspiring images and music in one's heart.

Ikeda: "Bodhisattva Wonderful Sound," the twenty-fourth chapter, which is the topic of our discussion this time, illustrates this well. A "wonderful sound" reverberates throughout the entire Lotus Sutra. It rings with music that stirs the spirit. In Japanese, the word for music is written with characters that mean to "enjoy sound"; a joyous heavenly song imbues the sutra.

Not only is it filled with music but also images of light, colors and fragrance. The earth shakes; flowers rain from the sky. It is a spectacular drama of life. It is like an opera performed on the stage of the cosmos.

It has philosophy and testimonials of personal experience. There are stories of struggles against villains, and the advance of the people. There is dance. It would inspire prodigious creativity even in someone who is not an artist.

The Lotus Sutra itself is an expression of the value of beauty. What is the foundation of this beauty? What is the basis of all great cultures? The answer is none other than the dynamism of human life, the struggle to draw upon and manifest the innate rhythm of the universe expressed by the line "winter always turns to spring" (WND-I, 536). It is the vitality to endure all, no matter how difficult or painful, and realize victory in the end.

Doesn't this zest for life pulse at the core of all high art, even if it seems to depict suffering? I would suggest that the "Wonderful Sound" chapter has as its core this great life force of hope.

Saito: Bodhisattva Wonderful Sound is described as being inordinately large in size. This had seemed peculiar to me before, but now it occurs to me that this may be intended to express the idea that he is overflowing with abundant life force, the wellspring of the universe.

Endo: He is said to stand forty-two thousand *yojanas* tall. [A Sanskrit text gives his height as 4.2 million yojanas.] Since the treasure tower in the Ceremony in the Air is five hundred yojanas tall, this makes Wonderful Sound eighty-four times the size of the treasure tower.

Suda: One yojana, a unit of measurement used in ancient India, is defined as the distance that the royal army could march in a day. While there are other explanations, a yojana can be conservatively calculated as 4.6 miles. This would give the treasure tower the enormous size of one-fourth the diameter of the earth.

Saito: And this bodhisattva is eighty-four times as tall.

Endo: Let's see. That would be about twenty-four times the diameter of the earth.

Suda: The arrival of such a gigantic bodhisattva would certainly cause a stir!

Ikeda: Indeed. This chapter, which is also called "The Coming and Going of Bodhisattva Wonderful Sound," describes Wonderful Sound making an appearance in the saha world and then taking his leave.

Bodhisattva Wonderful Sound is not only enormous in size but as the sutra explains, "a hundred, a thousand, ten thousand moons put together could not surpass the perfection of his face" (LSOC, 334). His body shines with a golden hue and is "adorned with immeasurable hundreds and thousands of blessings" (LSOC, 334).

And the sutra says that the lands he passes on his way to the saha world quake and tremble, and that in all of them "seven-jeweled lotus flowers" rain down and "instruments of hundreds and thousands of heavenly musicians" resound (LSOC, 334).

Endo: It sounds like a spectacular parade.

Ikeda: He is a magnificent bodhisattva of light and sound. Just showing his splendid form to the people of the saha world is part of the purpose of his visit.

Saito: A little earlier it was said that the words of the Lotus Sutra are expressions of the rhythm of the great life force that pulses at the very core of the universe. It seems to me that Wonderful Sound symbolizes the rhythm of this great life force.

Ikeda: The entire universe is playing a "wonderful sound." The universe itself is a symphony of life, a chorale sung by all beings and phenomena—a serenade, a nocturne, a ballad, an opera, a suite. The universe performs all "wonderful sounds."

The foundation of this is the Mystic Law. It is Nam-myoho-renge-kyo. Therefore, reciting the sutra is essentially a wake-up song that causes the sun to rise in our hearts, as well as a nocturne, a "Moonlight Sonata" that illuminates our hearts with the light of the moon.

Reciting the sutra is like reading a poem. And chanting Nam-myoho-renge-kyo is like singing a musical masterpiece. Our daily practice is the most cultural of activities.

CULTURE IS AN EXPRESSION OF PEOPLE'S STATE OF LIFE

Suda: Why does Bodhisattva Wonderful Sound come to the saha world? Let's consider the outline of the chapter.

Shakyamuni produces a light from between his eyebrows, which illuminates the worlds in the eastern direction. There, among the infinite number of Buddha lands, is a world called "Adorned With Pure Light" where a Buddha named Pure Flower Constellation King Wisdom dwells. Wonderful Sound lives in this land.

Saito: The sutra says that he has waited upon and made offerings to infinite numbers of Buddhas and attained all manner of *samadhis*, including the "Lotus samadhi" (LSOC, 330).

Ikeda: The statement that he has waited upon the Buddha is very important. From our standpoint, this means steadfastly praying to the Gohonzon. On another level, it means serving and supporting SGI members who are taking action for kosen-rufu, or simply meeting with other members. Through such actions we can increase our life force and expand our state of life.

Endo: A samadhi is a state of intense concentration. There are such samadhis as the "samadhi that allows one to understand the words of all living beings" and the "wisdom torch samadhi" (LSOC, 332).

Ikeda: A samadhi is a state of life that is abundant in wisdom, a state of inner peace. It indicates a rock-solid condition that nothing can perturb. From this inner peace, the great song of the spirit capable of moving people's hearts surges forth.

Inner peace is not born of indolence. It is exactly the opposite. Just as a top appears unmoving when rotating at full speed, an immense life state of composure is sustained by the earnestness of practicing at one's full capacity.

Suda: When the light from Shakyamuni's forehead illuminates Wonderful Sound, Wonderful Sound says to the Buddha Pure Flower Constellation King Wisdom, "World-Honored One, I must journey to the saha world to do obeisance, wait on, and offer alms to Shakyamuni Buddha, and to see . . . [various bodhisattvas]." The Thus Come One replies:

> You must not look with contempt on that land or come to think of it as mean and inferior. Good man, that saha world is uneven, high in places, low in others, and full of dirt, stones, mountains, foulness, and impurity. The Buddha is puny in stature and the numerous bodhisattvas are likewise small in form, whereas your body is forty-two thousand yojanas in height and mine is six million eight hundred thousand

yojanas . . . Therefore when you journey there, you must not look with contempt on that land or come to think of the Buddha and bodhisattvas or the land itself as mean or inferior! (LSOC, 332)

Endo: Certainly, nothing can compare with his enormous size.

Saito: And the Buddha of this other world is even larger than Bodhisattva Wonderful Sound.

Ikeda: Still, he tells Wonderful Sound that he must respect the Buddha and the bodhisattvas of the saha world, saying in effect: "You must not look down on those who expound the Law and spread the teaching under the most difficult of circumstances! You mustn't judge them by their appearance! You should treat them with the utmost respect!" This is an important teaching.

Those fighting with all their might amid the harshest of conditions are the noblest. Those who receive benefit and earn the respect of others due to the power of Buddhism and then look down on and seek to distance themselves from such a place of struggle, however, are guilty of the worst kind of arrogance.

Suda: Through the inherent power of the Thus Come One, Bodhisattva Wonderful Sound, without moving an inch, causes eighty-four thousand beautiful lotus flowers to appear on distant Eagle Peak.

Endo: He does this through his supernatural powers. In modern terms, this would be comparable to a satellite transmission.

Suda: The lotus flowers he causes to appear have golden stems, silver leaves, diamond stamens and calyxes of rubylike gems.

Endo: And they appear next to where Shakyamuni is preaching at Eagle Peak.

Ikeda: They are jewels of the spirit, jewels of good fortune and virtue and jewels of wisdom. These are the jewels that exist eternally throughout past, present and future.

Saito: Yes, for no matter how many actual diamonds you accumulate in this lifetime, you cannot take them with you when you die.

Suda: The people on Eagle Peak are stunned. Representing the assembly, Bodhisattva Manjushri asks Shakyamuni to explain the appearance of the lotus flowers.

When Shakyamuni replies that this is a sign that Bodhisattva Wonderful Sound is going to pay them a visit, Manjushri expresses the wish to meet Wonderful Sound.

Saito: In other words, he arouses a seeking spirit, longing to meet and learn from him.

Suda: Then, with the assent of Many Treasures Thus Come One, who says, "Come, good man" (LSOC, 333), Wonderful Sound appears aboard a "dais made of seven treasures" (LSOC, 334) accompanied by eighty-four thousand bodhisattvas.

Endo: This image reminds me of a brilliantly sparkling spaceship.

Ikeda: The sight would have caused everyone to gasp in amazement.

Through his august form and with his music, Wonderful Sound lets all present know of the incredible benefit of the Lotus Sutra. He expresses the invisible state of life he has attained in such a way that anyone can understand, in both a visible and an audible form.

It comes down to expression; unless we express ourselves

clearly, others will not understand. Take love as but one example. If you keep your feelings to yourself, the other person will never know! Only by conveying to others in some way the state of life we acquire through faith will they receive our light.

Culture is a good example of this. Bodhisattva Wonderful Sound represents cultural activity. I think we can say that Bodhisattva Wonderful Sound's actions symbolize the SGI's movement for peace, culture and education. We are moving forward, giving rise to a brilliant heavenly song.

Saito: I associate Bodhisattva Wonderful Sound with those engaged in our broad-ranging SGI cultural activities, especially those of the youth division fife and drum corps and music corps, as well as those of the Min-On Concert Association.

Ikeda: We are advancing in perfect accord with the Lotus Sutra's basic principles. Religion is like the earth. But without flowers or trees, the earth would be barren. Conversely, culture that is not grounded in the "earth" of religion is rootless.

Using the analogy of the body, if religion is the skeleton, then culture would correspond to the muscles, skin and clothing. The value of beauty is born when the two complement and support each other.

THE BEST FIFE AND DRUM CORPS IN THE WORLD

Endo: The corps was inaugurated on July 22, 1956, with a membership of just thirty-three young women. You, President Ikeda, used money out of your own pocket to present them with instruments. Shigetake Arishima, the leader of the brass band, which at that time was like an elder sibling to the corps, made every effort to round up instruments: he came up with forty fifes and ten drums. The drums were U.S. Army surplus and were decorated with flashy red and blue stripes.

Although they began practicing right away, the corps members did not even know the proper way to hold the drumsticks nor had any of them ever before laid hands on a fife. After blowing on them for five minutes straight, they all became dizzy. But you took every opportunity to encourage them, urging them to become the foremost fife and drum corps in the world.

They performed for the first time at a young women's leaders meeting on September 3, 1956 [held at the Nakano Public Hall in Tokyo]. Although they had practiced daily, on the day of their debut nearly half the members could not produce any sound on their instruments. So they lined up with those who could play in front and those who could not in back. The program for the performance consisted of three popular songs. Because it was their first performance, their legs were quivering, their fingers would not move properly, and they could only produce the faintest of notes. The drums were placed flat on the stage floor, and they struck them from a kneeling posture.

At this peculiar scene, hushed giggles could be heard in the hall. But the earnestness of the corps members finally brought tears to people's eyes. As one participant described it, by the time the performance was drawing to a close, the performers and the audience had become one.

Twenty days later, the corps performed at the third youth festival. Standing to the left side of the main reviewing stand, they performed on a makeshift stage of thin straw mats. The second Soka Gakkai president, Josei Toda, went to them and asked gently, "Are we going to hear some music today?" At these words, everyone gathered around him joyfully.

They were wearing cream-colored shirts with black ribbons and black skirts. On their feet they wore gym shoes they had coated with white chalk or toothpowder. This was their most festive attire. Someone told me that it had never even occurred to them to wear white socks, so meager were their means.

Afterward, you gave each of the members a pair of white

socks as a present. I understand that all were moved to tears by this gesture.

Ikeda: This brings back many fond memories. The fife and drum corps has now truly become the foremost body of its kind in the world. These emissaries of peace are today active around the globe.

Those who hear them perform are invariably moved, exclaiming "How bright!" and "How wonderful!" Since they are bringing people joy, they are bodhisattvas. They are expanding a spirit of friendship. They are creating waves of peace.

Music knows no boundaries. It directly bridges the gap between people's hearts. By causing the innate rhythm of the universe to reverberate through a single fife or a single drum, the corps is causing a prayer for peace to ring out in the depths of the hearts of humankind.

Saito: The heart is key. It's about heart-to-heart communication.

Ikeda: Beethoven was fond of the expression "from heart to heart." If I remember correctly, in the margin of the score for his resplendent Mass in C Major, he jotted down the words:"[Music] comes out of my heart. My wish is that it reaches the hearts of others." It is culture and fundamentally religion that nourish the heart.

Suda: One person who was moved by the spirit of the fife and drum corps was the late jazz great Art Blakey. On January 18, 1965, he performed in Tokyo. Even after the curtain came down following an intense two-hour concert, the audience remained electrified and showed no sign of leaving.

At that moment, several members of the fife and drum corps who were in the audience darted backstage with their drums in hand. In halting English, they explained that they were members of a fife and drum corps and entreated him to give them a lesson. So impressed was he by their spirit that he began instructing them right then and there.

Ikeda: It's hard to imagine that they did such a thing.

Suda: While Mr. Blakey must have been quite surprised, he promised to give them a lesson on another day as well, perhaps because he was struck by their sincerity.

On January 26, several brass band and fife and drum corps members met with Mr. Blakey, who gave them a basic lesson in drumming rhythm. The youth played in earnest, prompting the jazz artist to take off his jacket, pick up some sticks and start drumming away ferociously. He told them: "Your playing shouldn't be stiff and formal. You must play from your heart!"

Without even wiping the sweat from his brow, he continued to move to the rhythm and beat the cymbals. He seemed the embodiment of a tremendous force.

This practice session, in which teacher and students became one, went on for about an hour. Even after they had gone beyond the time that he had promised for the lesson, he would not stop. Finally, dripping with sweat and tears, he told them: "I feel like I have glimpsed the true image of Japan. Japan is my home." Then, going over to the edge of the stage, he tearfully embraced the manager.

Many capable people emerged from the corps through contact with such leading figures in the world of music and other fields.

THE VOICE OF COURAGE

Ikeda: We cannot become first-rate individuals without coming into contact with exemplary people ourselves. The point is not to start off familiarizing oneself with the amateurs of any given field, whether it be art, philosophy, religion or even life in general, but to aim straight for the top. By so doing, we begin to see clearly what is second- and third-rate. If we only acquaint ourselves with mediocrity, we will not know what is truly great.

In any case, the fife and drum corps, brass band and chorus groups of the SGI have all developed splendidly. I am particularly proud to witness the growth of all those capable people who accomplished their human revolution through such musical training.

There are many artists about whom people say, "Their art is incredible, but their life is a failure." Some even romanticize such tragedy. But I think that if an artist—as the entity of the art that he or she creates—becomes spoiled and decadent, then that person's art will also lack true brilliance.

On a different note, while there are various explanations of the meaning of "wonderful sound," I recall that one of these is "to stutter."

Saito: Yes. Wonderful sound is a translation of the Sanskrit *gadgada-svara*, which means to stammer, indicating a person whose voice is hard on the ear.

Ikeda: How did this come to mean a person of "wonderful sound"? Since there is no indication of this in the sutra, we can only use our imaginations. But I think it may have to do with the drama of one person's human revolution.

When Bodhisattva Wonderful Sound appears in the saha world, the scene is so fantastic that a bodhisattva named Flower Virtue asks, "what good roots has he planted, what benefits has he cultivated, that he possesses these supernatural powers?" (LSOC, 335).

Endo: That's right. Shakyamuni then reveals details of Wonderful Sound's previous existences. In the past, the Buddha explains, he made an offering to a Buddha called Cloud Thunder Sound King of a hundred thousand types of musical instruments and of eighty-four thousand alms bowls made of the seven treasures. As a result, he was born as Bodhisattva Wonderful Sound and endowed with various supernatural powers and all manner of good fortune and benefit.

Ikeda: Nichiren Daishonin says that the number eighty-four thousand stands for the "eighty-four thousand dust-like cares" (OTT, 177), meaning all manner of hardships and delusions. Life is an endless succession of struggles, struggles as innumerable as particles of dust. But when we chant Nam-myoho-renge-kyo, he teaches, these toils all become the "eighty-four thousand teachings."

Every difficulty we encounter becomes a life lesson; wisdom and the ability to help and guide others develop. Interpreted from the standpoint of Nichiren Buddhism, Bodhisattva Wonderful Sound toiled repeatedly to overcome many sufferings, chanted Nam-myoho-renge-kyo and carried out his human revolution. This is comparable to making an offering to the Buddha of "eighty-four thousand alms bowls made of the seven treasures." We are no different. No matter how tough things may get, we chant and continue moving forward without giving up.

Though invisible to the eye, there are paths in the universe and currents in life. If we dedicate our lives to kosen-rufu, we will absolutely enter the current of a supreme life. We will enter the path of the river of true happiness, the river of treasures. Those who exert themselves for kosen-rufu enter the golden current of the Mystic Law. By working wholeheartedly on the supreme path of kosen-rufu, we ourselves, along with our family and relatives, will all become happy without fail.

Didn't Bodhisattva Wonderful Sound, while battling a painful destiny, in the end sing a song of victory? As he struggled and suffered, he warmly encouraged those around him, singing a courageous tune. This is the image that comes to mind. A sincere voice encouraging a friend, words of conviction that move a person's heart, cries of justice to refute evil—these are truly "wonderful sounds."

King Ashoka's "Culture Festivals"

> *The Record of the Orally Transmitted Teachings states: The Bodhisattva Wonderful Sound represents the living beings of the Ten Worlds. The word "wonderful" means inconceivable. The word "sound" refers to the sounds uttered by all living beings, the voice of the Wonderful Law. These are the wonderful sounds that are constantly present in the three existences. It is pity and compassion that make it possible for Wonderful Sound to recognize and meet the various needs of the living beings [by assuming various forms]. This is what is expressed by the word "bodhisattva."*
>
> *Or again, we may say that the words "wonderful sound" refer to the unfathomable and wonderful sound made at the present time, in the Latter Day of the Law, when Nichiren and his followers now chant Nam-myoho-renge-kyo. (OTT, 176)*

Suda: The sutra says that Bodhisattva Wonderful Sound makes "musical offerings" (LSOC, 335). This is a characteristic of Mahayana Buddhism.

It seems that music and dancing were prohibited by Hinayana clerical orders as obstacles to one's practice. Practitioners were not only forbidden from engaging in such activities themselves, but they were also not supposed to enjoy them.

Endo: But when we come to Mahayana Buddhism, it's exactly the opposite.

Ikeda: The "Teacher of the Law" chapter includes a directive to make offerings of music to the Lotus Sutra (see LSOC, 200). And King Ashoka, a strong believer in Buddhism and once a king of ancient India is said to have made musical offerings.

Saito: This took the form of festivals that took place around stupas.

Ikeda: It's known that people would gather around stupas singing songs and playing various musical instruments. They acted out dramas, performed dances and read poetry.

Merchants stood by, hawking their wares.

Endo: Sounds like quite a party!

Ikeda: Children would sit watching acrobatics. Performances of juggling and magic brought enthusiastic applause. There were boxing, wrestling matches and other competitions. Young women danced in brightly colored costumes, and young men sat enrapt, unable to take their eyes off them. Processions of torches filled the streets.

Saito: What a brilliant display of culture and music!

Ikeda: It was an offering of music in praise of the Dharma. It was an offering of joy. When the people expressed their pure joy to live based on the Law with their entire being, song poured forth and their bodies sprang into action.

Those "waves of peace" spread out far and wide. Ashoka's offerings of music and dance could be thought of as the precursor to our great cultural movement.

Endo: It's a brilliant image.

Ikeda: It's brightness and beauty. It is peace.

Peace and culture are like two sides of a coin. Without peace, there can be no culture. When culture flourishes, peace unfolds. I'm not talking about fleeting or hedonistic culture but culture that brings out the most noble qualities in human beings; lofty culture created by people who believe in the innate goodness of humankind and strive together to approach something eternal.

Dr. Jutta Seifert once remarked to me that "Art is the expression of something sacred existing within us."[1]

Saito: According to one source, when the Lotus Sutra was being compiled in its present form, the musical offerings of King Ashoka were common knowledge; and this is reflected in the makeup of the "Wonderful Sound" chapter and the other chapters in the transmission section. Whether this explanation is true or not, it is clear that music is inseparable from the Lotus Sutra.

Ikeda: Come to think of it, the birthplace of the Buddhist scholar Kumarajiva was famous for its music.

Endo: He was born in what is known today as Kucha. This is part of China's Sinkiang Uighur autonomous region. He was from a town in the southern foothills of the Tienshan Mountains.

Ikeda: During the Han period, this was the largest kingdom in western China, with a population of more than eighty thousand.

It seems that Kucha music, noted for its outstanding singing and the use of wind and string instruments, was very popular. In Chang-an, the capital of Tang China, people vied with one another to hear such exotic melodies. The famous five-stringed *biwa* (Japanese balloon guitar) preserved at Shosoin[2] is thought to originally derive from the Kucha lute. The music of Kucha also greatly influenced the music of Japan's imperial court.

At the same time that it was a kingdom of music, Kucha was also a kingdom of Buddhism. When the seventh century's Learned Teacher Hsuan-tsang visited the area, he was surprised to find Buddhism flourishing there.

Suda: He was a great traveler who became the model for the "Learned Teacher" in *Journey to the West,* a sixteenth-century Chinese epic by Wu Ch'eng-en.

Saito: It is probably no coincidence that the Lotus Sutra's great translator was from this area.

Ikeda: Kumarajiva must have had quite an ear for music. Otherwise the text of the sutra surely would not have such exquisite rhythm.

Incidentally, many different musical instruments are mentioned in the Lotus Sutra.

Endo: Yes. Starting with the wind instruments, there are the horns, conch shells, pipes and flutes.

Ikeda: What about stringed instruments? The balloon guitar is one that the Sutra mentions.

Endo: Yes. In addition, there is the zither that is played with either a pick or the fingers, and the lute with many strings (see LSOC, 173).

Saito: There is the expression, "Like the harmony of zither and lute" (indicating conjugal harmony).

Endo: The harp is also mentioned.

Suda: As for percussion instruments, there are cymbals and gongs.

Ikeda: Music fills the Lotus Sutra.

Sheet music of Tang China, an age when the Lotus Sutra flourished in the country, has been excavated at Dunhuang. It is more than a thousand years old, and experts are still trying to determine just what kind of music it is. Not only does it indicate the pitch of each note, but it even indicates the rhythm. Some have even tried performing it.

At any rate, the Lotus Sutra encompasses the great sound of the universe. It contains the fundamental rhythm, the melody and the chords of the universe.

According to another explanation, Bodhisattva Wonderful Sound's name comes from a word meaning "thunder." This is interesting.

Saito: Yes. We earlier interpreted the Sanskrit term *gadgada-svara* as meaning a stuttering voice. But an explanation suggests that *gadgada* is a variant of *gargara*, which is the sound of the drum that precedes Shakra Devanam Indra into battle.

Suda: Since Shakra is originally the god of thunder, the sound of this drum could be thought of as the sound of thunder.

Ikeda: The term for thunder in Japanese, too, is said originally to indicate the roar or appearance of a god. It is the rumble of the heavens, the roar of the universe.

Endo: I am reminded of an incident that took place in Cuba [on June 25, 1996] when you were awarded an honorary doctorate from the University of Havana. I heard about this from a *Seikyo Shimbun* correspondent who accompanied you. On the day of the event, a rain fell, driving off the intense heat and soon turning into a heavy downpour.

During the ceremony, just when you began to deliver your address, it became a thunderstorm. The sound of thunder rang through the auditorium. This made some of the Japanese present a little worried, concerned that it might interfere with your talk.

But you stopped what you were saying and said: "What marvelous thunder! It is the music of the heavens, the resounding drum, the resplendent symphony of the skies, congratulating the progress of humanity toward the victory of peace. And what wonderful rain! The skies are telling us that we must not allow ourselves to be defeated by trouble! We must advance courageously through the storm of adversity!"

I was told that with these words you captured the hearts of all those in attendance.

Saito: I think that I, for one, would be hard-pressed to come up with such reassuring words on the spot.

Ikeda: The Buddha whom Wonderful Sound served in the past was called Cloud Thunder Sound King. In other words, he represents the sound of the universe, the voices of all beings.

All activities, from the movement of the planets to the motion of atoms and molecules, are governed by some kind of rhythm or musical principles. This is an important point. Why don't we take it up when we discuss the "Dharani" chapter?

It is up to us how much we can internalize this universal music. The sculptor Auguste Rodin said that art is the reflection of nature in human beings. It is vital that we polish our inner mirror that reflects the natural world.

When we tune and practice the instrument of the self, we cause the wonderful sound of the universe to pulse in our lives; we cause it to reverberate and ring out. Buddhist practice teaches us how to do this.

Historically, people have believed that musical training cultivates character. The ancient Greeks subscribed to this notion as did the people of ancient China. Plato placed great importance on musical education. He believed that rhythm and harmony foster outstanding people. And Confucius's emphasis on manners and music is also well known. He seems to have thought that balanced character could be cultivated through the study of music.

In early Buddhism, too, while there were prohibitions

against singing and dancing, music was not completely out of the picture. Originally, the sutras themselves were recited in a musical fashion. In this way, they first touched people's hearts.

According to an early sutra, Shakyamuni described the benefits of using one's voice, saying that it prevented fatigue, improved the memory, rejuvenated one's spirits and aided cognition.

BRINGING HOPE TO SOCIETY

Saito: I think that music has the power to infuse our lives with the harmony of the universe. It brings our lives into perfect balance.

Ikeda: Music liberates the heart. It eases the heart's blockages.

The English word *play*, in the sense of *perform*, also means to frolic or have fun. It implies a relaxing and liberating experience.

In Japanese, we also speak of "playing" wind and string instruments. Performing is play in the best sense of the term. Music makes our hearts free.

Suda: One of the samadhis that Bodhisattva Wonderful Sound attained is the "samadhi of the sport of transcendental powers" (LSOC, 332).

Endo: It must be the aim of music therapy to clear the heart of obstruction.

Ikeda: Since music is soothing as well as liberating, wherever there is song, there is growth. President Toda used to say, "Wherever people have prospered throughout history, song could always be heard."

In the SGI, too, as long as we cherish music and song, our organization will continue to develop. The same is true of society. It could be said that a society in which the people hum beautiful songs has a rhythm of advancement. On the other hand, the future of a society plagued by moans and cries must be bleak.

Endo: I believe that shortly after the Great Kanto Earthquake (1923) there was an author who argued that such an unprecedented natural disaster in the region of the capital must have been somehow related to the desolation, as well as arrogance, of people's hearts.

Ikeda: That was in an essay by the Japanese writer and poet Rohan Koda.

Endo: A song that was popular before the quake went, "I am the withered eulalia grass of the dried riverbed, and you, too, are the withered eulalia grass." In that essay, I recall Koda revealing that he had felt something ominous in the lines of that song.

Suda: He must have heard it as a melancholy sound.

Ikeda: Of course this cannot be proven empirically nor can we apply this to every circumstance, but I think that culture and music and the tendency of the times mutually influence one another. As the saying goes, "Songs follow the times, and the times follow the songs."

Suda: Are you referring to the difference between melancholy sounds and wonderful sounds?

Ikeda: "Melancholy sounds" does not refer strictly to sad tunes. I think they include any kind of melody, music or culture that causes people to have feelings of resignation. No matter how lively and spirited something may seem, music and culture that guide people toward nihilism, toward thinking, "There's nothing I can do to affect the outcome," are melancholy sounds.
    On the other hand, culture that, while perhaps unostentatious,

appeals to beautiful human emotion and elevates the mind qualifies as "wonderful sound." It inspires trust and hope within people.

The SGI movement brings hope to all, not only through music but through all endeavors. In that sense, it can be described as a wonderful sound movement.

It is a movement to pluck the strings of goodness in people's hearts. Isn't this perhaps what is signified by the thirty-four forms of Bodhisattva Wonderful Sound?

Saito: Yes. Wonderful Sound, like Bodhisattva Medicine King and Bodhisattva Perceiver of the World's Sounds, has acquired the samadhi to manifest all physical forms. In this state of life, one can assume any form in order to lead people to happiness.

Endo: The sutra describes him appearing alternately as King Brahma, Lord Shakra, the heavenly being Freedom and so on. It states:

> This bodhisattva manifests himself in various different bodies and preaches this sutra for the sake of living beings in various different places. At times he appears as King Brahma, at times as the lord Shakra, at times as the heavenly being Freedom, at times as the heavenly being Great Freedom, at times as a great general of heaven, at times as the heavenly king Vaishravana, at times as a wheel-turning sage king, at times as one of the petty kings, at times as a rich man, at times as a householder, at times as a chief minister, at times as a Brahman, at times as a monk, a nun, a layman believer, or a laywoman believer, at times as the wife of a rich man or a householder, at times as the wife of a chief minister, at times as the wife of a Brahman, at times as a young boy or a young girl, at times as a heavenly being, a dragon, a

yaksha, a gandharva, an asura, a garuda, a kimnara, a mahoraga, a human or a nonhuman being, and so preaches this sutra. The hell dwellers, hungry spirits, beasts, and the numerous others who are in difficult circumstances are thus all able to be saved. And for the sake of those who are in the women's quarters of the royal palace, he changes himself into a woman's form and preaches this sutra. (LSOC, 336)

Saito: Nichiren Daishonin says, "It is pity and compassion that make it possible for Wonderful Sound to recognize and meet the various needs of the living beings [by assuming various forms]. This is what is expressed by the word 'bodhisattva'" (OTT, 176).

Ikeda: Bodhisattva Wonderful Sound is completely free to adjust to the capacity of another person. This is total liberation. Buddhism is not a religion that tries to force people into a mold or to create a bunch of automatons. It emancipates the lives of those who have been living robotically.

The thirty-four forms of Wonderful Sound are proof of the correctness of the multifaceted activities SGI members carry out in all sectors of society. While we may exert ourselves in different areas, we are all motivated by compassion and humanity. We should burn with a spirit and determination to become the foremost ally of those who are suffering. If we lack this spirit, we are not behaving like Bodhisattva Wonderful Sound.

Saito: Dr. Alexander Yakovlev (a leading architect of perestroika), once remarked with respect to your activities, President Ikeda: "When Dostoevsky says 'beauty will save the world,' by beauty he must mean humanity."

He was referring to the importance of working continuously for society within society, always upholding a spirit of compassion toward humankind.

Ikeda: This is what is meant by beauty, by "wonderful sound." This is the spirit of the Lotus Sutra. The SGI is on the correct path.

Suda: The documentary *Knight of the Rising Sun*, introducing your activities for peace, won the Special Prize at the 1998 Religion Today Film Festival in Bologna, Italy. Judges said they were impressed by its portrayal of religion contributing to society.

Endo: For us as SGI members, this seems perfectly natural. But I guess that outside the SGI it strikes people as a novel concept.

Saito: That's because while many people spout theories, there are very few who in fact take action while standing up to the pressures of life. With regard to the problem of environmental degradation, I have heard someone lament, "Compared to the number of people who speak out, how few are those who take any action!"

Ikeda: Tsunesaburo Makiguchi, the first Soka Gakkai president, asserted that "religion must not exist for the sake of religion." He argued that the existence of a religion has no significance if it does not create the values of beauty, gain and good. Herein lies the decisive difference between the SGI and the Nichiren Shoshu priesthood.

President Makiguchi strongly asserted that religion must not remain confined within the world of religion but must work to transform the present world into a place of value. And he died a martyr to his beliefs. We need to change this world into a land of beauty, a land of gain, a land of good. And we need to create lives of beauty, gain and good. This is what it means to lead a life of value creation.

THE INVISIBLE BRIDGE
OF CULTURAL EXCHANGE

Suda: When Shakyamuni explains the thirty-four forms of Bodhisattva Wonderful Sound, the people listening all attain the samadhi enabling them to manifest all kinds of bodies.

Wonderful Sound then greets Shakyamuni and returns to his land. On the way back, the lands he passes through quake and tremble, jeweled lotus flowers rain down, and hundreds, thousands, ten thousands, millions of different kinds of music are played.

Ikeda: This scene concludes the "Bodhisattva Wonderful Sound" chapter. It describes his coming and going, which fills the universe with music. It is a bridge of music spanning the universe. Through this process, the lives of the beings at Eagle Peak open up to the vast universe. The eighty-four thousand bodhisattvas that accompany Bodhisattva Wonderful Sound also attain the same great state of life as he.

Opening the finite self to the infinite—this is the purpose of faith. Through faith, the self embraced in the universe comes to encompass the universe. This is what happens when we perform the gongyo and daimoku of "wonderful sound." Between the self and the universe, we extend an invisible bridge. This is the function of wonderful sound. Broadly speaking, this is the power of art. This bridge of life also bridges the gaps between people.

Endo: Dr. Petrosyan of Russia said that cultural exchange means building an invisible bridge between nations and people. Although other bridges (political or economic) are destroyed in an instant by war, he continued, the invisible bridge of culture will never crumble. He said that you, President Ikeda, are the architect of such cultural bridges.

Saito: I was very moved to hear these words. The unifying power of culture, transcending the divisive power of evil, is necessary.

Dr. Kychanov said that the world requires the power of good. He expressed hope that SGI members will bring about the victory of good.

Ikeda: The Great Teacher T'ien-t'ai of China says of Bodhisattva Wonderful Sound: "With wonderful sounds, he roars in the ten directions, spreading this teaching. Therefore, he is called Wonderful Sound."[3]

In Dharmaraksha's *Lotus Sutra of the Correct Law* (Jpn *Sho-hokke-kyo*, a Chinese language translation of the Lotus Sutra), the bodhisattva's name is rendered "Wonderful Roar," referring to the roar of the lion.

Right up to his death, President Toda maintained the spirit to fight on no matter what. His determination to expend every last ounce of energy was expressed in each word he spoke and in his appearance. Now, summoning all my thoughts into a single phrase, I would like to cry out just as he did, "Let's fight with all our might!"

The Daishonin states: "Even if you are not the Venerable Mahakashyapa, you should all perform a dance. Even if you are not Shariputra, you should leap up and dance. When Bodhisattva Superior Practices emerged from the earth, did he not emerge dancing?" (WND-1, 1119).

This is the vibrant spirit of the Lotus Sutra.

Let's enjoy. Let's advance cheerfully and with composure.

Let's struggle with all our might, holding our heads high!

NOTES

1. Dr. Jutta Seifert: President of the European Youth Cultural Initiative for the Young Generation and former undersecretary of the Austrian Federal Ministry of Education, Art and Sports.

2. A storehouse at Todai-ji Temple in Nara, built in the eighth century to preserve national treasures.

3. *Hokke mongu* (Words and Phrases of the Lotus Sutra), vol. 10.

PART III

"The Universal Gateway of the Bodhisattva Perceiver of the World's Sounds" Chapter

3 Developing the Compassion and Wisdom "To Perceive the World's Sounds"

Ikeda: What touches a person's heart most deeply? While there are various possible answers to this question, I would suggest that it is compassion and kindness. People who genuinely share the worries of others, who pray to overcome another's problem as if it were their own, who really treasure others, who are compassionately strict, who are kind—these are the people others never forget.

Compassion is the basic prerequisite of a leader. This is all that really matters. To be a leader is to cherish and protect each person. The "Universal Gateway of the Bodhisattva Perceiver of the World's Sounds" chapter calls to mind the image of such a compassionate leader.

Saito: Indeed, Perceiver of the World's Sounds[1] displays a kindness that resembles motherly love.

A MOTHER'S WORDS CAN PROVIDE LIFETIME SUPPORT

Endo: This bodhisattva is also sometimes referred to as the "merciful mother Perceiver of the World's Sounds."

Ikeda: We all think fondly of our mothers. I once heard someone recount the following: When he was a child, he was one of many siblings in a poor family.

His father drank heavily every day. His mother worked extremely hard, and she scrimped and saved even to cover the cost of his father's drinking. What's more, the father would frequently beat his wife and children.

Though very young, he was always being sent out to buy alcohol. One cold evening, when he was seven or eight, he was walking home alone with a fairly large bottle that he had had filled at the liquor store. Although he hated his father, he carried the bottle very carefully, telling himself, "This is sake that was wrung from my mother's hard work." The bottle was large, and eventually his hands became numb from the cold. He was so close to home that he could see the lights. He must have been distracted, and the bottle slipped from his numb hands. The glass shattered, spilling the sake everywhere. He didn't know what to do.

With tears in his eyes, the boy approached the entrance to the house, but he could not go inside. Within he could hear his father shouting, "What's taking that boy so long!"

At that moment, his mother, perhaps hearing his sobbing, went outside looking very concerned. Thinking that he would be scolded, the boy instinctively retreated a step. Yet, upon learning what had happened, his mother simply hugged him and asked: "Did the bottle hit your feet? Are you injured? Since you're not hurt, there's nothing to cry about." And she gently rubbed his back.

The man reflected that his mother's kindness at that crucial moment became a source of support for him whenever he encountered a difficult situation. He added, "If at that time I had instead been scolded, I might have been deeply hurt."

It seems that the awareness that someone loves and cares about us unconditionally gives us the will to live.

Endo: I think this quality of motherly compassion explains why Bodhisattva Perceiver of the World's Sounds has enjoyed such popularity.

Suda: The SGI treasures each member with a kindness that is, in a sense, even greater than that of a parent. No matter what a person is going through, SGI members support one another, sharing one another's worries and offering encouragement.

Endo: The examples of this are literally countless.

Saito: That's why the SGI is so strong.

Ikeda: It is not because the SGI is held together by an organizational structure that it is strong, but because it is made up of heart-to-heart human bonds.

Bodhisattva Perceiver of the World's Sounds is so named because he[2] listens with great compassion to all sounds and voices in the world, to the voices of suffering people, and he embraces and responds to them. He listens, understands and takes action in response to the true feelings of each person. Isn't this boundless kindness exactly what identifies Bodhisattva Perceiver of the World's Sounds? This is why he is so widely revered.

Saito: This bodhisattva is so well known that, in the East, even people who have never heard of the Lotus Sutra are familiar with Perceiver of the World's Sounds.

Suda: In India, China, Korea, Japan and many other Asian countries, no bodhisattva is better known. The number of shrines built to him also far exceeds those built to any other bodhisattva. People have continually entrusted their hopes to Perceiver of the World's Sounds.

Endo: That's because he is said to save people from all dangers and difficulties at all times and in all places.

Suda: Bodhisattva Perceiver of the World's Sounds is a superstar of the Buddhist world.

Saito: He is so famous that in China he is revered as a Tao-ist deity. It seems that the attraction people have toward this bodhisattva transcends even the boundaries of religion.

KINDNESS IGNITES PEOPLE'S HEARTS

Endo: It must be his kindness that people are drawn to.

Suda: His face definitely displays warmth and gentleness.

Ikeda: Nothing is as powerful as kindness. Nothing can better win over a person's heart. No eternal flame is as strong or bright. Its brilliance illuminates people's hearts. It ignites the light of hope. Kindness is true soft power.

Suda: Yes. Hard power clearly does not attract people.

Ikeda: Soft means compassion, *power* is force. It is the force of compassion. The foundation of culture, peace and education is compassion—kindness toward human beings. The *soft* of soft power implies limitless kindness, which gives rise to limitless strength.

Also, underlying kindness is strength; without strength, we cannot be kind to others. Behind the beautiful kindness of Perceiver of the World's Sounds is his courage to seek and spread the Mystic Law without begrudging his life.

Saito: Nichiren Daishonin in *The Record of the Orally Transmitted Teachings* and other writings cites the Great Teacher T'ien-t'ai of China, who said that Perceiver of the World's Sounds and the Lotus Sutra are simply different names for the same thing. This implies that while the bodhisattva's name and the title of the Lotus Sutra are different, their spirit is one and the same. Both are expressions of the Mystic Law.

Ikeda: In fact, Bodhisattva Perceiver of the World's Sounds represents one aspect of the life of the original Buddha from time without beginning revealed in the "Life Span of the Thus Come One" chapter. He is symbolic of the boundless compassion of the original Buddha at one with the universe. Therefore, the life of Bodhisattva Perceiver of the World's Sounds is not separate from that of the original Buddha from the remote past. If it were, he would be nothing but a lifeless shell.

Endo: To pray to Perceiver of the World's Sounds without believing in and accepting the Mystic Law would be putting the cart before the horse.

Ikeda: Bodhisattva Perceiver of the World's Sounds is encompassed in the life of the original Buddha from the remote past; that is to say, in the Gohonzon. The function of Perceiver of the World's Sounds is just a small aspect of the beneficial power of the Gohonzon—of the Mystic Law.

From ancient times, no chapter of the sutra has been as widely discussed or written about as the "Perceiver of the World's Sounds" chapter. There is even a history of people placing their faith in this chapter as an independent sutra. To this day people in various places continue to build statues of this bodhisattva. The Heart Sutra (Skt *Prajnaparamita-hridaya*), which enjoys particular popularity in Japan, adopts a form of the preaching by Perceiver of the World's Sounds.

Despite the bodhisattva's popularity, many have misunderstood the source of his power, which is the Mystic Law. In the transmission section of the Lotus Sutra—which includes the "Perceiver of the World's Sounds" chapter—people are urged to propagate the Mystic Law after Shakyamuni's passing.

Of all Buddhist scriptures in which Bodhisattva Perceiver of the World's Sounds appears, the "Universal Gateway of the Bodhisattva Perceiver of the World's Sounds" chapter of the

Lotus Sutra is the oldest. Here the function of this bodhisattva is clearly established. The power of Bodhisattva Perceiver of the World's Sounds to lead people to enlightenment derives from the Mystic Law; from Nam-myoho-renge-kyo in the depths of the "Life Span" chapter.

Endo: It would be pointless to worship Perceiver of the World's Sounds apart from the Mystic Law, the source from which his power derives. In fact, it would go against the bodhisattva's intention.

THE THEORETICAL IS "LIGHT," THE ESSENTIAL IS "SOUND"

> *His pure light, free of blemish,*
> *is a sun of wisdom dispelling all darknesses.*
> *He can quell the wind and fire of misfortune*
> *and everywhere bring light to the world.*
> *The precepts from his compassionate body shake us like thunder,*
> *the wonder of his pitying mind is like a great cloud.*
> *He sends down the sweet dew, the Dharma rain,*
> *to quench the flames of earthly desires.*
> *When lawsuits bring you before the officials,*
> *when terrified in the midst of an army,*
> *think on the power of that Perceiver of Sounds*
> *and hatred in all its forms will be dispelled.* (LSOC, 346–47)

Suda: Let's look at the chapter's summary. While Bodhisattva Wonderful Sounds of the previous chapter comes from a land to the east, Perceiver of the World's Sounds has by tradition been held to dwell in the west. Also, while Wonderful Sound produces sounds, Perceiver of the World's Sounds listens to voices. It seems that the two are therefore complementary.

Ikeda: In the essential teaching (second half) of the Lotus Sutra, we find many names that relate to sounds or voices. It's a very vocal group! Besides Wonderful Sound and Perceiver of the World's Sounds, there is Awesome Sound King Thus Come One ("Bodhisattva Never Disparaging" chapter), Cloud Thunder Sound King ("Bodhisattva Wonderful Sound" chapter) and Cloud Thunder Sound Constellation King Flower Wisdom ("Former Affairs of King Wonderful Adornment" chapter). Voices also figure prominently in the "Dharani" chapter. By contrast, in the theoretical teaching (first half) of the Lotus Sutra, there are many names that relate to "light."

Saito: These include the Buddhas Sun Moon Bright and Burning Torch ("Introduction" chapter), Flower Glow Thus Come One ("Simile and Parable" chapter), Light Bright Thus Come One ("Bestowal of Prophecy" chapter), Universal Brightness Thus Come One and Law Brights Thus Come One ("Prophecy of Enlightenment for Five Hundred Disciples" chapter) and Endowed With a Thousand Ten Thousand Glowing Marks Thus Come One ("Encouraging Devotion" chapter).

Ikeda: Light represents the truth of the true aspect of all phenomena. It is the eternal and unchanging truth. Sound, on the other hand, represents action as an emissary of the original Buddha of the remote past. It is inexhaustible wisdom, which functions in accord with changing circumstances.

Also, according to one explanation, the fact that Perceiver of the World's Sounds is supposed to dwell in the west suggests that the bodhisattva's roots are with an ancient goddess thought to reside in lands to the west of India.

At any rate, the "Perceiver of the World's Sounds" chapter begins with an inquiry into the origins of this bodhisattva, who has been present at the preaching of the Lotus Sutra from the beginning.

Endo: That's right. A bodhisattva named Inexhaustible Intent rises and asks Shakyamuni, "World-Honored One, this Bodhisattva Perceiver of the World's Sounds— why is he called Perceiver of the World's Sounds?" (LSOC, 339).

Shakyamuni replies that if there are beings experiencing suffering of any kind and they hear of this bodhisattva and single-mindedly call his name, "then at once he will perceive the sound of their voices and they will all gain deliverance from their trials" (LSOC, 339). In other words, they will be saved just by intoning his name. The fact that his help can be gained so easily would seem to be one reason for the spread of belief in him.

INCONSPICUOUS BENEFIT
IS INCOMPARABLY GREATER

> *Suppose someone should conceive a wish to harm you,*
> *should push you into a great pit of fire.*
> *Think on the power of that Perceiver of Sounds*
> *and the pit of fire will change into a pond!*
> *If you should be cast adrift on the vast ocean,*
> *menaced by dragons, fish, and various demons,*
> *think on the power of that Perceiver of Sounds*
> *and the billows and waves cannot drown you!*
> *Suppose you are on the peak of Mount Sumeru*
> *and someone pushes you off.*
> *Think on the power of that Perceiver of Sounds*
> *and you will hang in midair like the sun!*
> *Suppose you are pursued by evil men*
> *who wish to throw you down from a diamond mountain.*
> *Think on the power of the Perceiver of Sounds*
> *and they cannot harm a hair of you!*
> *Suppose you are surrounded by evil-hearted bandits,*
> *each brandishing a knife to wound you.*
> *Think on the power of that Perceiver of Sounds*
> *and at once all will be swayed by compassion!*

Suppose you encounter trouble with the king's law,
face punishment, about to forfeit your life.
Think on the power of that Perceiver of Sounds
and the executioner's sword will be broken to bits!
Suppose you are imprisoned in cangue and lock,
hands and feet bound by fetters and chains.
Think on the power of that Perceiver of Sounds
and they will fall off, leaving you free!
Suppose with curses and various poisonous herbs
someone should try to injure you.
Think on the power of that Perceiver of Sounds
and the injury will rebound upon the originator.
(LSOC, 344–45)

Ikeda: Of course, from the standpoint of Nichiren Buddhism, calling the name of Perceiver of the World's Sounds means chanting the name of the "Nam-myoho-renge-kyo Thus Come One," the original Buddha of the remote past who is the source of Perceiver of the World's Sounds' power. It is the practice of chanting daimoku.

It is to single-mindedly pray "as earnestly as though to produce fire from damp wood, or to obtain water from parched ground" (WND-1, 444). Prayer that is not earnest to the Gohonzon will not elicit a response. But when we pray to the Gohonzon with our entire lives, a path forward cannot help opening.

Nichiren Daishonin says, "Those who attained enlightenment by listening to the six chapters from the 'Medicine King' chapter on are merely those who had remained unenlightened after gaining blessings from the verse section of the 'Life Span' chapter" (WND-1, 516). Citing this passage, President Toda would often say, "The 'Perceiver of the World's Sounds' chapter is really nothing but the leftovers from the 'Life Span' chapter."

Nam-myoho-renge-kyo is the source from which Perceiver of the World's Sounds derives his strength. Therefore, the

Daishonin declares, "Now that we have entered the Latter Day of the Law, the benefits Nichiren and his followers enjoy in their chanting of Nam-myoho-renge-kyo are as far above those conferred by Perceiver of the World's Sounds as heaven is above earth or clouds are above mud" (OTT, 180).

Suda: The Daishonin is saying that even though the benefits enumerated in the "Perceiver of the World's Sounds" chapter are vast beyond belief, they cannot compare with the benefit of chanting Nam-myoho-renge-kyo. This is quite a statement.

Endo: The "Perceiver of the World's Sounds" chapter starts out by expounding the benefit of being saved from the seven disasters. These are fire, flood, *rakshasa* demons, attack by swords and staves, attack by *yaksha* and other demons, imprisonment and attack by bandits.[3]

You will not be burned even in a great fire, it says. Even if carried away in a flood, you will be saved from drowning. Though you may set out on the sea in search of treasure and are washed ashore by a storm in a land of human-eating rakshasa demons, if one person on the vessel intones the name of Perceiver of the World's Sounds, everyone on board will be free from harm.

Ikeda: It is teaching the principle of standing alone. If even one person stands up in earnest, if one person of sincere and solid faith appears, it will benefit everyone who is part of the community in which that person resides, as their lives are interconnected. They can lead their families, their relatives, their communities, society and the people in the groups they are part of, all in the direction of happiness.

Suda: The chapter also says that if you are about to be attacked with swords and staves, then Perceiver of the World's Sounds will break those weapons.

Ikeda: This pretty much describes what took place during the Tatsunokuchi Persecution (in 1271). The contemptible officials took Nichiren Daishonin to the beach at Tatsunokuchi where he was to be executed, but they were unsuccessful in their attempt. For that matter, in each incident the Daishonin faced, whether the Matsubagayatsu Persecution (in 1260), the Izu exile (in 1261) or the Komatsubara Persecution (in 1264), he wondrously escaped serious harm.

Of course, just as he counseled his disciples to do, the Daishonin himself exercised prudence in his activities (see WND-1, 1000). Also, listening with the ears of Shih K'uang and observing with the eyes of Li Lou (see WND-1, 33),[4] he remained abreast of the happenings of society.

Carelessness Is a Form of Arrogance

Ikeda: To think that just because you are practicing faith everything will be automatically all right or that things will somehow work themselves out is a careless attitude. It is also arrogant. Rather, we need to have the awareness: "Because I am practicing faith, I will make things work out. I will win!" "Because I am practicing faith, I will ensure that there are no accidents." Otherwise, we will run into problems.

It is probably inadvisable, for example, for women to walk home alone late at night. We live in unsafe times. Women should exercise every precaution and be sure to get home as early as is reasonably possible. In the event that they cannot avoid being out late, I hope they will use common sense to avoid placing themselves in a dangerous situation, perhaps calling someone who can come meet them. Also, it is important not to cause one's family members to worry.

Men, too, should be mindful of the need for women to get home safely. I hope they will show them every consideration, perhaps seeing them home if the hour is late.

Saito: Being protected by the Buddhist gods means protecting ourselves. As the Great Teacher Miao-lo of China indicates when he says, "The stronger one's faith, the greater the protection of the gods" (WND-1, 614), it is strong, fearless faith that spurs the Buddhist gods into action on our behalf. By possessing the determination of a lion king, we cause the Buddhist gods to function.

Suda: The "Perceiver of the World's Sounds" chapter says, "This bodhisattva can grant fearlessness to living beings" (LSOC, 340). In other words, he gives them courage.

Ikeda: That's right. Strictly speaking, it is not the Buddhist gods, or for that matter Perceiver of the World's Sounds, that actually protect us. We protect ourselves with courageous faith to not shrink back from anything in fear. We are protected by the power of Bodhisattva Perceiver of the World's Sounds functioning within our own lives. It is faith, chanting Nam-myoho-renge-kyo, and taking action for kosen-rufu that bring forth this power.

President Toda often said, "To simply yearn for benefit without devoting yourself to the Gohonzon is lazy and irresponsible." Those who pray with all their heart and struggle for kosen-rufu construct a bulwark of safety and tranquillity in their lives. Absolutely no effort in SGI activities is wasted. While it may not be immediately apparent, this is definitely borne out in time. We can appreciate this at the end of our lives. This is Nichiren Buddhism.

Suda: The "Perceiver of the World's Sounds" chapter next explains that, even if an evil demon should try to harm you, you will not be injured. It also says that if a person, whether guilty or not, has been imprisoned in fetters and chains, his bonds will be severed and broken and he will be freed. It also assures that a merchant who is guiding a band of merchants carrying valuable treasures over a steep and dangerous road will be protected from attacking bandits (see LSOC, 340).

Saito: The verse section describes various other benefits, such as being saved even if pushed off a high mountain. It also says that, if someone tries to injure you with curses and poisonous herbs, "the injury will rebound upon the originator" (LSOC, 345).

Endo: This is the well-known principle of bad causes returning to the one who perpetrated them.

AN ACCIDENT-FREE AND TRANQUIL LIFE

Now that we have entered the Latter Day of the Law, the benefits Nichiren and his followers enjoy in their chanting of Nam-myoho-renge-kyo are as far above those conferred by Perceiver of the World's Sounds as heaven is above earth or clouds are above mud.

In general we may say that the element kan, *or Perceiver, in the name Kanzeon represents enkan, or "perfect perception." The element* ze, *or World, means "miraculous," while the element* on, *or Sounds, refers to the capacity for attaining Buddhahood. Kan is another name for the Dharma-realm; hence, as already stated, it stands for perfect perception. And because Perceiver of the World's Sounds is a perceiver of the true aspect of all phenomena, he can see and understand the different realms, such as those of hell, hungry spirits, animals, etc. that make up this miraculous world.*

On, or Sounds, refers to the sounds of the true aspect of all phenomena, and hence it means that there are no living beings that do not possess the true aspect of Buddhahood. This has been referred to, in the "Life Span" chapter, as the original state endowed with the Ten Worlds, the three bodies with which the Buddha is eternally endowed.

The bodhisattva Perceiver of the World's Sounds has

already accepted the Lotus Sutra reverentially. And now the practitioners who accept and uphold this sutra, can enjoy benefits that surpass even those of the bodhisattva. (OTT, 180)

Ikeda: All of these could be summed up as the benefit of achieving an accident-free and tranquil life. This is why the "Perceiver of the World's Sounds" chapter is also referred to as the "Chapter for Removing Misfortune and Prolonging Life."

President Toda described these benefits in terms that we can easily understand, saying:[5]

1. If you are running a business and trying to earn a profit, some calamity may befall you. At such a time, if you place your trust in the Gohonzon, you can avert disaster.

2. If someone decides to cause you trouble or you experience a major loss, trouble will instead befall that person and your loss will turn into gain.

3. When you are suffering due to earthly desires or illness, if you place your faith in the Gohonzon, earthly desires will turn into enlightenment and the devil of illness will be powerless.

4. Should you fall from a cliff or have a car accident, if you believe in the Gohonzon, you will not be injured.

5. If someone tries to get you fired from your job, if you believe in the Gohonzon, that person will instead be forced to quit and you will keep your job.

6. If someone hates you or tries to harm you, if you have strong faith, he or she will have a change of heart.

7. Even if you face execution, if you have strong faith, you will be let off. This is what is meant by "the executioner's sword will be broken to bits." This is the principle that the Daishonin himself demonstrated.

8. Even if you face imprisonment, if you have strong faith, you will be exonerated and sent home.

9. If someone tries to poison you or if you are vilified, the perpetrator will find himself in the exact same situation. This is what is meant by the principle that the injury rebounds upon the originator.

10. Even in a powerful storm, those who have strong faith will not be harmed.

Endo: Mr. Toda's explanation is very clear.

Ikeda: It is considerate to put things in a way that people can understand.

Anyone can make things complicated, but then no one will grasp what you are trying to say. This is not "perceiving the world's sounds." This is not what the Lotus Sutra teaches.

As is clear from President Toda's explanation, the "Perceiver of the World's Sounds" chapter is documentary proof that we can receive benefit in this lifetime. When we practice the Mystic Law, we receive all of these benefits without fail. This is the promise of the original Buddha. All these fall into the category of conspicuous benefit. That is, benefit that suddenly materializes at a critical moment. In this Latter Day of the Law, however, it must be stressed that while we certainly experience conspicuous benefit, it is inconspicuous benefit that is central to our faith.

Just as a seed will grow into a great tree with the passage of time, the branches of good fortune and benefit in our lives will thicken and produce abundant flowers and fruit as we continue to practice. This is inconspicuous benefit. A tree of good fortune and benefit that is thus rooted in the earth of life will not fall over. It stands firm even when buffeted by a fierce storm.

Suda: This must be what is meant by benefits that are "as far above those conferred by Perceiver of the World's Sounds as heaven is above earth or clouds are above mud."

Ikeda: And that can be interpreted as the great benefit of attaining Buddhahood. President Toda characterized the state of Buddhahood as absolute happiness and as powerful life force.

To reiterate, when we practice Buddhism, we will absolutely experience conspicuous benefit of the kinds mentioned earlier. In particular, we gain wonderful benefit when we first embrace faith and see our immediate sufferings resolved without fail. When we then advance in faith with confidence gained from this initial experience, we can receive immense benefit. Next to this, our earlier benefit pales in comparison. This is the benefit of absolutely flourishing vitality.

Endo: This is the human revolution.

Ikeda: Yes, our lives are revolutionized. We become stronger and more vigorous. Instead of being controlled and pulled this way and that by hardship, we develop the fortitude to face our suffering head-on, take hold of it and overcome it with composure.

To illustrate, if our life force is a magnitude of one, and we encounter a problem that measures a magnitude of two or three, we will likely be discouraged. If we strengthen our life force to a magnitude of a hundred, a thousand or ten thousand, however, such difficulties will be merely minor distractions we toss aside as we joyfully move ahead.

President Toda said: "In this world, we are restricted by all kinds of conditions—our relationship with our parents, our siblings, our friends, as well as material things such as clothing, housing and taxes. This is the reality of our day-to-day existence. But when we tap into boundless life force, these cease to cause us suffering, and we can instead actually enjoy them. This is what we call 'emancipation.'"[6]

EMANCIPATION MEANS ABUNDANT LIFE FORCE

Endo: When we use the term *emancipation*, we are not talking about anything unusual, are we?

Ikeda: We mean obtaining the life force necessary to cast off the chains of suffering. Such abundant life force encompasses compassion and wisdom, as well as good fortune and benefit. It is to be infinitely bright and kind. It is to live a life of boundless wisdom.

When your entire being overflows with vitality, this painful saha world turns into a world of brilliant joy. That is Eagle Peak. That is Mount Potalaka—the place where Perceiver of the World's Sounds is said to reside. Incidentally, since ancient times, a number of countries have designated certain sites "Mount Potalaka."

Suda: Potala Palace in Tibet, for example, is named after this Mount Potalaka. The successive Dalai Lamas are held by their followers to be incarnations of Perceiver of the World's Sounds.

From the standpoint of the original intent of the "Perceiver of the World's Sounds" chapter, any place where we take action with the immeasurable life force of the Mystic Law is Mount Potalaka.

Ikeda: This great life force is itself what is meant by "peace and security in the present existence," and it also becomes proof of "good circumstances in future existences" (see LSOC, 136). Nichiren Daishonin says, "When one practices the Lotus Sutra under such circumstances, difficulties will arise, and these are to be looked on as 'peaceful' practices" (OTT, 115).

"Peace and security in the present existence" indicates the state of life to courageously battle and overcome any ordeal that might confront us and thereby to secure faith that shines with still greater brilliance and force than before.

Saito: Such benefit is truly unparalleled.

Ikeda: Though this wonderful state of life is available to all, many people don't seem to want it! Instead, they seem desirous of anything else and content themselves with pursuing immediate gain! And then if they are subjected to the slightest insult, they begin to doubt the Gohonzon!

Praying with doubt is like trying to keep water in a bathtub with the plug pulled. Your good fortune and benefit will drain away. A passage from the "Perceiver of the World's Sounds" chapter reads, "from thought to thought never entertaining doubt!" (LSOC, 347). A confident prayer will reverberate powerfully throughout the entire universe.

The benefit we receive when we initially take faith is comparable to a small mountain. The boundless life force of Buddhahood is like a large mountain. On the way from this small mountain to the large mountain you have to pass through a valley. This indicates the three obstacles and four devils and other obstacles of all kinds. Only by passing through this valley can we ascend the great mountain of Buddhahood.

THE UNIVERSAL GATEWAY OPEN TO ALL

Saito: The full title of the chapter we are discussing is "The Universal Gateway of the Bodhisattva Perceiver of the World's Sounds." *Universal Gateway* means a gate that anyone can enter. It is open to anyone. It is not a narrow passage; it is a broad and expansive portal.

Ikeda: Perceiver of the World's Sounds recognizes the "sounds" of all people's suffering. A leader should listen to people carefully. Men, in particular, ought to pay heed to what women have to say. A leader who doesn't listen humbly and attentively to others is not qualified to be called a leader. The same goes for men who don't listen to women. It is important that leaders listen with patience and equanimity.

Endo: There are certainly those whose remarks come across as nothing but complaints.

Ikeda: The Latter Day of the Law is a time when people are filled with complaint. A leader must simply hear people out. This is part of our Buddhist practice.

It is also important to create an environment where people feel free to talk about anything. No one will be happy if they find themselves in an environment where, as the saying goes, "not even demons will draw near."

Suda: Good leaders in all fields, including politics and business, listen to the opinions of others.

Ikeda: One such leader in Japan was the great industrialist Konosuke Matsushita, the founder of Panasonic. Although he would excuse himself as lacking a formal education, he was in fact extremely erudite. He always lent an ear to what others had to say. In fact, it is well known that he would seek out the views of employees on matters in the workplace.

Suda: For example, if he learned that a new product his company was selling was getting an unfavorable reception, he would go directly to the factory to investigate the cause with the technicians. If there were no problems with product quality, he would go to retail outlets and even meet with consumers to get to the bottom of the trouble.

Once when someone suggested that, given his standing, he ought to summon the responsible engineers or marketing staff to take care of such matters, Mr. Matsushita replied: "If I called in my subordinates, they would be nervous and would likely prepare their replies before coming in to see me. They might dress up reports to humor me. Without any independent knowledge of the situation, I would have no alternative but to accept what they said. That's what I'm afraid of. Therefore, I go out to assess the situation for myself."[7]

Saito: Spoken like a true leader. While it is easy to listen to opinions that agree with one's own, it is difficult to listen to opposing viewpoints. The tendency is certainly to try to avoid views that we don't like.

THE IMPORTANCE OF LISTENING TO "BAD NEWS"

Ikeda: It would seem that the ability to readily hear bad news is a key point that distinguishes a true leader from a tyrant. Tyrants appear proud in their power, but most often they are actually quite timid. For this reason, they cannot listen to others' opinions.

Endo: History offers countless examples of people who failed precisely because they could not take bad news.

Suda: Such accounts would fill hundreds of volumes.

Endo: To take an example from Nichiren Daishonin's time, one reason given as to why the Mongol invasions weren't successful was that information on the actual state of affairs never reached the Mongol emperor, Kublai Khan. Those around him, fearing his wrath, did not accurately inform him that Japan had no intention of acknowledging fealty to the Mongols and that assembling sufficient ships to undertake the invasion of Japan would require enormous effort. So when he was instead told simply that the invasion could not take place because the sea between Japan and China was too rough, he was determined to prove otherwise. This is what led to his launching an ill-advised invasion.

Suda: An outstanding leader actively seeks out contrary opinions.

Tai-tsung, the second emperor of China's T'ang dynasty, is known for his outstanding reign. His discussions with his ministers are collected in the work *Chenkuan Cheng-yao* (Essentials of Government in the Chen-kuan Era).

Ikeda: This work is quite famous. Some have even said that it should be required reading for all leaders in East Asia.

Suda: It is said that Tai-tsung could rule so benevolently because he had devised a system for actively gathering unfavorable reports.

He created an official post, the holder of which was asked to actively identify mistakes on the part of the dynasty or regime. He also made it possible for people to express harsh criticism without fear of retribution.

Ikeda: If people simply sit on negative information, it will never reach the leader. Therefore, a leader must actively seek out such feedback.

Saito: In Japanese history, too, there are similar examples. The case of the Kuroda clan in Hakata, Kyushu, is well known. The Kuroda clan made it a practice to hold unofficial conferences known as "divergent opinion meetings" where, in a departure from standard protocol, participants were allowed to say anything, even to criticize the lord of the clan. To have had such a system in a feudal age is unusual.

Ikeda: Of course, it is likely that many of the opinions voiced in such a forum will be off the mark. But simply knowing that people have certain views becomes an important factor in reaching decisions.

I reiterate that someone who does not have the magnanimity

to listen willingly to even harsh opinions is disqualified as a leader. In that sense, I think we can interpret the "Perceiver of the World's Sounds" chapter as a doctrine of leadership.

GOOD HEALTH THROUGH LISTENING AND SPEAKING

Ikeda: For those who are suffering, just being heard can help lighten their burden. Having someone warmly listen to what one has to say is in itself encouragement to go on.

Psychologists have clinically verified such effects. Studies have found that, among those who have been deeply affected by stress from the death of a loved one or some other incident, the percentage of people who can continue living in good health is extremely high for those who have someone in whom they can confide. By contrast, a high percentage of those who have no one with whom they can discuss their grief suffer from a variety of illnesses ranging from headaches to internal diseases.

Harvard psychologist David McClelland showed that people in crisis who are disposed to keep their deepest feelings buried inside release hormones that actually lower their immune system's resistance to disease.[8] And Hebrew University psychiatrist Gerald Caplan concluded that "when the stress level is high, people without psychological support suffer as much as ten times the incidence of physical and emotional illness experienced by those who enjoy such support."[9]

Endo: Human relations are quite literally lifelines.

Suda: I think it's also important to meet people face to face. One study found that the more time people spend on the Internet, the greater their chances of becoming depressed or feeling isolated.

Saito: That's ironic since one of the Internet's main selling points is that it enables exchange of information and communication around the world.

Suda: It seems that the purpose of this study, which was conducted in the United States, was to establish that the Internet is a viable and effective medium of exchange.

Endo: But the results that they got were not at all what they expected.

Ikeda: I suppose that without human contact, there is no stimulation for our lives.

Saito: How fortunate we are to have the SGI organization!

Ikeda: We must not become isolated, nor must we isolate others. It's important that we listen to what is in the hearts of those beset with worries. By doing so, we ourselves are in fact healed. When we welcome and encourage others, we ourselves are encouraged and our hearts expanded.

Suda: It is certainly true that, even if your spirits are low, when you help others, your mood is naturally uplifted.

Ikeda: That's because we are connected to those around us. When we start practicing Nichiren Buddhism, most of us are consumed just with solving our own problems. In a sense, our faith at this stage may be comparable to that of someone turning to Perceiver of the World's Sounds for help. Of course, the fundamental difference here is that we put our faith in the Gohonzon.

At first, though, we essentially just want to be heard. Gradually our state of life grows to where we can listen to the troubles of others. We go from depending on Perceiver of the World's Sounds to ourselves becoming the bodhisattva Perceiver of the World's Sounds.

Endo: This is a remarkable transformation.

Ikeda: That's the wondrous power of the Mystic Law.

BUDDHAHOOD EMERGES FROM THE SWAMP OF SUFFERING

Ikeda: Why does this change occur? In fact, the world of Buddhahood has already begun to bud within the lives of those who earnestly cry, through their suffering, "I want to become happy!" To discern this is the original meaning of "perceiving the world's sounds."

As we touched on earlier, with regard to the name Perceiver of the World's Sounds, Nichiren Daishonin says that *perceive* means perfect perception, *world* means wondrous and *sounds* refers to the capacity for attaining Buddhahood. He also says that *world* refers to the beings of the Ten Worlds:

> [The element *kan*, or Perceiver] is another name for the Dharma-realm; hence, as already stated, it stands for perfect perception already attained. And because Perceiver of the World's Sounds is a perceiver of the true aspect of all phenomena, he can see and understand the different realms such as those of hell, hungry spirits, animals, etc. that make up this miraculous world. (OTT, 180)

The groans of beings in the world of hell are also the sounds of a wondrous world. They are sounds of the world of the Mystic Law. Because of the mutual possession of the Ten Worlds, the world of hell, just as it is, is an entity of the Ten Worlds and an entity of the world of Buddhahood. To recognize this is the perfect perception of Perceiver of the World's Sounds.

The Daishonin continues:

> *On*, or Sounds, refers to the sounds of the true aspect of all phenomena, and hence it means that there are no living beings that do not possess the true aspect of Buddhahood. This has been referred to, in the "Life Span" chapter, as the original state endowed with the Ten Worlds, the three bodies with which the Buddha is eternally endowed. (OTT, 180)

We need the ability to recognize the true aspect of Buddhahood in the sounds of suffering of all people. It is precisely within the swamp of reality of all phenomena that the beautiful lotus flower of the true entity blossoms. All beings are lotus flower Buddhas, entities of Myoho-renge-kyo. To recognize this is to "perceive the world's sounds."

Endo: Come to think of it, Perceiver of the World's Sounds is often depicted in statues as holding a lotus flower in his hand.

Ikeda: The lotus flower could be said to be a symbol of compassion.

The "Perceiver of the World's Sounds" chapter says, "He views living beings with compassionate eyes" (LSOC, 347). Viewing people with "compassionate eyes" is not the same as simply looking on them with pity. It is to view people with the awareness, "This person is in fact a Buddha, but he is suffering because he doesn't realize this."

People often suffer with such thoughts as: "This is too much," "It's all over," "I am the worst person" and "There is no point in living." We suffer because we seek happiness. The original desire of all people is to live a happy life. What is the purpose of a religion if it ignores these voices and discriminates among people?

If someone is suffering because of a failing business, for example, Bodhisattva Perceiver of the World's Sounds responds to these desperate "sounds" and does everything he can to help that person. He guides the person to a more profound state of absolute happiness, to the world of Buddhahood. Perceiver of the World's Sounds expresses this compassion of the original Buddha from the remote past.

Saito: He doesn't look down on the concerns of someone hoping for his business to prosper as "commonplace" or as "geared to immediate benefit."

Ikeda: He simply does not look down on others. Instead, he uses people's earthly desires to lead them to the enlightenment of Buddhahood, changing those desires into the energy to advance. He clearly perceives the essential truth that the bud from which the tree of enlightenment grows is contained in the desperate cries of someone trapped in the painful throes of earthly desires.

Saito: From this we can well understand the significance of the word *perceive* in his name. He doesn't merely listen to the world's sounds but perceives their true significance.

Endo: He doesn't listen with just his ears. He perceives with the wisdom of his whole life.

Ikeda: Bodhisattva Perceiver of the World's Sounds is described as having "the true gaze, the pure gaze, / the gaze of great and encompassing wisdom, / the gaze of pity, the gaze of compassion" (LSOC, 346). Because he has such faculties, he earnestly embraces all people without disparaging the voices of any.

Suda: In their voices, he perceives the capacity to become a Buddha, the "faculty of Buddhahood."

RESPONSIBILITY MEANS TO RESPOND

Ikeda: In any event, it is not easy to listen. Someone who knows how to listen humbly is by that virtue alone very wise. The Chinese character for *sage* means to listen with open ears to the sounds uttered by the universe. The virtue to be able to do this is called *so* and is made up of a Chinese character that also includes the element for "ear." This means that someone who can listen is wise.

In particular, SGI leaders must sensitively respond to the voices of all the members. We must not be insensitive. And we have to respond promptly.

The English word *responsibility* is derived from the word *respond*. A responsible person is someone who responds with great sincerity to the voices of the people.

Endo: In that sense, it occurs to me that there are all too many irresponsible politicians.

Suda: I can only imagine that their ears are basically clogged.

Ikeda: For precisely this reason, the people have to speak up.

Nothing is stronger than the voices of the people. Nothing is more real than the cries of the people. Nothing is more formidable than the anger of the people.

Bodhisattva Perceiver of the World's Sounds is said to freely manifest thirty-three forms. The sutra explains that he can manifest as Brahma, Lord Shakra or in the person of a ruler. This indicates that there will appear without fail politicians with the mercy of Perceiver of the World's Sounds who perceive and hear the voices of the people. Again, we have to see to it that such leaders appear.

When the cries of the people influence and move society, true democracy will be born.

NOTES

1. Jpn Kan'non or Kanzeon, Chn Kwan Yin or Kuan-yin, Skt Avalokitesvara.

2. While there are indications that this bodhisattva is a woman, and, indeed, the bodhisattva's origins can be traced to fertility and water goddesses, there are very few references to female Buddhas or bodhisattvas in the entire Buddhist canon. Furthermore, images of the bodhisattva reveal facial hair, and the bodhisattva's name in Sanskrit, Avalokitesvara, is a male name. According to some views, while Perceiver of the World's Sounds was originally a goddess, the bodhisattva was turned into a man when inducted into Buddhism. Some argue that, in exhibiting both female and male qualities, the bodhisattva transcends sexuality.

3. Mythological beings who work to protect Buddhism.

4. Shih K'uang and Li Lou: Legendary figures in China famed, respectively, for their extraordinary hearing and vision.

5. *Toda Josei zenshu* (Collected Writings of Josei Toda) (Tokyo: Seikyo Shimbunsha, 1983), vol. 3, pp. 162–63.

6. Ibid., 164–65.

7. *Yonosuke miki, ketsudanryoku* (Power of Decision Making) (Tokyo: Kobunsha, 1968), p. 28.

8. Julius Segal, *Winning Life's Toughest Battles: Roots of Human Resilience* (New York: Ivy Books, 1986), p. 20.

9. Ibid., 20–21.

4   Kosen-rufu Is the Ultimate Path in Life

*At that time the bodhisattva Inexhaustible Intent immedi-
ately rose from his seat, bared his right shoulder, pressed his
palms together and, facing the Buddha, spoke these words:
"World-Honored One, this Bodhisattva Perceiver of the
World's Sounds—why is he called Perceiver of the World's
Sounds?"*

*The Buddha said to Bodhisattva Inexhaustible Intent:
"Good man, suppose there are immeasurable hundreds, thousands, ten thousands, millions of living beings who are undergoing various trials and suffering. If they hear of this bodhisattva
Perceiver of the World's Sounds and single-mindedly call his
name, then at once he will perceive the sound of their voices and
they will all gain deliverance from their trials."* (LSOC, 339)

Ikeda: Incidentally, do you suppose Bodhisattva Perceiver of
the World's Sounds is a woman or a man?

Suda: Outwardly, there is every indication that this bodhisattva
is a woman. There are even statues of the bodhisattva holding
a baby.

Endo: But there aren't many references to female Buddhas or
bodhisattvas in the sutras. They are usually male. That's because
ancient India was a male-dominated society.

Also, if you closely examine an image of Bodhisattva Perceiver of the World's Sounds, you will find that it depicts facial

hair, a masculine characteristic. Furthermore, the bodhisattva's name in Sanskrit, Avalokitesvara, is a male name.

Suda: Some argue that in exhibiting both female and male qualities, the bodhisattva transcends gender.

Saito: According to the Buddhologist Yutaka Iwamoto, who taught at Soka University in Tokyo, while Perceiver of the World's Sounds was originally a goddess, the bodhisattva took on a male form when inducted into Buddhism.

Ikeda: That seems to be the case. I guess that settles it! The original Indian goddess was probably connected with the idea of a Great Mother or Earth Goddess.

Saito: So it appears.

Ikeda: Just as Mother Earth sustains, nourishes and fosters all living beings, Perceiver of the World's Sounds represents the compassion to lead all people to happiness.

Saito: That's right. Scholars tracing the bodhisattva's origins suggest connections with the Persian goddess Anahita and with fertility and water deities.

Suda: The origins of life can certainly be traced to water, as well as to the earth.

Endo: There are statues of Perceiver of the World's Sounds that depict the bodhisattva holding a water jar.

Ikeda: This bodhisattva is said to freely manifest thirty-three bodies (forms) or states of existence. This is analogous to the way that water naturally assumes any shape. Like water, life is not static; it is essentially non-substantial.[1]

Belief in Perceiver of the World's Sounds

Ikeda: So Bodhisattva Perceiver of the World's Sounds can take the form of either a man or a woman. Moreover, the secret of the bodhisattva's popularity lies in having retained the original characteristics of a goddess.

In the conclusion of *Faust*, Goethe says: "Woman, eternally, / shows us the way."[2] This is a principle of humanity common to both East and West.

Suda: It seems to me that worship of the Virgin Mary in Christianity has much in common with faith in Perceiver of the World's Sounds.

Ikeda: People tend to pray to Mary about their immediate hopes and aspirations.

Suda: Yes, they pray to Mary for many things in life, such as recovery from illness, easy childbirth and a peaceful death.

Endo: While belief in Jesus is the main pillar of Christianity, it might be that many Christians find Mary more approachable.

Suda: Some say that Mary is like a bridge between the absolute world of divinity and the world of human beings. It is believed that no matter how great a sin one has committed, by sincerely praying to Mary, Mary will intercede with God on that person's behalf without passing judgment.

Saito: She is like a gentle mother who stands by her delinquent child as the child apologizes to its father for misbehaving.

Ikeda: Mothers are great. Children feel absolutely secure when embraced by their mother. Fathers, on the other hand, are no match for mothers, as their embrace sometimes leads to more tears.

Scholars of religion suggest that faith in Mary reflects belief in the Earth Goddess. But according to Jungian research in the area of depth psychology, in addition to the positive aspects of giving birth, nourishing and embracing, the Great Mother also tends to hold her children too tightly and sometimes devours them. This latter aspect might be comparable to the function of the Goddess Mother of Demon Children in Buddhism who killed the babies of others to feed her own children. Though Goethe alludes to an eternal benevolent femininity, it can be represented in ways that are exact opposites, such as in the form of Bodhisattva Perceiver of the World's Sounds or in the Goddess Mother of Demon Children, who both appear in the Lotus Sutra.

Suda: Dependency on a "comfortable" way of faith is infantile regression.

One researcher on the cult of Mary has pointed out that past images of Mary as a fragile girl have in more recent times been replaced by images of an adult woman exuding self-confidence and dignity. At the same time, the scholar notes, believers have regressed to a childlike state. She writes, "They gather together within the mantle of the holy mother like baby chicks, and simply intone prayers with their rosaries and await a miracle, creating a relationship based solely on sentimentality."[3]

Ikeda: When Christians in Japan went underground [as a result of persecution during much of the seventeenth, eighteenth and nineteenth centuries], it is said that they would conceal their faith in Mary by praying to Perceiver of the World's Sounds as a kind of surrogate. The compound proper name "Mary Perceiver of the World's Sounds" (Maria Kannon) that came into use in Japan as a result of this dramatically shows the similarity of belief in Perceiver of the World's Sounds to the cult of Mary.

In any event, history seems to show that both faith in Perceiver of the World's Sounds and faith in Mary developed and spread not because the clergy promoted them but as a result of the people's own desire.

Saito: Concerning the inclusion of Bodhisattva Perceiver of the World's Sounds in the Lotus Sutra, there seems to have been a very popular Indian goddess from whom Perceiver of the World's Sounds derived.

Ikeda: It's interesting that a goddess people at the time believed in and treasured was actively inducted into and brought to life in the Lotus Sutra. That in itself is an expression of the compassion to perceive the world's sounds—to know the hearts and minds of the people. Buddhism does not exist apart from the realities of the age and the people.

Saito: I think that the "Perceiver of the World's Sounds" chapter's clear promise of benefit in the present life conveys this same spirit.

Ikeda: Reality is reality, and theory is theory. Life is reality. Buddhism focuses on reality, and we practice faith to win in reality.

The saha world is itself the Land of Eternally Tranquil Light. To escape from reality is not the spirit of the Lotus Sutra. The Lotus Sutra teaches how to make our reality ideal. Buddhism is about winning in life.

Some might think it shallow to speak of attaining benefit in the present life, but I believe a religion that does not enable people to transform their lives is powerless. The Mystic Law exists so that we may enjoy "peace and security in the present existence" and "good circumstances in future existences" (see LSOC, 136). Creating value in daily life is the heart of the Lotus Sutra.

A World Religion Must Enable People To Gain Benefit in the Present

Endo: Professor Jan Van Bragt of Nanzan University in Japan argues that a true world religion must serve society's needs, have the ability to influence society, contribute to world peace, be thoroughly humanistic and respond to people's expectations for attaining benefit in this lifetime.

Ikeda: Reality is what matters. Mahatma Gandhi proclaimed, "Religion which takes no count of practical affairs and does not help to solve them, is no religion."[4] A religion that cannot respond to the problems and worries people are facing right now, he declared, is a religion in name only.

The fact is that many Japanese religions craftily take advantage of people's religious ignorance and have managed to endure by promising benefit in the present life. Their approach might be compared to luring children with candy. From the early days, the Soka Gakkai has been criticized as preaching benefit in the present in much the same way as these other schools. But the Lotus Sutra, humankind's supreme spiritual legacy, authoritatively teaches the gains to be had in this lifetime from Buddhist practice. It does so because the most important function of religion is to enable people to be truly happy.

The Soka Gakkai has fought against all manner of human suffering, giving hope to those struggling with illness, financial problems, domestic discord and so on. This itself is the spirit of the Lotus Sutra. We have been the greatest ally of the suffering and the poor. I take great pride in this.

Religion has no meaning if it avoids the serious question of how to encourage those suffering and how to help them out of it. I discussed this point from various angles with Dr. Bryan Wilson of the University of Oxford.[5]

PRAYER IS SUBLIME PROOF OF HUMANITY

Saito: Suppose a child becomes deathly ill. In addition to seeking the help of a physician, the parents would surely pray wholeheartedly for their child to recover. I'm certain that even if they didn't practice a particular religion, they would offer some kind of prayer. Prayer is not to be taken lightly. It is a natural human response.

Suda: I think it would be cold and inhumane to dismiss the desire to pray.

Ikeda: Prayer is unique to human beings. Animals do not have the ability to pray. It is sublime proof of our humanity.

In ancient times, people stood in awe of the immensity and boundlessness of nature. It may be that they deeply revered what they saw as a great presence beyond their human intelligence to fathom, and from this the desire to pray naturally emerged.

When people face a crisis, such as, for instance, any of the seven disasters[6] described in the "Perceiver of the World's Sounds" chapter, they desperately wish to be protected. Prayer is the crystallization of those earnest feelings. This is what gave birth to religion.

Endo: Religion did not come before prayer; prayer in fact came first.

Ikeda: How do we have our prayers answered? Buddhism clarifies this in terms of the law of life. It expounds the Mystic Law, the key that causes the gears of the microcosm—the self—to mesh perfectly with the macrocosm—the universe.

Worrying About Children

Saito: Along those lines, the "Perceiver of the World's Sounds" chapter says:

> If a woman wishes to give birth to a male child, she should offer obeisance and alms to Bodhisattva Perceiver of the World's Sounds and then she will bear a son blessed with merit, virtue, and wisdom. And if she wishes to bear a daughter, she will bear one with all the marks of comeliness, one who, having planted the roots of virtue in the past, is loved and respected by many persons. (LSOC, 340)

Ikeda: This is saying that the prayers of parents definitely affect their child's birth. Through the faith of parents, children will develop outstanding attributes.

Many parents worry over their children. Nichiren Daishonin in fact teaches that children may either be a blessing or a bane, saying: "There is a sutra passage that says that children are one's enemies" (WND-1, 1043); and "There is also a sutra passage that says that children are a treasure" (WND-1, 1044).

While people without children may long to have them, I hope that when they do have children, they will remember that they will suffer unless their children are good. Also, it is important to treat our fellow members with the same concern we would our own children, for nobler than the connection of blood is the connection between people brought together by lofty ideals and the fostering of spiritual heirs.

People who suffer because of their children can use that obstacle to strengthen their faith. It could even be argued that this is the reason that children cause their parents to worry. Children will become happy without fail when their parents attain Buddhahood.

While the "Perceiver of the World's Sounds" chapter speaks

of the benefit of offering obeisance and alms to Bodhisattva
Perceiver of the World's Sounds, this of course means praying
and making offerings to the Gohonzon. As evidence of this,
Perceiver of the World's Sounds presents the offerings made to
him to the Buddhas Shakyamuni and Many Treasures.

Endo: Bodhisattva Inexhaustible Intent offers a necklace
adorned with numerous precious gems to Perceiver of the
World's Sounds. But Perceiver of the World's Sounds declines
to accept it.

After Shakyamuni entreats Perceiver of the World's Sounds
to accept the gift, the bodhisattva complies. He then divides
the necklace into two parts, which he presents to Shakyamuni
and the tower of the Buddha Many Treasures (see LSOC, 344).

Suda: In terms of the implicit meaning of the sutra, Shakyamuni
and the tower of the Buddha Many Treasures represent the
Mystic Law, the Gohonzon. In other words, this teaches that
we should make the Mystic Law, not Perceiver of the World's
Sounds, our foundation.

Endo: I would really like for the many people who place their
faith in Perceiver of the World's Sounds to pay attention to
this passage.

Saito: In "Repaying Debts of Gratitude," the Daishonin says:

> If one chants Nam-myoho-renge-kyo, then the
> power of the words Namu Amida Butsu, the power
> of the mantras invoking Mahavairochana, the power
> of Bodhisattva Perceiver of the World's Sounds, and
> the power of all the Buddhas, all the sutras, and
> all the bodhisattvas will without exception vanish
> before the power of Myoho-renge-kyo.
> Unless these other sutras manage to borrow the

power of Myoho-renge-kyo, they will all become worthless things. (WND-I, 732–33)

THE BENEFICIAL POWER OF PERCEIVER OF THE WORLD'S SOUNDS IS NAM-MYOHO-RENGE-KYO

Ikeda: To embrace the Gohonzon is to embrace the entire universe. It is to tap the source of the power of the universe. One who does so is worthy of the utmost respect. Such a person is hundreds, thousands, tens or hundreds of thousands of times nobler than the founders of the various religious schools who are revered as gods and Buddhas. People don't realize this.

It is vital that we treat our fellow members exerting themselves for kosen-rufu with the highest respect and honor. This is the fundamental spirit of the SGI. As long as we uphold this spirit, we will never become deadlocked.

Endo: With regard to prayer, people frequently bring up the problem of extraneous thoughts occurring to them while they are chanting.

Ikeda: There is nothing wrong with having an active mind while chanting. This is a natural human tendency. The important thing is to face the Gohonzon just as we are, without affectation.

Having extraneous thoughts is an inherent part of our lives in that we are entities of the principle of three thousand realms in a single moment of life. Therefore, through daimoku we can turn even those thoughts into benefit.

There are no rules governing how we should pray. There's no need to be something we aren't. Even if we were to try to control our thoughts by making our prayer rigid and forced, our minds would still tend to wander. As we deepen our faith, we also strengthen our ability to concentrate.

Actually, since the thoughts or ideas that come to mind as we chant represent issues that concern us at that moment, we should not consider them extraneous. Instead, we should pray earnestly about each one, whatever it may be. Rather than chant only about large issues, we should pray specifically about every issue we face, winning over each one and strengthening our foundation as we go.

There is of course no need to be tense or nervous when praying. What matters is that we are completely ourselves.

Endo: People also wonder whether it is all right to chant for many things at the same time, or if they should concentrate on one issue at a time.

Ikeda: There's no limit to how many things we can pray about. It just means that the more desires we have, the more sincere and abundant our prayer will be. It's just like if you want to do a lot of shopping, you need a lot of money. Buddhism is reason.

Saito: It occurs to me that questions such as this one might arise from the misconception that the Gohonzon "hears" our prayers and then solves them supernaturally.

Ikeda: Who answers our prayers? We do—through faith and effort. No one does it for us.

Returning to the shopping analogy, it is the same as using our own money when we go shopping. Having our own money is a prerequisite. The "currency" of prayer is our practice of faith.

"No Prayer Goes Unanswered"

Suda: Some people have expressed concern because some of their prayers have not been answered.

Ikeda: We are practicing a faith in which no prayer goes

unanswered. We must first and foremost be convinced of this. There will be times, however, when our prayers seem to be answered and times when they do not. As long as we continue to pray, in the end everything will go in the best possible direction. This will be clear when we look back later.

More than anything, it is the struggle we go through to have our prayers answered that makes us stronger. If we were to immediately get everything we prayed for, we would become spoiled and decadent. We would lead indolent lives, devoid of hard work or struggle. As a result, we would become shallow human beings. What, then, would be the point of faith?

Life is a series of events and problems. We face all manner of troubles. This is the way life goes. But this variety enables us to lead a fulfilled and joyful existence, to grow and to develop an expansive and strong state of life.

Endo: Certainly, if all SGI members were to pray to win the lottery, it would be impossible for everyone to have their prayer answered!

Ikeda: If everything that we prayed for came true instantly, it would be no different than magic. This goes against reason. You can't make steamed rice by simply turning on the rice cooker if you haven't put in any rice.

Buddhism is common sense. It teaches the correct path in which our faith is expressed in how we live. There is no such thing as faith that ignores reality. Our desires will not be realized without making any real effort.

A Religion That Cannot Reply to People's Prayers Is Useless

Endo: Religions that promise immediate benefit are often criticized as inferior. Along those lines, I certainly feel that religions that make people dependent ought to be refuted.

Suda: Faith that seeks selfish gain by invoking some sort of mysterious force could well be described as magic.

Saito: On one side, there are religions that preach only inner fulfillment; on the other, there are those that promise mysterious benefit in the present life without any real effort. Both of these depart from the reality of human life, the reality of the oneness of body and mind. On that level, they are similar.

Endo: One is abstract, the other, preposterous.

Suda: I think we could also say that one lacks compassion, and the other lacks wisdom.

Ikeda: True religion is found in neither way of thought. True religion does not depart from reality; it reveals the fundamental law based on which people can improve their lives in reality. The first Soka Gakkai president, Tsunesaburo Makiguchi, termed this *value creation.* In refuting a view on religion articulated by an eminent scientist[7] of the day, Mr. Makiguchi declared that a religion that does not produce value in response to prayer is useless.[8]

This scholar had argued that while people sense the divine in wondrous laws of nature, things that cannot be understood through the natural sciences ought to be left unknown. And he asserted that it therefore defies good reason to pray to the gods for personal gain.

Suda: That's a typical criticism.

Ikeda: By contrast, President Makiguchi asserted that a religion not concerned with creating value in human life is useless. To ignore the reality of life is to ignore the human being.

Wondrous phenomena are not limited to the realm of nature. Mr. Makiguchi believed that human life itself and day-to-day occurrences are also wondrous, and that one ought to seek the wondrous power of life force that enables people to create value and realize victory. He stated that the natural sciences alone cannot lead people to happiness, and that what is needed is a science of value. His insight penetrates the basic flaw of modern civilization.

Saito: President Makiguchi also opposed the idea that the sacred is exclusive to religion. He argued that religion that exists merely for the sake of religion has no meaning.

Concerning such values as the sacred and inner peace: these accord with the value of gain, or benefit, where the individual is concerned and the value of good[9]—moral and ethical value—with respect to society. Mr. Makiguchi posed the question: "What is the significance of a religion if not to help people become happy and improve the world? Isn't the act of helping people become happy the value of gain? Isn't improving the world the value of good?"[10]

Ikeda: In short, it is hypocrisy to avoid the actual struggle of helping people become happy and improving the world while preaching the sacred as though it existed on another lofty dimension.

Helping people become happy and improving the world—this is kosen-rufu. This great struggle to grapple with reality is itself value creation and true religion. The sacred exists only in the midst of such struggle. Isn't peace also a form of benefit in this life?

There is profound meaning in the term *world* of "Bodhisattva Perceiver of the World's Sounds." We cannot separate ourselves from reality. The world is society. We are engaged in a struggle to create a happy society. *Sounds,* on the other hand, means the cries of individual living beings, their personal desire for happiness. It is Bodhisattva Perceiver of the World's Sounds, in other words, the Lotus Sutra, that unifies these two goals of social prosperity and individual happiness.

Endo: Certainly, those who care only about their own happiness become egotistic. By contrast, an exclusive preoccupation with the demands of society at the expense of the individual readily lends itself to totalitarianism and nationalism. The balancing of these two is most difficult.

Balancing the Individual and Society, Freedom and Equality

Suda: When Vice Chancellor Vrajendra Mehta of the University of Delhi visited Japan [in January 1999] to present you with an honorary doctorate in literature, President Ikeda, I recall that in his remarks the Indian educator emphasized the Middle Way.

Ikeda: That's right. He is a great philosopher and a distinguished political scientist. He remarked:

> The traditional way of thinking in the modern West has swung to the extremes of individualism and collectivism. This has unfortunately resulted in loss of the self. In contrast to these two "isms," Gandhi and other Indian thinkers have tried to respond by returning to traditions that have existed from ancient times. This is the thought of the Dharma, which views all things as mutually related, and the thought of nirvana, which is the ultimate transcendent ideal. Similarly, Mr. Makiguchi and Mr. Toda emphasized that individuals create value through their relationship with society.

From the standpoint of the philosophy of value creation, individual happiness and social prosperity are definitely not opposed. They are actually closely related, like the rotation and revolution of the earth. Through exerting oneself for the well-being of society, one becomes happy. And society must strive to bring happiness to each person.

Suda: It's a case of "one for all, and all for one."

Ikeda: Dr. Mehta also said:

> The universe is held together by organic relations. By this I mean the relations between man and nature, man and man, and man and the cosmos. This is not the relation between "part" and "whole." Man and nature and the universe—each of these is itself a totality. It is something irreplaceable that has a purpose.

What a profound view of life! To live based on the Law or Dharma, the correct path in life, means to advance along the Middle Way.

Endo: This surely does not mean taking the path of least resistance.

Ikeda: It means to find and stay on the right path—to hit the mark or target. Never to stray from the correct path as a human being, to live always on course and in accord with the law of life—that's what is meant by the Middle Way. It is humanism.

Dr. Mehta characterized the nineteenth century as a century in pursuit of freedom, and the twentieth as a century in pursuit of equality. And he said that the twenty-first must be a century that pursues justice.

Freedom and equality, individualism and collectivism—it is justice that balances these opposing forces. It is the Dharma. It is the Middle Way. This is how we must usher in the "third civilization."

Endo: This is a clear manifesto for the twenty-first century.

Ikeda: Returning to the earlier topic of prayer, following the Middle Way is to steadfastly advance along the correct path in which daily life equals faith and faith manifests itself in one's efforts. It is neither abstract "placebo faith" nor effortless "magical faith."

Saito: We need to continue chanting and taking action until our prayers are realized. Then, in the end, we will attain a state of ultimate fulfillment. Life is about such struggle.

Ikeda: Whether our prayers are answered depends on our faith. The depth of our karma also affects the result of our prayer. Sometimes it just takes time. Whether and when our prayers are answered can have a variety of meanings. But there is no doubt about the fact that our lives begin to change in a favorable direction from the very moment we begin to pray.

Suda: Is this true even of self-centered prayer?

Ikeda: It is human nature to think of oneself. The important thing is that we go to the Gohonzon just as we are. If we put on an air of nobility, as if all our concerns are lofty ones, then we are presenting a false self. The Gohonzon does not respond to lies.

When we chant daimoku about our greatest worries and our deepest wishes, our state of life improves, and we gradually develop the mind to pray not just for ourselves but for the happiness of our friends and for kosen-rufu. Also, I think it is vital to challenge ourselves to pray for such lofty goals. It is all up to us—we are free to pray about anything we wish.

ENEMIES ON EVERY SIDE

Ikeda: Each day, I pray only for the attainment of kosen-rufu and for the health, longevity, prosperity and happiness of all SGI members. I believe that this is my fundamental responsibility and mission.

To be the one bearing all the responsibility is no easy task. I will never forget the words of Madame Deng Yingchao (widow of the Chinese premier Zhou Enlai): "We had enemies on every side. That was the situation every single day. It was like that for years, for decades. We really fought hard."

It is the same with the Soka Gakkai. We have been surrounded by enemies. Politicians, priests, the media, traitorous former members—all have united their forces with the aim of stamping out the people's advance and attacking me personally. They have resorted to all kinds of base ploys.

Alone, I have fought and surmounted these attacks and protected all the members. I have not let down my guard for a single moment. I could not afford to. As a result, the Soka Gakkai has developed into a dignified international organization. I have prayed single-mindedly to the Gohonzon to open a boundless, hope-filled path toward the spread of this Buddhism and a peaceful world. I wish for all leaders to have this same spirit, without which our organization will succumb to bureaucratism.

Leaders must work wholeheartedly with the prayer and determination to help every member in their areas become happy without fail. To wage a genuine struggle, we must abandon our egos. To win or lose, to live or die—everything is a decisive battle. Terrible things can happen when people take their responsibilities lightly.

One month before his death, Professor Yudo Takada, the founder of my alma mater, Fuji College (formerly Taisei Gakuin), said: "Education means imparting life to students." What noble words! He firmly believed that education meant devoting oneself completely to one's students. What distinguishes a truly humane educator is the ability to treasure, love and work hard on behalf of students as though they were one's own children.

The same applies to leaders of kosen-rufu. In this world, only the SGI is working to achieve a peaceful world through the spread of Nichiren Buddhism. The SGI is the sole body of people dedicated to the sublime goal of fulfilling the Buddha's will.

In a sense, the course or orbit along which the SGI is advancing kosen-rufu is itself the Dharma. As we live in accord with this Dharma, or Law, we can accomplish our own human revolution and attain enlightenment. The relation between our individual enlightenment and the propagation of Buddhism is like that of a planet's rotation on its axis and revolution in its orbit around the sun. Those with a self-centered practice may be compared to a planet that only rotates on its axis and does not revolve around the sun. While such people might appear to enjoy good circumstances, they actually wind up falling out of rhythm and becoming lonely and isolated. Instead of being self-centered, we should center on the Dharma, or the Law. This is what is meant by the phrase "Rely on the Law and not upon persons" (WND-1, 105).

TAKING ACTION FOR KOSEN-RUFU ALLOWS OUR LIVES TO BLOSSOM

Ikeda: Our lives are like a flower. They are entities of Myoho-renge-kyo. Only by taking action for kosen-rufu can we cause this lotus flower to blossom. To just pray without taking action for kosen-rufu is like trying to raise a flower on water without sunlight. Under such circumstances, there is no true blossoming of the self.

When we exert ourselves for kosen-rufu, we are protected without fail. We must not separate ourselves from our friends and comrades in the SGI. The SGI is a castle of peace and tranquillity, a treasure land. The degree to which the SGI has served to protect us is truly remarkable.

President Toda used to say, "The Soka Gakkai organization is more precious to me than my own life." Those who treat the organization dedicated to kosen-rufu lightly only invite the same treatment by Brahma, Shakra and all the Buddhist deities. They have no time for such people.

At any rate, ordinary SGI members who are painstakingly carrying out activities for kosen-rufu are treasures more precious than any celebrity.

Endo: President Ikeda, I recall the episode involving King Ashoka that you brought up in your discussion with visiting scholars from the University of Delhi. Ashoka at one time placed offerings before stupas erected in tribute to the Buddha's disciples. He made offerings and prayed at the stupas honoring Shariputra, Maudgalyayana, Mahakashyapa, Ananda and others. But before the stupa to Bakkula he made only a small offering. Thinking this peculiar, an attendant inquired: "This person is equally a disciple of the Buddha. Why do you make such a distinction?" The king replied, "It is because while it seems that he wholeheartedly exerted himself in his practice, he did not expound the Law to others and did not contribute to society." The king took as a standard for Buddhist practitioners those who exert themselves for the widespread propagation of Buddhism and for the good of society.

Suda: When Professor Seba Singh Rana, a leading authority on King Ashoka, heard you relate this story, he remarked, "If people simply keep knowledge to themselves, not sharing it or putting it to use for the benefit of others, it turns into 'poison.'" His words impressed me deeply.

Ikeda: Poison symbolizes a cold and hellish heart. People whose lives are dominated by the worlds of hell and hunger resent and envy the happiness of others, and they are consumed by the desire to cause others to fall into the state of hell.

By contrast, those who dwell in the worlds of bodhisattva and Buddhahood are overwhelmed by the desire to help others become happy. The SGI is a compassionate group whose members are dedicated to becoming happy themselves and helping others do the same. Kosen-rufu is a movement to expand this life current of compassion—the very thing that society needs most—and with it to nourish the world.

Even if it seems that our individual impact is very small, by moving we can create waves. The continuous flow of one wave after another is itself kosen-rufu.

Endo: I think that this is the means for detoxifying a society poisoned with mercilessness and brutality.

SEEING THROUGH THE "POISON" OF NATIONALISM

Saito: This conversation calls to mind the words of a scholar who had investigated the history of persecution of the Jewish people. How was it possible that a person such as Adolf Hitler could become the supreme leader of a country of such rich cultural heritage as Germany? How could people have been so totally taken in by the ridiculous idea that the Jewish people were the fundamental source of all evil and misery, and that it was only natural that they be slaughtered? This scholar writes:

> Many answers have been given and perhaps many are needed, for no single theory can satisfactorily explain Hitler's phenomenal success with the German people. They were mesmerized by his voice, and they responded to his message. Was it because their moral sense, at least with regard to the Jews, had become

atrophied under the effect of generations of virulent anti–Semitism? Had the German people already become mithridatized by anti–Semitic poison, so that they had become immune even to Hitler's deadly brand?[11]

Her remarks drive home just how dangerous and frightening it is if people are "mithridatized"—desensitized to such poison.

Ikeda: It's the same in Japan. People are losing their sense of human rights. There is a nationalism growing that has no qualms about making people victims of the state. It is a dangerous situation. We therefore have no alternative but to stand up.

Endo: Although Japan's constitution is founded upon the ideal of creating peace through soft power, this ideal is now being trampled upon.

Suda: Justifications for Japan's past war of aggression in Asia are being advanced with tremendous vigor. Most alarming is the prominence in the media of such propaganda that appeals to members of the younger generation.

Saito: At the same time, the spirit of resistance has all but disappeared, resulting in an atmosphere where people think it is best simply to leave everything up to those in power. This certainly goes for the media. The abject tendency of the public to follow the prevailing current without question is truly pathetic.

THE LEGACY OF JAPANESE RELIGION AS A SLAVE TO POWER

[Concerning the thirty-three bodies that Bodhisattva Perceiver of the World's Sounds manifests in order to benefit living beings,] the Record of the Orally Transmitted Teachings says: The number "thirty" stands for the doctrine of

three thousand realms [in a single moment of life]. The "three bodies" stand for the doctrine of the three truths.

Again, we may say regarding the thirty-three bodies or bodily transformations that, if one is endowed with the three bodies in each of the Ten Worlds, this constitutes thirty bodies, and if the original three bodies are then added in, we have a total of thirty-three bodies.

Generally speaking, [concerning thirty or "three multiplied by ten"], the number three stands for the three categories of action, namely, actions of the body, mouth, and mind or physical, verbal, and mental actions, while the number ten[12] stands for the Ten Worlds. The number three [of thirty-three] may stand for the three poisons of greed, anger, and foolishness. The word "bodies" represents the bodies of all living beings.

Now when Nichiren and his followers chant Nam-myoho-renge-kyo, they are enjoying the benefits of the thirty-three bodies or bodily transformations. (OTT, 182–83)

Ikeda: The primary reason the spirit to oppose authority among Japanese is so weak is that religion in the country has long been spineless. This is what the nineteenth-century leading thinker and educator Yukichi Fukuzawa argued in his work *An Outline of a Theory of Civilization.*

Endo: I recall that in this work he harshly denounced priests as "slaves of the government."

Ikeda: He writes:

> Religion works within the hearts of men. It is something absolutely free and independent, not controlled in any way by others or dependent upon their powers. But while this is the way religion ought to be, such has not been the case here in Japan . . .

Buddhism, too, has belonged to the ruling class and has depended upon the patronage of the ruling class ever since its introduction . . . The worst of [the Buddhist monks] even felt proud when the government made them peers. . . .

Buddhism has flourished, true. But its teaching has been entirely absorbed by political authority. What shines throughout the world is not the radiance of Buddha's teachings but the glory of Buddhism's political authority . . .

Thus we can say that the Buddhist monks were slaves of the government. More recently, the government has passed a law that permits Buddhist priests throughout the country to eat meat and get married. The fact that prior to this law these priests were unable to eat meat or get married was not because they were keeping some kind of religious precept. Rather, they refrained from these things because they did not have the government's permission. From this, then, we can conclude that the monks have been slaves of the government; indeed, we can even conclude that at present there is no real religion in Japan.[13]

Saito: Religion, which ought to become a mainstay of people's spiritual independence, has long been in such a deplorable state that it is quite natural the Japanese people's spirit to fight authority remains weak.

Ikeda: For precisely this reason, the Soka Gakkai movement in Japan is a cultural, human and spiritual revolution on the most fundamental level.

Nichiren Daishonin, while enduring a barrage of attacks from priests who had become slaves to power, calmly described the sovereign of Japan as a "ruler of this little island country" (WND-1, 765). In society, everything has its limits. Buddhism is unlimited. The Daishonin knew that even the most powerful person is no match for the Mystic Law and that the powerful therefore ought to humbly seek the true teaching.

A little earlier we talked about President Makiguchi's theory of value. Mr. Makiguchi's decree that "religion is worthy of the name only if it can lead people to happiness and improve society" is linked directly with Nichiren Daishonin. Our movement is continually tapping the wellspring of religion to send a fresh spiritual current into society. It is ever engaged with society. This is also the spirit of Bodhisattva Perceiver of the World's Sounds, who has the ability to manifest any form he chooses.

The sutra describes him as assuming thirty-three bodies to preach the Law and lead people to happiness. These bodies include the forms of a Buddha, a cause-awakened one, a voice-hearer, King Brahma, Lord Shakra, the heavenly being Freedom, the heavenly being Great Freedom, a great general of heaven, Vaishravana, a petty king, a rich man, a householder, a chief minister, a Brahman, a monk, a nun, a layman believer, a laywoman believer, the wife of a rich man, of a householder, of a chief minister or of a Brahman, a young boy or a young girl, a heavenly being, a dragon, a *yaksha*, a *gandharva*, an *asura*, a *garuda*, a *kimnara*, a *mahoraga*, a human or a nonhuman being and a *vajra*-bearing god (see LSOC, 342–43).

Saito: He can manifest all forms, including even those not mentioned in the sutra.

Ikeda: This indicates the importance of respecting all individuals, whatever their station. There are occasions when any person may fulfill the function of a Buddha or bodhisattva. We must never judge a person based on status, line of work or appearance.

"Politics Without Religion Is Dead"

Suda: The Lotus Sutra is a teaching directed toward society.

Ikeda: It is indeed. From the fundamental level of religion, the Lotus Sutra constantly purifies, refreshes and revitalizes society.

With regard to the relationship of religion and politics, Dr. N. Radhakrishnan[14] related to me [in 1994] that Gandhi once said: "Politics that is bereft of religion is dead and lifeless!" Gandhi also said: "It is a noose that will hang the nation."[15]

Saito: I completely agree.

Ikeda: While Yukichi Fukuzawa said that Japanese religion is a slave of the government, Gandhi, by contrast, called for transforming politics by infusing it, through religious spirituality, with moral compassion.

In late sixth- or early seventh-century Japan, the Seventeen-Article Constitution of Prince Shotoku includes the exhortation to "devoutly revere the three treasures."[16] There was thus the idea that the political authorities, too, should behave in accord with universal truth.

Some religions collaborate with power and become its slaves. There are also those who isolate themselves from society, turning a blind eye to politics. But this only passively supports the growth of pernicious power, ultimately allowing it to thrive. There is also a third path in which religion neither unites with power and assists it, nor abets power through a hands-off approach. This is the path of establishing the correct teaching for the peace of the land, which Nichiren Daishonin espoused.

It aims, from the standpoint of the eternal truth of the correct teaching, to engage in and revolutionize reality. This is the sole noble path by which religion can avoid becoming a slave to power. Yet for precisely this reason, it is a path occasioned by persecution and difficulties, which means it is the genuine article.

Establishing Ethics in Economics

Saito: We have already discussed the principle in the "Perceiver of the World's Sounds" chapter of attaining benefit in the present. An abstract religious view that rejects the creation of value in daily life will not become a vibrant force in society.

Conversely, an easygoing teaching of immediate gain will neither help people open up their inner lives nor give them the ability to transform society even at great personal sacrifice. These are opposite extremes, and I think that both would be very convenient for those in power.

Ikeda: In Japan, not only have priests become slaves to power but so have most intellectuals, leading members of the business world and ordinary citizens. By rights, the powerful and society's leaders should serve as the hands and feet of the people. They are a means for the people's happiness; they are public servants. This concept, however, has been turned on its head.

Endo: While such people may call themselves public servants, "public" here does not mean the people but the state or the present system. The idea that public servants are supposed to serve not the people but the system is frightening.

Suda: I guess that nothing will change in Japan unless the basic tenet of democracy that the state is a means that has the people's happiness as its end is really driven home to the Japanese people.

Ikeda: People who are without the invisible authority of the spiritual realm (i.e., religion) readily adhere to visible authority (i.e., the political and social hierarchy).

The Buddhism of value creation that seeks to breathe life into society is not limited to politics. Just as Perceiver of the World's Sounds can manifest all manner of forms, the stage on which we carry out our Buddhist activities encompasses all spheres of society, including, for example, economics.

Gandhi espoused an economics of justice, saying:

> An economics that inculcates mammon worship and enables the strong to amass wealth at the expense of the weak, is a false and dismal science. It spells death. True economics, on the other hand, stands for social justice, it promotes the good of all equally, including the weakest.[17]

The worship of wealth makes the strong arrogant and the weak servile, corrupting the spirit of both. The essence of economics lies in fostering the wisdom to bring happiness to all people, particularly the destitute. This is what is meant by an "economics of justice." It accords with the true meaning of economics, which in Japanese is a contraction of a phrase literally meaning to "govern society and save the people."

Saito: Professor Amartya Sen of Cambridge University's Trinity College in England, who received an honorary doctorate from the University of Delhi at the same time as you, President Ikeda, is also an advocate of ethics in economics.

Ikeda: Professor Sen was the first Asian to win the Nobel Prize for economics. He was born in the village where the great Indian poet Rabindranath Tagore ran an academy, and he was in fact given his name by Tagore.

Saito: When he was nine, Professor Sen experienced the Great Bengal Famine of 1943, in which approximately three million people died of starvation. He explains that this experience inspired him to study economics so he could help the poor. He has consistently advocated ethical standards in economics.

Ikeda: How noble!

In his theory of value, President Makiguchi included gain among the three major values of beauty, gain and good. He clearly stated that gain that does not benefit the public interest is evil and antivalue.

Without a system of values to guide economic activity, economics becomes devoted to nothing more than money-making for the sake of making money and economic growth for the sake of economic growth. There is the danger that such a situation will spin out of control.

Endo: Japan's bubble economy [in the late 1980s] would be a classic example of this.

Ikeda: President Makiguchi's theory of value could therefore be said to aspire toward an economics of justice.

Suda: These days in Japan all one hears people talking about is "restoring prosperity." It's as though people think that returning to economic expansion will solve all the country's problems.

While economic growth is of course very important, nothing would be more wasteful than for Japanese society to simply pursue past dreams of economic prosperity without changing its underlying values.

Saito: It would mean that the country had learned nothing from the bursting of the economic bubble, which resulted in such turmoil that it has been dubbed the second defeat in war.

Nichiren Buddhism Is Based on Making a Vow

> *He views living beings with compassionate eyes.*
> *The sea of his accumulated blessings is immeasurable.* (LSOC, 347)

This passage is saying that because both the objective and subjective aspects of the Dharma-realm are part of the Wonderful Law, the Buddha looks on every living being equally, as though he or she were his only child. The blessings and wisdom of the objective and subjective worlds are immeasurable. Nam-myoho-renge-kyo has these two elements of blessings and wisdom. (OTT, 218)

Ikeda: The kosen-rufu movement in Japan is an effort to transform this land devoid of philosophy and culture into one that is rich with humanism. If the struggle for kosen-rufu is forgotten, then even Nichiren Buddhism will become no better than the selfish religions that have heretofore prevailed.

Suda: The Nichiren Shoshu priesthood is a case in point.

Ikeda: When we take action for kosen-rufu with a selfless spirit, the microcosm of our lives fuses with the macrocosm of the universe and our prayers are answered. The Daishonin says, "It could never come about that the prayers of the practitioner of the Lotus Sutra would go unanswered" (WND-1, 345). So the issue becomes whether one is a practitioner of the Lotus Sutra.

Nichiren Daishonin's teaching is about making a vow. In our present situation we need to pledge to the Gohonzon: "I will advance kosen-rufu to the best of my ability! I will realize victory without fail!" Our prayer starts from this vow.

In explaining the origins of Bodhisattva Perceiver of the World's Sounds, the sutra says, "His vast oath is deep as the ocean" (LSOC, 344), meaning that his pledge to spread Buddhism is profound. It further states that, as a result of this oath, "The sea of his accumulated blessings is immeasurable" (LSOC, 347).

Nichiren Daishonin says regarding this passage, "The blessings and wisdom of both the objective and subjective worlds are immeasurable. Nam-myoho-renge-kyo has these two elements of blessings and wisdom" (OTT, 218). In other words, both we and our immediate environment gain tremendous good fortune and wisdom.

Some people tend to be wise while others possess good fortune. Everyone is of course unique, but if we have wisdom yet lack good fortune then our efforts will come to nothing; we cannot create happiness for ourselves. If, on the other hand, we have good fortune but no wisdom, then we will find it difficult to earn others' trust and cannot help those around us become happy. A supreme life encompasses both good fortune and wisdom.

To walk the essential path of humanism throughout life, the path of kosen-rufu, is to lead an unsurpassed existence. Therefore, we need to forge ahead on this path without retreating a single step. There is no need to hold back.

All leaders should take their places in the vanguard of our movement, working with the persistence of beavers and engaging in dialogue with the fortitude of lion kings, while putting their whole lives into creating a history of the victory of kosen-rufu. To the extent that we do so, our own eternal journey over the three existences will shine with brilliance.

NOTES

1. Non-substantiality: Along with the truth of temporary existence and the truth of the Middle Way, one of the three truths formulated by the Great Teacher T'ien-t'ai of China to clarify the essential nature of phenomena. The truth of non-substantiality is that phenomena have no absolute or fixed existence of their own.

2. *Goethe's Collected Works*, vol. 2, Faust I & II, ed. and trans. Stuart Atkins (Cambridge, MA: Suhrkamp/Insel Publishers Boston, Inc., 1983), p. 305.

3. Setsuko Takeshita, *Seibo Maria* (Holy Mother Mary) (Tokyo: Kodansha, 1998), p. 113.

4. *The Collected Works of Mahatma Gandhi*, vol. 26 (New Delhi: The Publications Division, Ministry of Information and Broadcasting, Government of India, 1967), p. 557.

5. Dr. Wilson was the first president of the International Religious Society Association. His discussions with President Ikeda are collected in the volume *Human Values in a Changing World*.

6. The seven disasters: fire, flood, *rakshasa* demons, attack by swords and staves, attack by *yaksha* and other demons, imprisonment and attack by bandits.

7. Dr. Jun Ishihara (1881–1947): A professor of physics who taught at Tohoku University, Japan.

8. *Makiguchi Tsunesaburo zenshu* (Collected Works of Tsunesaburo Makiguchi) (Tokyo: Daisan Bummeisha, 1988), vol. 9, p. 88.

9. Mr. Makiguchi posited the existence of three basic values: beauty, gain and good.

10. *Makiguchi Tsunesaburo zenshu*, vol.5, p.356.

11. Lucy S. Dawidowicz, *The War Against the Jews* 1933–1945 (New York: Holt, Rinehart and Winston, 1975), p. 22.

12. In writing Chinese and Japanese numbers, the character meaning ten represents multiples of ten. Therefore, the number thirty-three is written with the characters for three, ten and three, in that order.

13. Yukichi Fukuzawa, *An Outline of a Theory of Civilization*, trans. David A. Dilworth & G. Cameron Hurst (Tokyo: Sophia University, 1973), pp. 146–48.

14. Dr. N. Radhakrishnan: Director of the Gandhi Smriti and Darshan Samiti.

15. Haribhau Upadhaya, *Bapu monogatari* (The Story of Bapu), translated from Hindi by Hakobu Ikeda (Tokyo: Kodansha Shuppan Sabisu Senta, 1998), p. 22.

16. The three treasures: The Buddha, the Dharma (i.e., his Law and teaching) and the *sangha* (the Buddhist Order or community).

17. *The Collected Works of Mahatma Gandhi*, vol. 66 (New Delhi: The Publications Division, Ministry of Information and Broadcasting, Government of India, 1976), p. 168.

PART IV

"Dharani" Chapter

5 Those Who Devote Themselves to Kosen-rufu
   Receive the Benefit of Protection

Ikeda: In July 1960, an outdoor training session was held for the Suiko-kai[1] at Inubozaki, a cape with a well-known lighthouse in Chiba Prefecture. I hoped that participants in this event would themselves serve as lighthouses to illuminate the lives of all people. That was a little more than two years after President Toda's death. I had just succeeded him as third Soka Gakkai president [in May 1960]. Most of the organizational leadership was young.

I wanted Mr. Toda's spirit to be carried on eternally by generations to come. Not knowing how long my health would hold up, I hoped to pass on his spirit to these youthful successors.

At night, we built a fire. The youth gathered in a circle around the crimson flames.

We could have used flashlights instead, but I deliberately had them make a bonfire because I wanted to teach them that life is like a bonfire; that we ourselves need to burn bright so as to illuminate those around us. When the flame of faith is burning in the lives of leaders, all members can advance with peace of mind toward the same light. The day when people throughout Japan, throughout the world, will gather in pursuit of justice with a sense of hope is definitely near.

I wanted those young people to know that as long as the bonfire of their lives continues to burn, as long as the flame of the Soka Gakkai spirit continues to blaze, kosen-rufu can be accomplished without fail. Among the people there, some lived true to their pledge to uphold these words, while others betrayed it.

I now wish to call out again: "Let your faith burn brightly! For only then is Buddhism truly alive." Buddhism comes down to the human being; it is faith. It is not to be sought anywhere else. As long as the flame of faith burns in the SGI, the sacred enterprise of kosen-rufu to lead all people to happiness will continue to advance. How precious is the SGI! Let us dedicate our lives to protecting this wonderful organization! If this flame goes out, the future of humankind will be plunged into darkness.

We need also to be aware that all manner of obstacles will, as a matter of course, threaten like a strong gale to extinguish this flame. But the Daishonin says, "A strong wind makes a kalakula grow larger" (WND-1, 471). *Kalakulas* are mythical insects said to swell in the wind, using its force to grow larger. In this way, we, too, must move forward, causing the flame of faith to burn all the more powerfully, the greater the obstacles we face. Wind will extinguish a small flame, but it will cause a large flame to burn with even greater intensity. Kosen-rufu is an eternal struggle. It is a great battle between good and evil, between the Buddha and all kinds of opposing negative forces.

In "Dharani," the twenty-sixth chapter of the Lotus Sutra, bodhisattvas, Buddhist deities and even demons, discerning the great passion for kosen-rufu alive in the Buddha's heart, pledge one after another: "I will support this great struggle!"

"I will protect and serve with all my might those working to advance kosen-rufu!" Eagle Peak, where this scene takes place, is filled with their irrepressible enthusiasm. Such is the dramatic episode that the "Dharani" chapter describes.

Why don't we start our discussion by considering the chapter's basic outline?

THE UNFATHOMABLE POWER OF DAIMOKU

The Buddha said to Medicine King, "If there are good men or good women who offer alms to Buddhas equal in number

to the sands of eight hundred ten thousand million nayutas
of Ganges Rivers, what is your opinion? The merit they
gain will surely be great, will it not?"

"Very great, World-Honored One."

The Buddha said, "If there are good men or good women
who, with regard to this sutra, can accept and uphold even
one four-line verse, if they read and recite it, understand
its meaning, and practice it as the sutra directs, the benefits
will be very many." (LSOC, 348–49)

Saito: "Dharani" begins with Bodhisattva Medicine King asking Shakyamuni how much merit or benefit people can gain from accepting and upholding, reading and reciting, studying the meaning of or copying the Lotus Sutra.

Without replying to this query, Shakyamuni poses the following question to Bodhisattva Medicine King: "If there are good men or good women who offer alms to Buddhas equal in number to the sands of eight hundred ten thousand million nayutas of Ganges Rivers, what is your opinion? The merit they gain will surely be great, will it not?" (LSOC, 348).

When Medicine King says that the benefit of such people will be very great indeed, Shakyamuni instructs him: "If there are good men or good women who, with regard to this sutra, can accept and uphold even one four-line verse, if they read and recite it, understand its meaning, and practice it as the sutra directs, the benefits will be very many" (LSOC, 348).

Suda: He says that by accepting and upholding even a single verse of the Lotus Sutra, we will gain the same benefit as we would by making offerings to an infinite number of Buddhas. When you stop to think about it, this is remarkable.

Ikeda: How is this possible? It's because the Lotus Sutra is the source of the enlightenment of all the infinite numbers of Buddhas. In particular, the source of the enlightenment of all Buddhas is the implicit teaching of Nam-myoho-renge-kyo. This daimoku is the sutra's undiluted and pure essence.

Therefore, we mustn't try to gauge the power of daimoku with our own limited state of life, thinking, "This must be all there is." The sutra says that the benefit of daimoku is beyond even the Buddha to fathom. For us to suppose that we understand its full scope is arrogance. If we underestimate the infinite power of benefit of the Gohonzon owing to weak faith, then we can only tap a minute portion of the Gohonzon's power.

Speaking at Toshima Public Hall in Tokyo, Josei Toda would often say: "If the benefit that I have received is as great as this hall, then the benefit all of you have received is no more than the size of my little finger."

Japan today is facing a difficult economic situation. For precisely that reason, I hope all our members will now acquire immense benefit now. I would like to see each one gain inexhaustible good fortune. When times are good, anyone can do well. It is when things get tough that we see what we are made of. That is when our faith is put to the test. It is important that we patiently strive to create hope.

Saito: Bodhisattva Medicine King and the others present at the assembly are moved when they hear Shakyamuni expound the great benefit of the Lotus Sutra. Medicine King vows, "World Honored One, I will now give to those who preach the Law dharani spells that will guard and protect them" (LSOC, 348). With that, he begins to recite an incantation.

Endo: It begins, "anye manye mane mamane chitte charite shame . . ." (LSOC, 348) and so on, but I haven't the foggiest idea what it means.

Ikeda: After intoning this spell, Medicine King declares, "If anyone should assault or injure these teachers of the Law, then he will have assaulted and injured these Buddhas!" (LSOC, 349). In other words, to persecute those working to accomplish kosen-rufu is to persecute all Buddhas.

Suda: Hearing this, Shakyamuni praises him, saying: "Excellent, excellent, Medicine King! You keep these teachers of the Law in your compassionate thoughts, shield and guard them, and for that reason you pronounce these dharanis. They will bring great benefit to living beings" (LSOC, 349).

Endo: Essentially, protecting the practitioners of kosen-rufu brings great benefit to humankind.

Ikeda: That's right. The practitioners of kosen-rufu today are the SGI organization and its members. To protect the SGI and SGI members is to protect humankind. Since SGI members are spreading the Mystic Law, which brings great benefit to all people, they are treasures of humanity. I am not saying this out of self-aggrandizement or arrogance. This is what the Lotus Sutra teaches.

How truly fortunate we are! The key is whether we can fully awaken to this noble mission. When we do so, our lives undergo a complete transformation.

THE VOW TO PROTECT PRACTITIONERS

The "Dharani" chapter in the eighth volume of the Lotus Sutra says, "If you can shield and guard those who accept and uphold the mere name of the Lotus Sutra, your merit will be immeasurable." In this passage, the Buddha is praising the Mother of Demon Children and the ten demon daughters for their vow to protect the votaries of the Lotus Sutra, and saying that the blessings from their vow to protect those who embrace the daimoku of the Lotus Sutra are beyond even the Buddha wisdom, which completely comprehends the three existences, to fathom. While by rights

nothing should be beyond the grasp of the Buddha wisdom,
the Buddha says here that the blessings that accrue from
accepting and embracing the daimoku of the Lotus Sutra are
the one thing that wisdom cannot measure. (WND-I, 131)

If there are those who fail to heed our spells
and trouble and disrupt the preachers of the Law,
their heads will split into seven pieces
like the branches of the arjaka tree.
Their crime will be like that of one who kills father
    and mother,
or one who presses out oil,
or cheats others with measures and scales,
or, like Devadatta, disrupts the Order of monks.
Anyone who commits a crime against these teachers
    of the Law
will bring on himself guilt such as this! (LSOC, 351)

Saito: In the "Dharani" chapter, five parties vow to protect the practitioners of the Lotus Sutra. After Medicine King, a bodhisattva named Brave Donor says to the Buddha:

"World-Honored One, I too will pronounce dharanis to shield and guard those who read, recite, accept, and uphold the Lotus Sutra. If a teacher of the Law acquires these dharanis, then although yakshas, rakshasas, putanas, krityas, kumbhandas, or hungry spirits should spy out his shortcomings and try to take advantage of them, they will be unable to do so." (LSOC, 349)

Next, the heavenly kings Vaishravana and Upholder of the Nation individually recite *dharanis* to safeguard the practitioners of the Lotus Sutra.

Ikeda: So after the two bodhisattvas, two of the four heavenly kings also make vows.

Suda: Yes. After that, the ten demon daughters and the Goddess Mother of Demon Children and a whole host of demons pledge: "World-Honored One, we too wish to shield and guard those who read, recite, accept, and uphold the Lotus Sutra and spare them from decline or harm. If anyone should spy out the shortcomings of these teachers of the Law and try to take advantage of them, we will make it impossible for him to do so" (LSOC, 350–51).

Ikeda: What spirit! Women are really strong!

Endo: After intoning a dharani, they resolutely declare: "Though he climbs upon our very heads, he will never trouble the teachers of the Law! . . . Though only in a dream, he will never trouble them!" (LSOC, 351). They continue:

> "If there are those who fail to heed our spells
> and trouble and disrupt the preachers of the Law,
> their heads will split into seven pieces
> like the branches of the arjaka tree.
> Their crime will be like that of one who kills father
> and mother." (LSOC, 351)

Ikeda: The passage "If there are those who fail to head our spells / and trouble and discrupt the preachers of the Law, / their heads will split into seven pieces" is famous. It is paraphrased on the upper right-hand side of the Gohonzon as we face it.

Saito: This is the doctrine of punishment.

Ikeda: That's right. The important thing to understand about punishment is that it is not something someone else does to us; it is our effect when we act contrary to the Law. When we live based on the Law, however, we receive benefit. These go hand in hand.

In the upper left-hand corner of the Gohonzon are the words, "Those who make offerings will gain good fortune surpassing the ten honorable titles [of the Buddha]."

Saito: Still, the force of the ten demon daughters is tremendous.

Suda: In fact, their pledge goes on: "We will see that they [the teachers of the Law] gain peace and tranquillity, freeing them from decline and harm and nulling the effect of all poison herbs" (LSOC, 352). Shakyamuni delights at their words and praises the demon girls, saying:

> "Excellent, excellent! If you can shield and guard those who accept and uphold the mere name of the Lotus Sutra, your merit will be immeasurable. How much more so if you shield and guard those who accept and uphold it in its entirety . . . You and your attendants should shield and guard teachers of the Law such as these!" (LSOC, 352)

The sutra further says that the sixty-eight thousand persons in the assembly listening to this exchange attain the "truth of birthlessness," signifying a kind of enlightenment (LSOC, 352). This concludes the "Dharani" chapter.

Ikeda: The chapter exudes the passion to steadfastly protect those who carry out the practice for kosen-rufu.

According to one interpretation, Bodhisattva Medicine King's function is to protect practitioners of the Law in terms of health. He safeguards them from illness. Of course, since

Medicine King represents the bodhisattvas of the theoretical teaching, his vow can be taken to mean that all bodhisattvas of the theoretical teaching protect the Bodhisattvas of the Earth, or bodhisattvas of the essential teaching.

Also, Bodhisattva Brave Donor courageously and without begrudging his life offers the treasure of Buddhism to all living beings. While this primarily indicates making offerings of the Law, it can also mean supporting practitioners from a material standpoint.

Again, Vaishravana and Upholder of the Nation represent the four heavenly kings who protect Buddhism. Since they are kings of the world of heavenly beings, they have great power. In today's terms, they can be thought of as leaders of society. It is the duty of such leaders to protect all practitioners of kosen-rufu without exception.

Endo: Indeed, many leaders today around the world are praising the SGI.

CHANGE EVIL DEMONS INTO BENEVOLENT DEITIES

> *The Record of the Orally Transmitted Teachings says: The "name of the Lotus Sutra" means the daimoku. "Those" of the passage refers to all the practitioners of the Lotus Sutra among the living beings of the country of Japan.*
>
> *We may also say that, while the word "those" may refer either to men or women, here it is intended as praise for women in particular, and thus refers to women.* (OTT, 185)

Ikeda: The fact that the ten demon daughters pledge their protection indicates that practitioners of the True Law can change evil demons into benevolent deities.

Suda: After all, the Goddess Mother of Demon Children and her daughters are originally all evil demons.

Ikeda: In *The Record of the Orally Transmitted Teachings*, Nichiren Daishonin says: "In the case of the teachings that pertain to transmigration, the pre-Lotus Sutra teachings, the Goddess Mother of Demon Children is an evil demon. But in the case of the teachings that pertain to the extinction of transmigration, the Lotus Sutra teachings, she acts as a benevolent demon" (OTT, 184). With regard to the Goddess Mother of Demon Children, for example, the Daishonin teaches that the characters of her name in Japanese, Kishimojin, can be read in two different ways—from top to bottom and from bottom to top—as meaning either "evil demon" or "benevolent demon" (see OTT, 184).

Endo: The first interpretation is based on the top-to-bottom reading of the characters of *ki shi mo*. The Daishonin says, "*Ki*, the demon, is the father." This refers to the fact that Kishimojin is the wife of the evil demon Panchika. Panchika is said to carry a sack of jewels, and in Japan he came to be known as Daikokuten, who is revered as the god of rice and rice fields.

Suda: As to the middle character, read from the top, the Daishonin says, "*Shi*, the children, are the ten demon daughters." The Goddess Mother of Demon Children is said to have ten thousand children, and according to the Daishonin, these include the ten demon daughters.

Endo: Speaking of demons, isn't it interesting that male demons tend to have horrible faces, while female demons tend to be quite beautiful?

Saito: Images of the ten demon daughters produced in Japan show them as having plump faces. It seems that these were objects of devotion in ancient times.

Ikeda: Beautiful women who protect the votaries of the Lotus Sutra—today these are none other than the members of our women's and young women's divisions. But calling them demons will surely bring retribution!

Saito: Indeed, their fierce resolve to protect the SGI puts men to shame!

Ikeda: Men need to work harder so that women don't have to go to such lengths. It's inexcusable for men to take the efforts of women for granted.

Endo: Regarding the third character making up the name of the Goddess Mother of Demon Children, the Daishonin says, "*Mo*, mother, is Hariti." This is apparently her original name, and it seems that she was first revered in the Gandhara region of India (which is today in northern Pakistan).

Suda: In Buddhist texts, the Goddess Mother of Demon Children is described as a demon that steals and eats people's children. When Shakyamuni witnesses this, he hides her youngest child from her. Seeing the Goddess Mother of Demon Children's grief at the disappearance of her child, Shakyamuni reprimands her, saying: "If you are so sad at the loss of just one of your many children, you must be able to understand the enormous grief of the parents whose children you steal and devour!" This well-known episode causes her change of heart.

Ikeda: The Goddess Mother of Demon Children, who dotes on her own children while not the least concerned about the children of others, symbolizes the negative side of the maternal instinct. By contrast, to take the love one feels for one's own children and extend it into a love of humanity is the spirit of the merciful mother Perceiver of the World's Sounds, of a bodhisattva.

The Daishonin explains that the name of the "evil demon"

the Goddess Mother of Demon Children can also be read in reverse: "The word 'goddess' represents the ninth consciousness. The word 'mother' represents the eighth consciousness, the level at which ignorance appears. The word 'children' represents the seventh and sixth consciousnesses. The word 'demon' represents the first five consciousnesses, those of sight, hearing, smell, taste, and touch" (OTT, 184).

Simply put, the ninth consciousness is the world of Buddhahood. When the world of Buddhahood in the depths of our lives wells forth, the eighth consciousness changes, as does the seventh, the sixth (which corresponds to "mind") and the rest of the five consciousnesses. These are all purified and come to function positively.

Through the power of the Mystic Law, the Goddess Mother of Demon Children becomes a benevolent demon. When we fight resolutely for kosen-rufu, then even evil demons turn into benevolent forces. Our obstacles become our aids.

Saito: So, thanks to Shakyamuni, the Goddess Mother of Demon Children and her daughters became benevolent deities.

Ikeda: And those to whom these benevolent deities give their protection are primarily women. They protect those women exerting themselves for kosen-rufu.

This is why the Daishonin declares, "While the word "those" may refer either to men or women, here it is intended as praise for women in particular, and thus refers to women" (OTT, 185).

Endo: It occurs to me that among those whom the Daishonin encouraged by saying, "The ten demon daughters will protect you," the majority of them were women. These include Shijo Kingo's daughter Kyo'o, Oto Gozen, Lady Nichinyo and the wife of Myomitsu Shonin.

Ikeda: I like to see women protected. I am always praying, indeed imploring, all the Buddhas and heavenly deities throughout time and space to: "Guard and protect wholeheartedly the SGI women's and young women's division members. Keep them safe from harm and in good health, and fill their lives with good fortune and boundless happiness." I pray with the fervor of a roaring lion. I hope all leaders will have that same spirit.

BUDDHISM IS A GREAT STRUGGLE BETWEEN GOOD AND EVIL

Ikeda: In the "Dharani" chapter, two sages (the bodhisattvas Medicine King and Brave Donor), two deities (Vaishravana and Upholder of the Nation) and various demons all pledge their protection. They represent the Buddhist deities and bodhisattvas throughout the universe who all make the same pledge. They could be described as the alliance to protect the votaries of the Lotus Sutra.

Why is this? Why is their protection necessary? It's because kosen-rufu is a great struggle between the Buddha and all manner of negative forces. This saha world is the domain of the devil king of the sixth heaven. The revolutionaries who stand up and challenge this evil sovereign in the name of justice are Buddhas; they are the votaries of the Lotus Sutra. It is only natural that they will be attacked by the forces of evil. If this evil were allowed to persist, however, the world would remain shrouded in darkness. But the "Dharani" chapter states that the sutra's practitioners will be protected from this army of evil by an army of good.

The Daishonin says: "You people look to human beings to be your allies. But I, Nichiren, make the gods of the sun and moon, Shakra and Brahma, my allies" (WND-1, 1057). He says in effect: "You make allies of people. I will make an ally of the heavens." On a different level, I, too, have tried to live with the universe as my ally.

The Daishonin also says: "[Despite the personal interference of the devil king of the sixth heaven] it is because the heavenly deities came to my aid that I survived even at Tatsunokuchi and also emerged safely from other great persecutions. By now, the devil king must be discouraged" (GZ, 843).

Saito: What a remarkable state of life where you can say, "The devil king must now be discouraged." Certainly it is true that, even with the full power of the Japanese state behind them, the Daishonin's enemies could not do away with him. This is incredible! It's inconceivable!

Standing entirely alone, the Daishonin resolutely fought on with universal forces on his side.

Ikeda: In his later years, President Toda remarked: "The Soka Gakkai has managed to come to this point. This would have been unimaginable without the protection of the Buddhist deities." Only people who have put their all into the struggle for kosen-rufu can understand these words.

The Osaka Incident,[2] for example, was a ploy to crush the Soka Gakkai. Because of the organization's rapid growth, plans were made to suppress it. The principal targets were President Toda and myself. The authorities obviously intended to use my arrest as an excuse to investigate the Soka Gakkai and eventually haul in President Toda. Mr. Toda was getting on in years and I knew better than anyone how physically weak he was. Had he been put in jail, it could well have meant his life.

In response to their tactics, President Toda demanded: "Release Daisaku! I will come get him myself, club in hand, if I must." And he said, "I'm ready to spend fifteen more years in prison."

I absolutely had to prevent them from getting at President Toda and from trampling on the citadel of kosen-rufu. I prayed that I would bear the brunt of the attack and go to prison instead. I prayed to be a shield protecting President Toda. And so it was that I ended up going to jail.

Saito: You went in his place.

Ikeda: It has been my determination to become the roof of the Soka Gakkai. A roof has to withstand scorching heat, rain, storms and heavy snowfall. But if that's what it takes to be a true bulwark for others, then it's worth it. Nothing would be more lamentable, however, than if leaders were to grow spoiled and decadent due to such protection.

I am like a stake in the water. As long as the stake is firmly in place, the ship of the people tied to it can remain stalwart. Then, even on stormy days, everyone can rest assured. Meanwhile, as everyone enjoys their security, the stake, out of sight in the cold water, stands firmly to keep the ship in place.

Saito: My understanding of the "Dharani" chapter has until now been rather vague.

The vow of the ten demon daughters, "Though he climbs upon our very heads, he will never trouble the teachers of the Law!" (LSOC, 351), is also a pledge to bear the brunt of attacks and protect the practitioners of the Lotus Sutra, even if it means being attacked thimself.

I had interpreted this as simply the pledge of the Buddhist deities. But I now understand that it is an exhortation to me personally to embrace the same determination.

Suda: To protect the person is to protect the Law.

Ikeda: As the Daishonin says, "The Law does not spread by itself" (GZ, 856). Without people, Buddhism would perish.

Endo: That reminds me of the Daishonin's words of praise to

Joken-bo and Gijo-bo [who had been his seniors when he initially became a priest] for protecting him at a time of crisis. He says, "You have performed an unrivaled service for the Lotus Sutra" (WND-I, 729).

PEOPLE FUNCTION AS BUDDHIST DEITIES

Ikeda: That's right.

"You have performed an unrivaled service for the Lotus Sutra"—in other words, there is no greater offering to the Lotus Sutra than to protect its votary.

Gijo-bo and Joken-bo had not gathered together high-ranking priests and held a grand ceremony. Nor had they delivered fine lectures before many people or made contributions to Mount Hiei, which could be thought of as the head temple of the Lotus Sutra for that time. But when the Daishonin first proclaimed his teaching, these two priests protected him from attack at the hands of the local authority (the steward Tojo Kagenobu) and secretly helped him escape capture. It was this act that the Daishonin praised as "an unrivaled service for the Lotus Sutra" and that led him to declare that they were sure to attain Buddhahood.

He makes this statement in "On Repaying Debts of Gratitude" more than twenty years after the incident occurred. Even so long after the fact, the Daishonin never forgot his gratitude and continued to warmly encourage them.

The Daishonin was always appreciative and filled with praise for those who had protected him, saying things like, "You must be the incarnation of Bodhisattva Pure Practices"; and "Shakyamuni lord of the teachings must have entered your body prompting you to come to my assistance." He never expected nor took for granted the efforts of others on his behalf. Self-centered people tend to be arrogant, thinking it only natural that others support and protect them. But those who live centered on the Law will be filled with gratitude for such consideration, regarding it as an act for the sake of the Law.

The world of kosen-rufu is bound together by feelings of mutual respect and appreciation. I don't know how many times in a single day I say "thank you." It must be dozens or even hundreds of times.

Saito: I think that people who have lost such a beautiful spirit eventually find it impossible to stay with the SGI.

Suda: But they don't want to recognize that they have fallen from this pure world of faith. So to justify themselves they blame the SGI. This is most likely what goes on in the minds of those who abandon their faith and turn against the SGI.

Endo: When we read such words of the Daishonin, however, we can clearly see that while he speaks of Buddhist deities, which may conjure images of some mysterious invisible force, these actually take the form of real people.

Suda: Buddhist deities also represent natural phenomena, such as the power of wind.

Endo: That is also true, but I think it is above all the people in our immediate surroundings who function as Buddhist deities.

Working Together for Kosen-rufu Is Most Respectable

Ikeda: Exactly. In particular, our fellow members of the SGI are themselves Buddhist deities, something that should be treasured and appreciated to the utmost.

This is what the Daishonin tells his followers. For example, he says: "The heavenly gods and benevolent deities will assume various forms such as those of men and women, and present offerings to help the persons who practice the Lotus Sutra" (WND-1, 35); and "I cannot help wondering if you are not a reincarnation of my departed parents, or perhaps a manifestation of the ten demon daughters! (WND-2, 774). The Daishonin wrote this to a follower who had brought offerings for him all the way to remote Mount Minobu at a time when his priestly disciples of many years had ceased to visit him.

Today, those who support kosen-rufu and the SGI, the organization of kosen-rufu, can all be thought of as Buddhist deities. There are many such examples. They are bodhisattvas and the Buddha's emissaries. To forget this and instead admire only influential people in society, while thinking little of one's fellow members, is completely backward. Our fellow members are most precious and honorable. What is societal status? What is wealth? In light of the Lotus Sutra, no one is more respectable than SGI members working for kosen-rufu. I have said this many times. I would like this to be taken as my final injunction.

Kosen-rufu will advance to the extent that we sincerely treasure and support our fellow SGI members. Should the bonfire of this passionate spirit be extinguished, it would lead to bureaucratism, and the flame of kosen-rufu would die out.

Suda: I imagine there are some arrogant and cunning individuals within the SGI, as well.

Ikeda: For precisely this reason, I would like to see members establish a firm solidarity as true comrades and protect the SGI. This is the organization that President Toda declared more precious to him than his own life.

At any rate, those who treasure the Gohonzon will in turn be treasured by the Gohonzon, as well as by all Buddhas and Buddhist deities throughout the three existences and the ten directions, just as a mirror reflects our image. When we protect those struggling for the widespread propagation of the Mystic Law, we in turn will be protected by the Gohonzon. This is indicated in the "Dharani" chapter when Shakyamuni praises the two sages, two deities and the benevolent demons saying, "Excellent, excellent!" (LSOC, 352).

Those who treasure the SGI will be treasured by the Gohonzon. As long as we remember this one point, our lives will be rock-solid.

THE ONENESS OF MENTOR AND DISCIPLE

Suda: I understand that Mr. Toda also worked with great determination to protect President Makiguchi. He gave himself entirely to the publication of Mr. Makiguchi's *Soka kyoikugaku taikei* (System of Value-creating Education), from getting the manuscript into order to printing it.

Ikeda: Yes. That's why President Toda is listed in the book as both publisher and printer.

The name *Soka* was born from a discussion that took place between President Makiguchi and Mr. Toda. As is well known, it was Mr. Toda who came up with it.

Suda: Yes. It seems this happened around 1929 when Mr. Makiguchi and Mr. Toda were talking one night until after midnight at Mr. Toda's house, seated around the brazier.

President Makiguchi said to Mr. Toda: "Never before has even one elementary school principal published a theory of education. There is a chance that I will be forced to resign my post as principal of the Shirogane Elementary School. And while this is not a problem for me personally, I want to prepare my theory of education for those to come while I am still active as school headmaster." Mr. Toda replied, "Sensei, let's go ahead with it!"

"It will take money, Toda."

"I don't have very much, but I will gladly put in all I have—nineteen thousand yen," Toda said.

Mr. Toda then asked President Makiguchi, "What is the purpose of your theory on education?"

"It is to create value."

"Then let's call it *soka* [value-creating] education."

The name was thus decided.[3]

Ikeda: This is also the *Soka* of Soka Gakkai. In today's confused world, this is a name that brings hope to humankind. The creation of value—of beauty, benefit and good—this is a name filled with profound philosophy and character. It also reflects the character of these two great predecessors.

The name had been decided, but from that point on, the journey was long. Just scraping together the necessary capital to finance the project was a great struggle.

Suda: President Toda came up with the idea of holding practice examinations for students in Tokyo. Around this time the term *entrance examination hell* came into use, referring to the grueling process of gaining admission to high school. The process was made even more rigorous as examinees had no way of gauging their ability or the degree of difficulty of the exams in advance. By returning corrected answers on the practice tests, Mr. Toda gave students a way to determine which schools they should apply to based on their ability.

The first time, he administered the test for a group of about five hundred in a single hall. Several years later, he had approximately three thousand students taking the test at five sites. Through these efforts, Mr. Toda came up with the funds to finance the publication of President Makiguchi's *Soka kyoikugaku taikei*.

Ikeda: Mr. Toda later wrote a mathematics textbook titled *Suirishiki shido sanjutsu* (A Deductive Guide to Arithmetic), which became a bestseller. Again, he used the royalties to help President Makiguchi.

They decided on the book's title and managed to pull together the necessary funds to publish it, but a lot more was required to see it through to completion. That's because Mr. Makiguchi's busy schedule didn't allow him the time he needed to get the manuscript in order. He was always jotting down his thoughts on memo pads or scraps of paper. While these notes crystallized his profound thoughts, he simply hadn't the time to organize them. So Mr. Toda offered to do it for him.

President Makiguchi hesitated, not wanting to burden Mr. Toda with such a task. It would be quite an undertaking, as his notes were in utter disarray. He probably even doubted whether it would be possible for another person to make sense of them.

But Mr. Toda insisted: "If *I* can't understand your theory, then who is the book going to be published for? Do you want leading scholars around the world to read it? If I read your notes and can understand them, then I am confident I will be able to compile them."[4]

When he came upon overlapping information, Mr. Toda would cut the memos apart, regrouping them by topic. He reportedly had an eight-tatami-mat room filled with such clippings, which he arranged in logical order and which became the basis for Mr. Makiguchi's book.

President Makiguchi's theory was extremely complex, and Mr. Toda's diligence in completing the project was a monumental endeavor. President Toda organized the first three volumes in this fashion, eventually publishing all four volumes himself.

Saito: From its inception, the *Soka kyoikugaku taikei* was the distillation of the principle of the oneness of mentor and disciple. This is truly moving.

Ikeda: Whenever Mr. Toda, who tended to be lighthearted and candid, spoke about Mr. Makiguchi, he always became very serious. He continued to talk about President Makiguchi to the very end of his life.

His life overflowed with the solemn determination to protect his mentor. This is itself the spirit of performing "an unrivaled service for the Lotus Sutra" (WND-1, 729).

THE MEANING OF *DHARANI*

Ikeda: I think it's time we clarified the meaning of *dharani*. This term is probably unfamiliar to many.

Endo: Earlier we looked at the dharani spell that Bodhisattva Medicine King intones. It begins, *"anye manye mane mamane"* and so forth. These are the first four words; altogether it is forty-three words long.

Suda: It sounds like a spell.

Endo: It *is* a spell.

Saito: And it has a literal meaning.

Endo: That's right. Referring to the original Sanskrit text and the Chinese translation appearing in the Dharmaraksha's *Sho-hokke-kyo*,[5] it basically goes like this:

> The state of tranquil extinction and emancipation that is the Buddha's enlightened state eradicates the sufferings of all people equally. With his gaze fixed on his inner aspect, which is pure, unchanging and inherent in all, he abides in peace and tranquillity. He causes people to believe and accept this and so enables them to experience peace and tranquillity. With skilled words that are inexhaustible, he develops boundless happiness and greatly advances without looking back.

This is the gist of it. It seems that quite a bit of research is being done on this passage.

Saito: These words are often discounted as merely being spells or incantations.

Ikeda: There must be some meaning in the fact that Kumarajiva did not translate this passage into Chinese.

Suda: He simply transliterated the Sanskrit sounds into Chinese characters.

Ikeda: The word *dharani* is itself a Sanskrit term.

Saito: Yes, and in Chinese the term is translated using characters that mean "upholding." It includes the idea of being "capable of upholding," as well as "able to ward off."

According to the explanation of the Great Teacher T'ien-t'ai of China, by firmly upholding the words of the Buddha, one can "thwart evil and give rise to good."

Originally, *dharani* meant to "remember and preserve," its roots meaning to "support" or "maintain."

Ikeda: Hence, it means "upholding"—to uphold and maintain all the teachings. In the *Sho-hokke-kyo*, the chapter is titled not "Dharani" but "Upholding."

Endo: Yes. It means to maintain the teaching in its entirety in one's heart.

The term *dharani* in fact appears in the Lotus Sutra about ten times in the preceding chapters. The "Introduction" chapter says of the bodhisattvas gathered at the assembly, "All had gained dharanis, delighted in preaching, were eloquent, and turned the wheel of the Law that knows no regression"

(LSOC, 35–36). *Dharani*, here, means "to remember and uphold the Buddha's preaching."

Ikeda: In ancient civilizations, important teachings were not recorded. It was customary instead to commit them to memory, carrying them always in one's heart. To deeply engrave the mentor's teaching in one's life for eternity—this is the original meaning of dharani. In short, it is to "remember and bear firmly in mind." It is to absolutely never forget the words of the mentor.

The expression "remember and bear firmly in mind" appears in the Universal Worthy Sutra. In his writings, the Daishonin says, "Many hear about and accept this sutra, but when great obstacles arise, just as they were told would happen, few remember it and bear it firmly in mind" (WND-I, 471).

This is the "dharani of retaining all that one hears" (see LSOC, 274). There is also a "dharani of retaining repetitions of teachings" (see LSOC, 274).

Suda: This means "repeatedly intoning." The "Distinctions in Benefits" chapter speaks of *dharani* to retain repetitions of teachings, saying that numerous bodhisattvas "gained dharani that allow them to retain hundreds, thousands, ten thousands, millions, immeasurable repetitions of the teachings" (LSOC, 274).

Endo: To chant daimoku that many times would bring incredible results!

DHARANI ARE THE BUDDHA'S SECRET WORDS

Ikeda: The Daishonin flatly states in *The Record of the Orally Transmitted Teachings*, "Dharani here means Nam-myoho-renge-kyo" (OTT, 183). He continues, "This is because dharani represents the secret words of all Buddhas."

He is saying that it is a secret language that only Buddhas understand. The Daishonin further says: "The five characters of the daimoku are the secret words of the secret of the Buddhas of the three existences" (OTT, 183). In other words, they are the secrets of all secrets.

Among secrets, some hide faults or evil deeds, and some veil hidden treasure.

We are of course talking about the latter kind of secret. Simply put, dharani may be described as an example of words imbued with spirit. They do not simply convey a meaning; they are infused with the energy of life. Therefore sound and rhythm are very important.

Endo: It seems like dharani are similar to poetry.

Ikeda: In a broad sense, poetry and dharani are alike. As a matter of fact, in ancient Japan, *waka* poetry was considered the dharani of Japan, and the art of poetry was considered the most direct way to enlightenment. This was the belief of such figures as Saigyo.[6]

The sound and rhythm of words infused with the energy of life were considered to be a kind of power.

Suda: It has traditionally been thought in Japan that words themselves when spoken have a mysterious power to bring about what they describe.

Saito: Throughout the ancient world, it was often believed that words that express truth possessed the power to dispel misfortune or cure illness.

Endo: It may be that the "Dharani" chapter was based on such beliefs. After all, the purpose of presenting the votaries of the Lotus Sutra with dharani spells is to afford them protection.

Ikeda: That's true. Still, we mustn't just accept at face value the concept that words have mysterious power; Shakyamuni himself prohibited the casting of spells and fortune-telling. That said, however, the sound and rhythm of words do have greater power than the meaning of words themselves. Words indeed have life.

The Japanese author Toson Shimazaki said: "Life is power. Power is voice. The voice is words. New words are therefore new life."[7] The voice more than anything expresses our life force. That is why the heart, the body and life itself can be transformed depending on one's voice and choice of words.

As the Daishonin says, "The voice carries out the work of the Buddha" (OTT, 4). The voice also has the ability to produce evil. Positive words create a healthy mind and body while negative words adversely affect our mental and physical well-being.

Endo: So dharani are words of truth infused with the greatest vitality.

Ikeda: In the world of art, there is an enormous difference between an original and a forgery. The original is filled with an indescribable force, a power that grabs people's hearts. That's because it has been infused with the artist's life itself. A forgery, on the other hand, no matter how close to the original, is infused with only the desire to make money. This cannot help being expressed in the work. It is the same with words. Words filled with life, that have life flowing through them, are like great art.

Saito: That must be why Kumarajiva did not translate the dharani.

Ikeda: We also do not translate Nam-myoho-renge-kyo, for this is the language of the Buddha.

If you go to an English-speaking country and you say "Thank you," you will be understood even if you don't understand the precise meaning of the words. Likewise, since daimoku is the language of the Buddha, when we chant Nam-myoho-renge-kyo, our prayers are communicated to all Buddhas throughout time and space.

The Daishonin says, "The voice of chanting daimoku cannot fail to reach all the worlds in the ten directions" (GZ, 808). The voice is what matters.

To illustrate, the sounds *ka ki ku ke ko*, of the fifty sounds in the Japanese phonetic system, are hard on the ear. There is a very solid feeling about them. But the sounds *sa shi su se so* are soft and airy, like the wind. *Na ni nu ne no* feels smooth, whereas *ma mi mu me mo* feels damp and moist.

Saito: The great violinist Sir Yehudi Menuhin remarked in his dialogue with you, President Ikeda, that the sound of daimoku is easy to hum and has a pleasant rhythm.

Ikeda: And this was coming from one of the most particular persons in the world when it comes to the nuances of sound!

Suda: He also said that he received an especially strong impression from the syllable *nam* in Nam-myoho-renge-kyo.

He described the sound of the letter "m" as the wellspring of life. Observing that it is present in the word *mother* and in *mama*, he said it is often the first sound that children learn to make. It is therefore a very important sound, he stated, adding that it was also deeply significant that the sound of "r" (in *ren*) occupies a central position.

Ikeda: Mr. Menuhin said he thought there were profound similarities between chanting Nam-myoho-renge-kyo and singing. He pointed out that the act of using one's voice has a positive influence on the human body.

Saito: I understand that in 1999 Rector Roberto Kertész of Flores University in Argentina expressed interest in finding scientific evidence of the effects of chanting daimoku. He explained that his interest had been piqued from seeing all the benefit that SGI members are receiving and that he wished to help people who either know nothing about Buddhism or have no interest in it understand its greatness and the greatness of daimoku.

Suda: So, to recapitulate, there are three kinds of dharani: the power to remember and bear firmly in mind (the dharani of listening and upholding), the repetition of a teaching engraved in one's life for the benefit of oneself and others (the dharani of retaining repetitions of teachings), and short phrases to protect those who correctly uphold the Buddha's teaching (the dharani spell). There are of course other dharani, too.

Endo: The "Dharani" chapter primarily concerns the third of these. The source and underlying power of these spells are of course the Mystic Law.

THE UNIVERSE SINGS A SONG OF SUPPORT

Ikeda: The Mystic Law is the fundamental rhythm of the universe. The entire universe is a grand orchestra, a choir. The great French writer Victor Hugo sings:

> *You must know that everything has its law, its goal,*
> *   its road;*
> *That from the star to the atom, immensity listens*
> *   to itself;*
> *That everything has a consciousness inside the*
> *   creation;*
>   . . .
> *Everything speaks;*
> *The air which passes, the seabird which sails;*
> *Each blade of grass, flower, germ and element.*

Did you imagine the universe differently?
 . . .

Everything in the universe says something to someone;
One thought fills with superb tumult.
God didn't make any sound without mixing a verb in it;
Everything speaks.
And now, man, do you know why everything speaks?
Listen.
It is because wind, waves, flames, trees, reeds, rocks—
Everything is alive.[8]

The poet's intuition is in fact being substantiated by modern science.

I have discussed this in the past, so I won't go into great detail here, but the point is that people's view of the universe is shifting. Whereas the universe was once thought of as a mere collection of silent matter, it is coming to be seen as dynamic—a place where, as Hugo describes, the "harp of the heavens" rings out and all things produce sound.

Everything from the microscopic world of elementary particles, atoms and molecules to the macrocosmic world of planets, the solar system and the galaxy—to say nothing of the world of living organisms—is oscillating and emitting sounds in accord with the principles of musical harmony.[9]

Saito: The Daishonin says, "In effect, we may say that, since these "true words," or mantras, are dharani of the Wonderful Law; then the words and utterances of the beings as the Ten Worlds are all dharani . . . The dharanis represent a function of Nam-myoho-renge-kyo" (OTT, 240).

Ikeda: All things produce sound. And all of these sounds, from the world of hell to the world of Buddhahood, are songs of support for the votaries of the Lotus Sutra. They are the pledge of the vast universe to protect the sutra's votaries without fail.

Endo: The Daishonin speaks of the "mantra of the dharani of the Mystic Law." There is also a dharani known as the "mantra dharani" (spells used by the True Word school of Buddhism). Mantra and dharani, which had different origins, seem to have grown closer in meaning.

Ikeda: One thing that distinguished them originally was that mantra referred to short spells and dharani to long spells.

Saito: Mantra means the true words of the Buddha. This ultimately means Nam-myoho-renge-kyo.

The Daishonin says that the five dharani pronounced by the two bodhisattvas, the two heavenly kings and the ten demon daughters in the "Dharani" chapter in fact correspond to the "five characters of the daimoku" (OTT, 183); and that "the five groups of supernatural spells represent our individual bodies [or Myoho-renge-kyo]" (OTT, 186).

THE BUDDHIST DEITIES RESPOND TO SELF-RELIANT FAITH

Ikeda: The macrocosm of the universe is an expression of the five characters of the Mystic Law, as is the microcosm of our lives and the protection dharani described in the "Dharani" chapter. This means that we, as votaries of the Mystic Law, will receive the universe's protection depending on how vibrant our lives are. The universe protects those whose lives burn with faith. The Great Teacher Miao-lo of China states: "The stronger one's faith, the greater the protection of the deities."[10] This is a passage that the Daishonin cites repeatedly.

If people who have faith in the Mystic Law become great leaders, then the Buddhist deities who are their supporters will work wholeheartedly on their behalf. If, on the other hand, they have weak faith, their supporters will not lift a finger. The

Daishonin says, "A sword is useless in the hands of a coward" (WND-I, 412). The Buddhist deities will work hardest to protect those striving most diligently for kosen-rufu.

Endo: We shouldn't be dependent on the Buddhist deities for protection but should work ourselves to spur them to action.

Ikeda: Otherwise, we will grow weak and spineless. Then what would be the point of faith?

Strong faith means self-reliant faith. The Daishonin says: "Let the gods forsake me. Let all persecutions assail me. Still I will give my life for the sake of the Law" (WND-I, 280). The solemn protection of the Buddhist deities is acquired through such unflagging faith.

With the kind of faith where we can say, "If I can work for kosen-rufu, I don't need anything else," everything will open up for us. Buddhism is a battle. Without victory, everything is meaningless.

DEDICATION TO KOSEN-RUFU BRINGS FORTH INCREDIBLE LIFE FORCE

Ikeda: At any rate, there is a fundamental difference in someone who strives to protect the SGI for the sake of kosen-rufu and someone who tries to use it for personal gain. It's incredible just how much energy, wisdom and compassion well forth from our lives and how much the Buddhist deities go to work for us when we truly stand up for kosen-rufu.

Exactly three years after I took faith, President Toda's business failed.[11]

While he was not accused of any criminal wrongdoing, he wound up owing several tens of millions of yen, the equivalent to tens of millions of U.S. dollars today. But I worked and worked, and I repaid it all.

There wasn't even enough money to buy Mr. Toda a bottle of sake, so I pawned my overcoat to get him some. For six months, I received no salary. My shoes were falling apart, I didn't have any proper clothes, and I was in poor health. But if it meant I could protect President Toda, I was even willing to suffer in the worlds of hunger and hell. I was determined to have no regrets. I knew that to protect President Toda was to protect kosen-rufu.

Among the more senior employees, who were also leaders in the Soka Gakkai, some deserted Mr. Toda when he was in the direst of straits. At the crucial moment, it becomes clear who are living true to the spirit of mentor and disciple and who are interested only in protecting themselves. Arrogant people above all view the mentor from the perspective of their own needs. They are like people gazing at the summit of a high mountain from below, unable to grasp what it is like at the top. Yet they pretend to understand it perfectly well.

The Daishonin says, "Among my disciples, those who think themselves well versed in Buddhism are the ones who make errors" (WND-1, 903). The kind of arrogance that feigns a complete understanding of Buddhism is most dangerous. When times get difficult, people with such arrogance will do what they can to stay out of harm's way and, acting as though they were mere observers, try to make themselves look good. They will manipulate things for their own protection. Because they never experience true hardship, they are completely unaware of the debt of gratitude they owe their mentor and the SGI.

When we practice humbly with the attitude that we will give our lives for kosen-rufu, incredible power wells forth from the depths of our lives. In every activity where I took responsibility, I produced results unmatched in the entire country. I have spread the Mystic Law around the world. I have made the impossible possible. There is therefore no way that my successors cannot manifest genuine strength!

Many leaders had been practicing longer than me and were

many years my senior. Also, I was not a top leader. But it's not a matter of position. It's not about appearances. Position in the organization and faith are entirely separate issues. Position does not make one worthy; strong faith is all that matters. This is why I have said that I want youth division members to be aware that they are each the president of the SGI.

The important thing is to stand alone and chant daimoku with the pledge, "I will accomplish kosen-rufu without fail." We need to pray to the Gohonzon, "Please allow me to fight with the intensity of a charging demon." With such prayer, we cannot fail to manifest power. We cannot fail to win.

No matter how difficult the circumstances, one who stands up in earnest for kosen-rufu will absolutely receive the protection of the Buddhist deities. The "Dharani" chapter teaches this passionate confidence in faith.

NOTES

1. Suiko-kai: A young men's special training group that studied directly under second Soka Gakkai president Josei Toda. They took their name from the Chinese novel *Suikoden* (The Water Margin).

2. Osaka Incident: On July 3, 1957, Daisaku Ikeda was arrested and imprisoned by the Osaka Prefectural Police on trumped-up charges of violating the election law. He was later cleared of any wrongdoing.

3. *Toda Josei zenshu* (Collected Writings of Josei Toda) (Tokyo: Seikyo Shimbunsha, 1983), vol. 3, p. 417.

4. Ibid., 418.

5. *Sho-hokke-kyo*: The earliest Chinese translation of the Saddharamapundarika-sutra (Lotus Sutra), consisting of twenty-seven chapters in ten volumes. This translation (dated 286) corresponds with the Myoho-renge-kyo (406) of Kumarajiva in most respects, except that it contains several parables that the latter omits.

6. Saigyo (1118–90):Waka poet and Buddhist priest of the True Word school.

7. Toson Shimazaki, *Toson shisho* (Personally Selected Poems by Toson Shimazaki) (Tokyo: Iwanami shoten, 1972), p. 4.

8. Translated from the French.Victor Hugo, "Ce que dit la bouche d'ombre" (What says the shadow's mouth), *Les contemplations* (Paris: Flammarion, 1995), pp. 361–63.

9. President Ikeda spoke about this at the first SGI World Youth Division Leaders Meeting, held in Tokyo on July 10, 1991.

10. The eighth volume of *Maka shikan bugyoden guketsu* (*Annotations on "Great Concentration and Insights"*).

11. Mr. Ikeda joined the Soka Gakkai on August 24, 1947, and became Mr. Toda's employee in 1948. On August 22, 1950, Mr. Toda was forced to shut down operation of his business.

PART V

"Former Affairs of King Wonderful Adornment" Chapter

6   The Victory of a Family Revolution

Ikeda: Once when some SGI members from Asia visited Okinawa, I referred to one couple who was there, commenting:
"Their daughter is now a senior in high school. In the future,
when she falls in love and marries, her father will miss her the
most. Mothers know that one day their daughters will get married, and so they take it in stride. Because fathers always cherish
their daughters above all, they lie awake at night in tears!

"The Lotus Sutra explains the enlightenment of the dragon
king's daughter. Her name is written in Chinese with two characters; the first, 'dragon,' corresponds to 'father,' and the second, 'woman,' corresponds to 'daughter.' The father-daughter
relationship is extremely profound.

"Therefore, even after a daughter falls in love and gets married, nothing makes a father happier than for his daughter to tell
him that she loves him most of all. There is no sentiment more
appreciated by a father. A family where the daughter cherishes
her father is a happy one."

Saito: That may seem simple, but I think it is a fundamental
principle of humanity.

Ikeda: This is Nichiren Daishonin's wisdom that "Women support others and thereby cause others to support them" (WND-1,
501). This is also Buddhist psychology; it reveals insight into
humanity.

While this guidance was directed at women, taking into consideration the social conditions of the day, it is wisdom that applies to both women and men, as well as to couples, parents and children.

Endo: The same would apply toward a father who does not practice.

Ikeda: Yes, it is the same principle—we should treat a father who does not practice with great care and sincerity, always asking after his health and encouraging him to live long. Becoming a good child, a good spouse—that is proof of our faith. If we instead let our families down because of our Buddhist practice, then what is the point of faith?

It is foolish to quarrel over matters of faith. Besides, often when family members are opposed to a person's faith, it is not so much because they have a problem with the practice itself but more with the behavior of the person. It is not uncommon for people to attribute their spousal problems to issues of faith.

Yet such problems are fundamentally due to our own karma. Sometimes they are the workings of the three obstacles and four devils, problems that test one's faith in Buddhism. That is why the Daishonin says to the wives of the Ikegami brothers, "You two wives should have no regrets even if your husbands do you harm because of your faith in this teaching" (WND-1, 502). He also states, "Whether tempted by good or threatened by evil, if one casts aside the Lotus Sutra, one destines oneself for hell" (WND-1, 280). The important thing is to maintain faith under any circumstances. This is the foundation of happiness.

We need to strengthen our faith. This is the basis for everything. Then we can lead our entire families to happiness. Steadfast faith does not mean projecting a heroic image. It means showing genuine concern and consideration for others' circumstances. Even the smallest act of consideration shines with a brilliant light.

"Treasure Your Wife and Children"

Ikeda: Josei Toda was frequently asked about family members who opposed the practice.

To someone whose children were against his or her Buddhist practice, he said, "You need to show how much you love your children . . . If parents treasure their children, there is no way the children will turn against them. Nothing can match a parent's compassion. It's because your children aren't getting enough affection that your family is in discord. It's not the children's fault; it's you, the parent's fault. If you try to blame your misfortune on the Gohonzon, you will only make matters worse."[1]

To someone whose wife opposed his faith, President Toda said: "You must fulfill your responsibilities as a husband. A husband should adore his wife and buy her a new dress on occasion. You need to resolve this problem yourself. Your wife is not the problem. You are. First, you must change. You must become an admirable human being. You are allowing yourself to be held back by your wife's opposition. It's up to you to develop an expansive state of life . . .

"As long as you are complaining to your wife, you are not practicing correctly. When you can show your wife the appreciation you would show the Buddha, she will have nothing to object to.

"There is usually no reason for a husband to complain about his wife. After all, she's not receiving a paycheck from you! And I bet you don't even buy her new clothes! So, rather than grumbling all the time, you should cherish her dearly. That is where faith begins. I can't stand to hear men complain about their wives not practicing or blame their wives for their problems when they themselves aren't doing much."[2]

This was usually the kind of guidance President Toda gave to people in such situations.

Endo: It's very clear, isn't it?

Suda: The guidance of the Soka Gakkai remains consistent.

Saito: It seems as if we've already reached our conclusion before even beginning our discussion of the "Former Affairs of King Wonderful Adornment" chapter.

Ikeda: Actually, we still need to provide ample evidence for our conclusions based on the sutra. Let's thoroughly clarify how to develop the kind of excellent faith that can create a harmonious family. This chapter contains a number of important points.

Endo: In the title, "Former Affairs of King Wonderful Adornment," "former affairs" indicates origins or history. So this chapter describes the kind of person King Wonderful Adornment was, as well as some of his experiences and episodes.

Ikeda: Yes, it's a well-known story.

Suda: The king was the only one in his family who did not practice Buddhism. It is a tale of how the wife and two children enabled the king to take faith.

THE CONFLICT BETWEEN CUSTOM AND PROGRESS

Endo: A long, long time ago there was a king named Wonderful Adornment. The king's wife was named Pure Virtue; and their two sons were Pure Storehouse and Pure Eye. As you can see, the names of the three all include the word *pure*.

The queen and two princes took faith in the teaching expounded by a Buddha named Cloud Thunder Sound Constellation King Flower Wisdom. The king alone remained deeply attached to Brahmanism.

Saito: We can surmise that Shakyamuni's India, in which Brahmanism had already become an established teaching and Buddhism was a new teaching recently introduced by the Buddha, provided the model for this story.

Ikeda: Fathers often tend to be conservative. Youth, on the other hand, are more likely to possess adventurous spirits. They purely seek the truth, favoring what is right and just over tradition. But fathers are likely to say, "Right or wrong, this is the way it's been done for years!" This is also a problem attributable to the generation gap.

Suda: The king is too proud and obstinate to listen to the advice of his children and wife.

Endo: He is surprisingly small-minded. Yet, as a man, I can understand him!

Ikeda: In the SGI, too, it is often the wife or children who begin to practice, with the husband joining last. It is just as the Lotus Sutra describes. The parallel is amazing.

Saito: At the time when Buddhism was spreading, the foundation of Indian society was a patriarchal system derived from Brahmanism. This meant that fathers had absolute control over all members of the family. In this context, women and the young were drawn to the new teaching of Buddhism. It seems this led to conflicts in many families. In fact, Buddhist texts describe such circumstances. This is probably the reason for the "King Wonderful Adornment" chapter.

Ikeda: We are looking at a clash between new and old ideas.
When new ideas are genuine, they usually cause quite a stir. Simple idealism or temporary youthful indulgences do not usually give rise to real generational conflict.

Endo: I imagine no one would be particularly upset with family members who decide to embrace that family's traditional religion.

Suda: Actually, they might be praised as pious.

Saito: But a revolutionary religion that enables people to change on the deepest level will invariably be opposed by old traditions. This is proof of its genuineness.

Ikeda: It goes without saying that movements that go against common sense or are antisocial in nature will be challenged. But even people who follow reason and strive for their family's happiness and the well-being of society are met with opposition. That is the fate of those who create a new age.

Overcoming the various conflicts at home one by one and building family harmony is the way to transform society. This reformation that is kosen-rufu can only be achieved through the collective transformation of individual families.

Saito: The "King Wonderful Adornment" chapter tells the story of a son who converts his father. I imagine that for the people of ancient India this must have been a landmark event. As the Japanese Buddhist scholar Hajime Nakamura points out, "The arbitrary and absolute obedience to the head of the household of traditional Brahmanism has no place in the Buddhist sutras."[3]

Ikeda: In Buddhism, all family members are equally respected as individuals. This is extremely progressive. Buddhism is therefore essentially incompatible with the traditional Japanese concept that people must adhere to the religion of their ancestors.

Suda: Buddhist thought has much in common with the modern concept of human rights. The Japanese modern constitution, which is based on humanism, guarantees freedom of religion to everyone.

Ikeda: From that standpoint, we are talking about a conflict between humanism and old customs that fail to recognize individual rights, rather than between Buddhism and the religions of one's ancestors.

CHANGING THE ERRONEOUS VIEWS
OF THE POWERFUL

> *World-Honored One, these two sons of mine have carried out the Buddha's work, employing transcendental powers and transformations to turn my mind away from erroneous views, enabling me to abide safely in the Buddha's Law, and permitting me to see the World-Honored One. These two sons have been good friends to me. They wished to awaken the good roots from my past existences and to enrich and benefit me, and for that reason they were born into my household.* (LSOC, 357–58)

Ikeda: The "King Wonderful Adornment" chapter is not just the story of a family. In telling the story of a royal family, a family that has power, it describes how enabling the powerful to embrace Buddhism may save a country. If the rulers of the land do not change, people's suffering will continue. It is said, in fact, that 70 to 80 percent of the world's problems exist because of the way governments are run.

Saito: I agree. In the "King Wonderful Adornment" chapter, it is the Buddha himself who first resolves to guide the king to Buddhism.

Suda: It says, "At that time that Buddha, wishing to attract and guide King Wonderful Adornment, and because he thought with compassion of living beings, preached the Lotus Sutra" (LSOC, 354). The Buddha aspires to lead a country founded on erroneous views to happiness through the supreme teaching of Buddhism.

Endo: Learning of the Buddha's spirit, the two sons Pure Storehouse and Pure Eye decide to introduce their parents to the Lotus Sutra.

Ikeda: Wishing to reply to the will of their teacher, the Buddha, they take resolute action.

Endo: They speak first with their mother, Pure Virtue. Their mother responds, "You should go to your father, tell him about this, and persuade him to go with you [to hear the Buddha preach]."
     At this, the two cry, "We are sons of the Dharma king, and yet we have been born into this family of erroneous views!" (LSOC, 354).

Ikeda: But their mother is strong, saying in effect: "What good will it do to lament your situation!" "Stop complaining!" She encourages them to change their reality.

Suda: Yes. She tells them to have compassion for their father.

Ikeda: This is an important point. Our strong concern for others' happiness is crucial. Without compassion, we will not be fulfilled and will tend to complain. We will find ourselves swayed and defeated by our circumstances.
     The brothers probably couldn't understand why their father would not embrace their faith even though they were practicing so hard. But that's nothing but self-pity. If we have a negative attitude, thinking, "Why am I not getting the results

I want when I have done so much already?" that is the reason we won't see results. Faith is not emotionalism. Faith is courage. To become happy, we must have courage.

Queen Pure Virtue possesses the wisdom that comes from compassion. Therefore, she knows that abruptly telling the king about Buddhism won't work. So she advises her children how to go about it.

Saito: She tells them: "You should manifest some supernatural wonder for him. When he sees that, his mind will surely be cleansed and purified and he will permit us to go to where the Buddha is" (LSOC, 354).

Ikeda: She knows how her husband's mind works! It is said that behind every great accomplishment there is a woman. True to these words, it is thanks to the boys' mother that their father changes and the entire land is transformed.

In other words, she understands that just asking their father to change would have no effect. So she instructs them instead to show through their actions how they themselves changed through their faith.

Suda: The two sons then go straight to their father to demonstrate their supernatural abilities. They leap high into the air where they freely walk around and even lie down; they produce water and fire from their bodies; they make themselves so huge that their bodies cover the sky and then they return to normal size.

Endo: They disappear into thin air and then suddenly reappear; they dive into the ground as if it were water, and walk on water as if it were land.

Saito: The sutra says that they manifest these various supernatural wonders out of genuine love and compassion for their father (see LSOC, 354–55).

In the Sanskrit text, the mother tells her sons, "If you treat your father with compassion, then he will respond with compassion and understand your intent."

Ikeda: In fact, King Wonderful Adornment is thrilled to see the supernatural talents of his sons. All parents delight at seeing the splendid growth of their children.

Endo: The king presses his palms together and says to his sons: "Who is your teacher? Whose disciples are you?" (LSOC, 355). The two proudly respond that the Buddha who expounds the Lotus Sutra "is our teacher and we are his disciples" (LSOC, 355).

Suda: At this, the king says: "I would like to go now and see your teacher. You can go with me" (LSOC, 355).

Endo: At this point he's on the verge of taking faith.

Saito: I think we can say that in his heart he has already accepted Buddhism.

Suda: The sons' strategy works, and they succeed in breaking down the walls in the king's heart.

Faith That Makes
the Impossible Possible

Ikeda: Such is the power of actual proof. Nothing is stronger. The king's sons offer proof of their human revolution. The Daishonin says: "Nothing is more certain than actual proof" (WND-1, 478); and, "even more valuable than reason and documentary proof is the proof of actual fact" (WND-1, 599).

Family members in particular need to see proof, for they know us best. No matter how great we may present ourselves outside the home, our families clearly see the reality of our situation. Of course, there are most likely also sides of us that our families are the last to know.

At any rate, parents can see the growth of their children, and a wife can tell when her husband has changed for the better. It is this human revolution that amounts to "supernatural abilities."

The fact that the Ikegami brothers of the Daishonin's time could guide their father, who had been adamantly opposed to their practice, to the Daishonin's teaching is surely a demonstration of their noble humanity. Such humanity enabled them to remain undaunted even in the face of their father's opposition.

Saito: Supernatural ability, as you mentioned, does not simply mean superhuman power; it refers to a human revolution. The Daishonin says, "Outside of the attainment of Buddhahood, there is no 'secret' and no 'transcendental powers'" (OTT, 125).

Suda: In saying that Pure Storehouse and Pure Eye display supernatural abilities, the sutra is speaking to the capacity of the people of the time.

Ikeda: That's probably a fair statement. The Great Teacher T'ien-t'ai of China calls this "preaching the Law in a way that accords with society." On that premise, it could also be said that the concept of supernatural abilities represents the principle of making the impossible possible.

We may casually say "actual proof" and "human revolution," but in reality these are not easy to achieve. Although many profess faith in Buddhism, those who carry out genuine faith and practice are very few. We cannot attain Buddhahood by practicing halfheartedly or out of force of habit. There's no such thing as a self-centered, egotistical Buddhist practice. That wouldn't be practicing the Buddha's teaching but practicing one's own teaching. Only by carrying out faith single-mindedly dedicated to the achievement of kosen-rufu can we change our karma.

The only way to cause a transformation in those running

a country is to demonstrate the true power of the people through courageous prayer and struggle to make the impossible possible.

To take on such a struggle with an easygoing attitude will only result in mishaps. We need to be keenly aware of how serious an undertaking it is.

Having a Husband Who Is Opposed to Buddhism

Suda: I heard a wonderful experience by someone who succeeded in changing the karma of her family. Her name is Chieko Yamashita of Chiba Prefecture, and her story was also published in the *Seikyo Shimbun*.

Although she is president of a company that operates a bicycle parking lot of approximately four thousand square yards, when asked what she does, she simply smiles and says, "I'm just the bicycle lot grandma."

Ikeda: I recall that she also has a private community center.[4]

Suda: That's right. She achieved her dream of building a private community center. You gave the center the name Yamashita Glory Community Center. When she received the calligraphy of these words written by you, she took the characters for community center to mean treasure house. She was very moved by your consideration.

Endo: Was her husband opposed to her practice?

Suda: Yes. And it was no ordinary opposition either.

They were married in the tumultuous period following the end of World War II. Her husband then failed in business and became obsessed with drinking and gambling.

She explains that eventually her family of four had no place to live and they were given shelter in the corner of a friend's kitchen. During the day, they would stay in a small park nearby, her infant child crawling around on the ground.

With help, they found a tiny one-room apartment; but they were still destitute. To make dinner, she would go out with two ten-yen coins and buy ten yen worth each of sardines and spinach. While shopping, the child she carried on her back would cry for candy. Wishing that she had just ten more yen to buy some, she would search the crowded streets of the outdoor market for dropped coins. She says that she will never forget the bitter pain of not even having ten yen to spare.

Ikeda: I recall that Mrs. Yamashita was from a well-known family.

Suda: That's right. She was born in Kagoshima, Kyushu, and apparently lacked for nothing growing up. There was constant discord between her father and mother, however, and not wanting to end up the same way, she approached marriage with extreme caution. Nonetheless, as Mrs. Yamashita puts it, "I wound up suffering the same destiny as my mother."

She left her husband and children. She could not watch the children and work at the same time, and, as her parents had died shortly after the war, she couldn't ask for their assistance. She couldn't rely on the help of her husband's family either, and her children, a boy and a girl, were put in separate foster care facilities. Overcome with anguish at the thought of this, she decided to gather her children and return to her husband. What followed were days of living in fear of physical abuse.

Endo: I hope that nowadays there are more options for someone in the same situation.

Saito: At that point she had not yet taken faith.

Suda: Mrs. Yamashita joined the Soka Gakkai in 1965. Her husband was unemployed and she supported him by selling insurance door to door. Her husband joined the Soka Gakkai as well, but only in name, and instead went to extraordinary lengths to keep his wife from practicing.

Every night he would beat her with whatever objects might be handy, demanding that she quit the Soka Gakkai. When drunk, he would rail on and on against her faith.

On one occasion, he destroyed her altar with an ax, doused the wood with kerosene and set it on fire. She ran out of the house barefoot, clutching the Gohonzon to her chest. She spent the night locked outdoors chanting daimoku until dawn.

Eventually her husband found work as a subcontractor for a major glass company. But he was reckless with his income and they continued to live in poverty.

Throughout this time, Mrs. Yamashita scrimped and saved with the dream of one day buying a house. But when she had finally saved four million yen and gleefully showed her savings passbook to her husband, he snatched it away from her. When she located the passbook in the apartment two days later, her account had a balance of zero. He had thrown all the money away at the racetrack.

Mrs. Yamashita remarked that her senior in faith told her that she was the one who must take ultimate responsibility for her own happiness. She was told, "Unless you change, you cannot accumulate good fortune."

She says that "When I heard this, I made up my mind to not give up. The Daishonin says, 'Buddhism is like the body, and society like the shadow. When the body bends, so does the shadow' (WND-1, 1039). I determined to stop swinging between joy and sorrow because of the chaos in my life and to stop complaining about what my husband was or wasn't doing. I decided that since this was my karma, I would take responsibility for overcoming it myself. I would accumulate good fortune. I realized that it was not about anyone else; everything depended on my life condition. I gained profound conviction in the principle of the oneness of life and the environment."

Ikeda: That's the kind of determination we need to have! Once we understand that everything that happens to us enables us to attain Buddhahood in this lifetime, all of our problems will be resolved.

On the other hand, the more we tend to complain and put the blame on others, the longer we delay the transformation of our karma.

If we pray to the Gohonzon through all our sufferings and sorrows and firmly resolve that: "This is my destiny. This is my life. I will do my human revolution first and foremost," then a path forward will open without fail.

APPRECIATION FOR THOSE WHO OPPOSE OUR FAITH

Suda: I think that's really true.

Realizing that feeling sorry for herself wouldn't do anything to bring her good fortune, Mrs. Yamashita exerted herself wholeheartedly in Soka Gakkai activities. In the process, she was unexpectedly approached about managing some land in front of a train station. In her seventh year of practice, 1972, she opened a bicycle parking lot.

More than anything else, Mrs. Yamashita's attitude, her frame of mind, began to change. She developed sympathy for her husband for not understanding the joy of faith and she began praying every day that he would change his ways. She came to view her husband as a truly good friend for enabling her to deepen her faith.

She explains: "It's amazing. As soon as my resentment toward my husband turned into appreciation, he suddenly lost his infatuation with gambling. And he began to pray to the Gohonzon."

In 1976, Mrs. Yamashita's husband was diagnosed with

cancer of the esophagus. Her prayer to the Gohonzon was: "Please take half of my life and give it to my husband. Let us fight for kosen-rufu together." Of that time, she says: "I wept at the love and appreciation I now felt for the man it seemed I had cared nothing for. For the first time I realized in the depths of my life that up until that point I lacked compassion."

When she went to see him at the hospital, her husband, who had not moved from the bed, sat right up. Soon he could get out of bed on his own, and, as Mrs. Yamashita describes, "For the first time, we became a true married couple, able to talk openly and honestly about anything, about kosen-rufu and the Soka Gakkai."

Her husband began to study Buddhism insatiably. The following year, as though he had completed his mission, he died. Seeing his beautiful countenance in death, two close friends decided to take faith, too.

"Through all the negative and positive experiences, my husband taught me about faith. He was truly a good friend in faith. I have now grown into a person who can feel incredible appreciation, knowing that I owe everything to the terrible hardship I experienced."

In addition to transforming her state of life, Mrs. Yamashita has transformed her financial fortune. As she puts it, "Money just keeps coming my way." As was already mentioned, she realized her long-standing wish of building a private community center. And the friend who had once loaned the Yamashitas the small one-room apartment they lived in has marveled at how happy Mrs. Yamashita has become since joining the Soka Gakkai.

Ikeda: What a wonderful experience! I have heard much about her family, and I have met Mrs. Yamashita at Soka University.

Nothing brings me more joy than seeing how happy members have become through faith. It is what I live for. Everything else is secondary.

Ideally, I would like to meet with every member and thank and encourage him or her. That is how I truly feel. However, as I am but one person, that is simply not possible. But I live each day praying with my entire being to the Gohonzon with that wish in my heart.

Therefore I hope that each leader will kindly and warmly care for the members in my stead, for they are all children of the Buddha.

Uncrowned Heroes
Who Serve the People

Ikeda: Leaders have no right to scold members. They should only serve and treasure them.

If you must be arrogant, then be arrogant toward the powerful. If you must scold people, then scold those who are evil and malicious. Leaders who cause their members to suffer are despicable. Leaders who lack compassion and consideration toward their fellow members cannot attain Buddhahood. Leaders who treat the Buddha's children with malice and spite will receive negative effects from their causes.

Each day, from morning to night, I am completely at the service of the people. That's the way it should be. I believe that this is the noblest way to live.

We are discussing King Wonderful Adornment. He is a king adorned with the wonderful benefit of the Mystic Law. In *The Record of the Orally Transmitted Teachings* Nichiren Daishonin says, "The benefits of the Wonderful Law are used to adorn the six sense organs" (OTT, 187).

We do not adorn ourselves with the trappings of power. Those who decorate themselves with authority, wealth, honor or fame are examples of the evil King Wonderful Adornment before he took faith in the Mystic Law. But when we discard these shallow adornments and dedicate ourselves to faith, knowing that there is no greater treasure than the Mystic Law, we become a good King Wonderful Adornment. An uncrowned king is the noblest of all.

There are those who become leaders and then, after gaining fame or recognition in society thanks to the SGI, grow arrogant, making something other than faith the most important thing in their lives. Such people function as devils.

Saito: I really think that vanity is the enemy of faith.

Problems Are Part of Life

Endo: Some leaders are ashamed that they have problems and avoid seeking guidance.

Suda: And some may look disparagingly at someone with problems and think, "And he calls himself a leader!"

Ikeda: Everyone has problems. We are all ordinary people, and because we suffer, we practice Buddhism. Such problems as having a child who refuses to go to school or a husband who doesn't work hard or a family member who has fallen ill, all exist so that we may advance in our lives. This is the Buddhist principle of earthly desires are enlightenment.

No one is perfect, and leaders are no exception. To try to be something we are not in order to make ourselves look good only results in our own suffering and does nothing for others.

It's important to be ourselves, so that we can say in all humility: "I have this problem. But I will overcome it. I will exert myself in SGI activities and show proof of my human revolution. This is my situation but I hope we can work together for kosen-rufu." The important thing is that we become happy in the end. It is only a matter of course that we will be beset with various obstacles along the way.

Suppose there is something wrong with your child. You will not have peace of mind. But you can't die and escape the situation either. That's why we have to do our best. That's what is meant by transforming earthly desires into enlightenment.

If there are those who want to make snide comments about your having problems, even though you are practicing or even though you are a leader, then let them. They are the ones who will receive retribution, whereas your negative karma will be erased in like measure.

The important thing is that our lives glow and that we live freely in a manner true to ourselves. This is what is meant by the wisdom to illuminate and manifest the true nature of all phenomena. We need to cause our lives to shine.

Those who put on airs are so out of touch that they don't even realize their own absurdity.

To live in envy of others is a life based on pre-Lotus Sutra teachings. The Lotus Sutra teaches that we live determined to follow our own paths. Faith means to achieve victory in life based on who we truly are, not a made-up image of ourselves. This is the teaching of the "King Wonderful Adornment" chapter.

APPRECIATION LEADS TO GREAT BENEFIT

> *The two sons then addressed their father and mother, saying: "Excellent, father and mother! And we beg you in due time to go to the place where the Buddha Cloud Thunder Sound Constellation King Flower Wisdom is, attend him in person, and offer alms. Why? Because encountering the Buddha is as difficult as encountering the udumbara flower. Or as difficult as it is for a one-eyed turtle to encounter a floating log with a hole in it. We have been blessed with great good fortune from past existences and so have been born in an age where we can encounter the Buddha's Law."* (LSOC, 356)

Saito: To continue with the story in this chapter, when the sons hear that their father, King Wonderful Adornment, has resolved to hear the Buddha, they announce that they will renounce their royal status and devote themselves to Buddhist practice. They do this because the "buddhas are difficult to encounter" (LSOC, 356).

Suda: A famous passage here says that encountering the Buddha is "as difficult as it is for a one-eyed turtle to encounter a floating log with a hole in it" (LSOC, 356). The Daishonin explains this analogy as follows: There is a turtle that lives at the bottom of the ocean. Once in a thousand years he can rise to the ocean's surface in hopes of finding a floating sandalwood log on which to float. But the log has to have a hollow that is just the right size to hold him. Also, because the turtle has only one eye, he cannot judge distances, making it difficult for him to reach a log that he happens to see. This analogy is used to describe the difficulty of encountering the Mystic Law (see WND-1, 957).

Ikeda: There are infinite life forms in the universe. The earth, and even the smallest garden, is home to countless living entities. Among all of these, we possess the good fortune to have been born as human beings. What's more, we can pray to the Gohonzon, an opportunity so rare that it might only be encountered once in a thousand, ten thousand or a million years.

Moreover, we have been born right in the time when the Mystic Law is spreading throughout the world. How deep are our karmic bonds! What an immense mission we possess! There are no coincidences in Buddhism. Truly, as the sutra says, "We have been blessed with great good fortune from past existences and so have been born in an age where we can encounter the Buddha's Law" (LSOC, 356). To live aware of this solemn fact is the greatest pleasure. It is to overflow with joy.

We should carry out faith single-mindedly, regarding each day as a treasure. When we practice with such excitement and enthusiasm, we receive benefit at once. The two brothers in the "King Wonderful Adornment" chapter express their determination to practice single-minded faith.

To spend life idling away time, never awakening to one's mission, is to be like a living corpse. The Daishonin admonishes us, "You must not spend your lives in vain and regret it for ten thousand years to come" (WND-1, 622).

THE POWER OF WOMEN AND YOUTH

Endo: King Wonderful Adornment goes to see the Buddha, taking his ranks of ministers and attendants along with him. He is joined by Queen Pure Virtue and the two princes, along with all of their respective attendants.

All the residents of the palace convert to Buddhism. Hearing the Buddha preach, the king is "exceedingly delighted" (LSOC, 357), and he makes sincere offerings to the Buddha. The Buddha predicts the king's future enlightenment, telling him he will become a Buddha named Sal Tree King.

The king then turns over his kingdom to his younger brother and, with his entire family, dedicates himself wholeheartedly to practicing the way.

Saito: With this, it could be said, the entire country changes from a land of erroneous views to a land of justice.

Suda: This is kosen-rufu.

Ikeda: In this story, the mother and children enable the father, who is in a position of authority, to mend his ways. In other words, a woman and youth stand up and accomplish kosen-rufu. A leader with political and financial power who upholds erroneous views that oppose the Law exemplifies the negative aspect of King Wonderful Adornment. By contrast, SGI members, who are without such political and financial power, can be likened to the queen Pure Virtue and her children Pure Storehouse and Pure Eye.

The Soka Gakkai began with absolutely nothing amid fierce storms of opposition. Solely through the power of the Mystic Law, we have shown actual proof, demonstrated the power of the people and the strength of unity, and progressed in reforming the erroneous views of society.

Endo: That is what I call miraculous.

Suda: It is an example of supernatural ability.

Ikeda: If this were something that anyone could do, there would be no need for faith. Faith in the Mystic Law enables us to achieve the impossible.

Endo: The sutra says that the king went on to practice the Lotus Sutra for eighty-four thousand years. This could also mean overcoming the so-called eighty-four thousand earthly desires. I think it indicates that he thoroughly adorns his life with the benefit of the Mystic Law, which teaches the principle of transforming earthly desires into enlightenment.

The king addresses the Buddha, saying, "These two sons have been good friends to me. They wished to awaken the good roots from my past existences and to enrich and benefit me, and for that reason they were born into my household" (LSOC, 358).

Ikeda: He has become a person who truly appreciates his children.

FAMILY MEMBERS ARE ALL "GOOD FRIENDS"

Saito: Isn't the gist of the Lotus Sutra's teaching on the family that one's family members are "good friends"? They are good friends who help us deepen our faith and develop our humanity.

In early Buddhist texts, too, we find such statements as, "Your wife is your foremost friend"[5] and "The mother is a friend to her family."[6]

Ikeda: Being members of the same family implies a deep karmic relationship. Speaking of his own family, the Daishonin says, "It is no doubt because of karmic forces that they became my parents, and I, their child" (WND-1, 993). And with regard to marriage, he says, "This is not a matter of this life alone" (WND-1, 501).

Since we became a family because of a profound connection, we should help one another become happy as good friends. A family whose members share the lofty goal of kosen-rufu and support one another, enabling each other to grow, is a creative family and a source of personal growth. A home should not be uninviting and closed off from the outside world like a fortress; rather, it should be an open home that contributes to the community and society by aiming to achieve lofty ideals.

Endo: Speaking of karmic relationships, there is an interesting account of the members of King Wonderful Adornment's family. This is from T'ien-t'ai's *Words and Phrases of the Lotus Sutra*.[7]

In the past, there were four Buddhists practicing austerities in the latter day of a particular Buddha. But they had nothing to eat and became deadlocked. At that time, one of the four said: "This will not work. I will take care of providing us with food so that the three of you can focus on your Buddhist practice." And that is what they did.

Thanks to the efforts of the one, the other three attained Buddhahood, accumulating benefit that endured for countless lifetimes. The benefit of the one whose efforts made it possible for the other three was that in every lifetime he became a king; but his benefit did not continue indefinitely. Eventually he was bound to fall into a state of suffering.

Seeing this, the three got together to discuss the situation: "Since we have attained enlightenment thanks to him, we must help him. But now he has become attached to desires and holds erroneous views. The only way to help him will be to persuade him through the power of family love." They decided that one of them would become his beautiful wife, and the other two would become his wise sons. In this way they became the royal family and led the king to happiness.

Ikeda: At the end of the story, T'ien-t'ai explains that Pure Virtue is the bodhisattva Wonderful Sound, who is present in the assembly where Shakyamuni expounds the Lotus Sutra; and that the king's sons are the bodhisattvas Medicine King and Medicine Superior. The king is Bodhisattva Flower Virtue. This is a family bound together throughout past, present and future—united as good friends.

Life is wondrous. From where have human beings come and to where do we go? These questions cannot be answered by science, politics or economics. Only Buddhism can resolve them.

Take someone who has a wonderful family or a wonderful partner.

Yes, the person seems happy. But, there is no escaping the four sufferings of birth, old age, sickness and death. At some point they will have to say good-bye. This is the suffering of having to part from those one loves.

But if we believe in the Mystic Law, then we can be together with our loved ones in lifetime after lifetime. Sometimes we may be related as parent and child, other times as husband and wife, other times as siblings or close friends. While the relationships may take various forms, we can be confident that we will be born near each other again and again. As the sutra says, this is "so that together [we] may reach the place where the treasure is" (LSOC, 180). The Mystic Law is truly amazing. This principle is taught to us by King Wonderful Adornment's family.

If, on the other hand, we never want to see certain people

again, then of course we will not have to be born together with them! We are completely free in this regard.

On Divorce

Suda: Getting stuck with someone you never want to see again is to experience the suffering of having to meet with those whom one hates. It happens sometimes that people who fall in love and get married reach a point where they can't stand the sight of each other! Such conflict may result in divorce, but in some situations it might be best to look at the problem as one's karma. Should married couples work hard at changing their karma by staying together?

Ikeda: This is something that only the people involved can decide. No one else has the right to say that anyone either should or should not get divorced. Nor can anyone say a person has no faith because he or she is divorced. Divorce is a matter of personal choice.

Whether or not people get divorced, the important thing is that they become happy, that they do their human revolution. Whether someone is married or has children, what is of utmost importance is happiness. This is what faith is about. For happiness exists within our own lives.

We are born alone and we die alone. We live so that we may transform ourselves in this lifetime. That's why we need to do our best, regarding those around us as good friends who help us develop our faith and viewing everything we do as part of our Buddhist practice.

Someone once asked President Toda this question: "Things are not going very well between my husband and me. Should I try to stick it out? Or do you think I ought to consider getting separated?"

He replied, "I can't tell you what to do about your marriage. I can neither tell you not to get divorced nor to get divorced.

The only thing I can say is that unless you break through your karma to have such a husband, then, even if you do separate, you are bound to experience the same kind of suffering in the future. And if you're going to have to go through the same suffering anyway, then perhaps it's not too late to do something about it in your present marriage."[8]

Endo: Personally, I think that where children are concerned, parents should carefully consider their options if their decision could cause the children suffering.

Saito: President Ikeda, you once told someone in answer to a question: "Whether people stay married or get divorced is a private issue, and it is up to them to decide. But it is important to remember that building one's happiness on the misfortune of others is not the way of Buddhism. This should be the basis for consideration."

Ikeda: It's ideal if the parents of a child get along well. But if they don't and end up in divorce, that doesn't necessarily mean that the child will turn out badly. There are many cases where children grow into fine, upstanding people precisely because of such hardships.

Suda: There are also people who get remarried and become happier than ever.

Ikeda: The bottom line is that we must look at ourselves closely and do our human revolution in the place we are now. Then we must make our own decisions.

As long as we have rock-solid faith, we will become happy without fail. No matter what happens, as long as we have the faith to continue advancing toward the achievement of kosen-rufu without giving up our practice, we will be victorious in the end. This is what we need to understand.

But if people do get divorced, rather than brooding over the past, it would be wonderful if they could look at the experience as a valuable lesson and work for kosen-rufu even harder than before. I would hope that those around them would provide warm support. I also hope that those who are in single-parent families will not feel lonely but will instead open their hearts and expand their circle of friends.

The fact is that most marriages are not 100 percent successful. Some have gone so far as to say that 99 percent of all marriages are unsuccessful!

In reality, many families who appear to have everything going for them actually have many problems. It was the French essayist Montaigne who said, "There is scarcely less vexation in the government of a family than of an entire state."[9]

Endo: Isn't it healthy for couples to quarrel?

Ikeda: Having the energy to argue is a sign of good health! When the two people in a relationship share similar conditions, it is only natural that they will lock horns from time to time. On the other hand, if one party begins to outgrow the other, then the two will probably not have serious confrontations, because their states of life are so different.

It would be great if we could live cheerfully, enjoying life to the extent that we regard our partner's nagging as a sign of his or her good health and proof that he or she is still alive and kicking. When we develop a broad state of life, then even our partner's ranting and raving will sound like the sweet song of a bird.

PATIENCE IS THE KEY TO HAPPINESS

Ikeda: At any rate, the important things are love and compassion. From that understanding, all a couple can do is chant daimoku together with their sights set on a lofty goal and strive for true happiness.

Even married people were strangers at one time. Without patience and the effort to understand each other, things are not likely to go well. Patience is necessary for a couple to live together, earn a living, protect their home and educate their children while dedicating themselves for others.

We need patience in order to become happy. There are many who dream about happiness without being patient. But that is merely a dream; it is a fairy tale. It is to wish for a childish, easy life. This illusion breaks up many marriages. The pursuit of such happiness can only end in misery.

It is important to make steady efforts to construct something together. From there, real love develops. Real love means wanting to live with the other person throughout eternity. Real marriage is when you have been married for twenty-five years and feel an even deeper love than you did when you first met. Love deepens. Love that does not is merely on the level of simple likes and dislikes.

Suda: Patience is necessary for happiness. This is a key point.

Ikeda: Daily life is reality. Therefore, it is necessary that we earn an income to support our families, and it is important for a couple to listen to each other. Men in particular should listen to what women have to say. It is also important for a couple to compliment and praise each other. It could be for anything—praising one another is what matters. Nothing comes from pointing out the other person's faults. That's just foolishness.

ALL IT TAKES IS ONE "SUN"

Ikeda: One person in the family must decide to brighten the home.

We have to decide, "As long as I'm around, any situation will be a bright one." If we become a "sun," there will be no darkness wherever we go in the world. If there is one person in the home who is like the sun, the entire family will be illuminated.

All we need to do is become people overflowing with good fortune who share their boundless fortune with their families. If that is our conviction, then our families will surely embrace faith as well.

In the event that only one person in a family practices, he or she will be protected on all sides by the four leaders of the Bodhisattvas of the Earth—Superior Practices, Boundless Practices, Pure Practices and Firmly Established Practices. In addition, the Buddhas and bodhisattvas in the ten directions, as well as all protective functions in the universe, will join forces and protect the person and the person's entire family. There is no need to feel lonely. The important thing is not to grow impatient but to be considerate of the feelings of others, thus leading them to Buddhism.

We must not be judgmental. If we give up on the person we are trying to share faith with because it is difficult, we will only inhibit the person's growth. It will inhibit our own growth as well. Rather, we should pray wholeheartedly that, "This person will change"; "Since he possesses Buddhahood within, it is sure to blossom in time. I will bring it to bloom."

If one's parents do not practice, then rather than getting frustrated, it is more valuable to decide, for example, "If Dad won't chant, I'll chant enough for the both of us." Regarding his own parents, the Daishonin says, "Before I die, I will transfer the great blessings deriving from my practice to my parents who gave me life" (WND-1, 402). There are many interpretations, but I think the Daishonin is teaching us that we should have the desire to enable our parents to take faith while they are still alive.

Endo: And if they should die without taking faith?

Ikeda: They'll be reborn quickly, so there's nothing to worry about! Life is eternal, and daimoku will reach them without fail. Anyway, we will be better off if we look at everything that happens as moving in a positive direction.

RAISING CHILDREN WHO LOVE THE SGI

Suda: How do we encourage our children to take faith in Buddhism?

Ikeda: The most important thing is to help them learn to respect and love the SGI without pressuring them. Since faith is a life-time issue, it's enough that they develop their understanding over time. It's probably not wise to be inflexible and try to force them to practice.

We need to teach our children the spirit to cherish and pro-tect the SGI. I hope parents will raise their children to really love the SGI. If children have that spirit, they will absolutely become fine people. To boast about one's children without teaching them this spirit is the attitude of the Goddess Mother of Demon Children depicted in the Lotus Sutra.

Saito: Unfortunately, in some cases, the children of senior leaders or of members who are celebrities do not participate in Gakkai activities. If parents are making it appear as though they are working for kosen-rufu, while at home they speak ill of and criticize their fellow members, and especially if they arrogantly belittle the SGI, it will be acutely reflected in their children.

Suda: One high school student remarked, "After my mom gets a phone call about activities, she always lets out a sigh. It doesn't seem like she is enjoying her practice. Is it OK to have that kind of faith?" Fortunately in this case, the child knew that there was once a time when the mother practiced enthusiastically.

Ikeda: Of course, the failure of children to practice cannot nec-essarily be attributed to a problem with the faith of the parents.

We have to view children in the long term. It is not uncommon for those considered to be problem children to turn out to be thoughtful and down to earth.

The bottom line, however, is that everything is ultimately decided by the parents' faith. In particular—and I say this based on the experiences of hundreds of thousands of people—the faith of the mother is crucial. This is what is meant by "consistency from beginning to end." "Beginning," may be interpreted as the faith of the parents; and "end" the faith of the children. There is essentially no separation between the two.

It is up to us to demonstrate through our example the spirit of treasuring the Gohonzon and the SGI, which is dedicated to kosen-rufu. As long as we have such a spirit, everything will work out in the end.

If parents practice joyfully, consequently receiving great benefit as they advance, their children will naturally understand. No matter how we might treasure and pamper our children, it will all count for nothing if we do not teach them this spirit. To raise decent human beings is no easy task.

If people ridicule the SGI even inwardly—the organization dedicated to realizing the Buddha's intent and decree—they will come to be ridiculed by their family and those around them.

Earlier we talked about "good friends." It is important to choose wisely the people with whom we associate. If we wish to seek the correct Law, we need to seek the right person. If we get involved with the wrong people, then no matter how hard we practice, we will not gain benefit. Herein lies the profound significance of the SGI.

At any rate, when it comes to faith, it is important that parents wisely guide their children. It is also helpful to ask for the support of the youth division leaders responsible for future division activities.

When it comes to matters other than faith, too, I hope that parents will be friends to their children and listen to what they have to say. In particular, while it may be OK for a mother to keep after her children, it's not a good idea for a father to shout at them. It's also important to note that if both parents scold a child at the same time, that leaves the child with nowhere to turn.

Endo: It's crucial to listen to children. Reflecting on my own situation, I can see that there have been times when I have allowed my busy schedule to keep me from listening to my own children.

Ikeda: I recall the case of a woman who was the only person practicing in her family.

Her husband was always condemning the Soka Gakkai. But she took it all and held it inside, never complaining to her children. She felt that grumbling to her children would only make them think that their parents were fighting over her faith.

She quietly took all her sufferings to the Gohonzon, praying by herself each day. Her children eventually grew up and awakened to faith. They realized that they could take faith because of the diligent prayers of their mother.

Sharing Our Hearts With Our Children

Endo: What about children who are lonely because their parents are always off doing SGI activities?

Ikeda: The issue is whether parents have the children's respect. I hope parents share their feelings about SGI activities by explaining that they are striving for the benefit of others and society. In this way, children can feel proud of their parents.

It is also vital that children know their parents love them, so that they realize the reason their parents are working so hard is precisely because of that love. I hope parents will be considerate of their children.

When there is no time, we should be diligent in leaving notes or communicating by phone. We should also use wisdom to come up with ways to spend time with our children. It's about letting our children know we care. Even just making a point to look in their eyes each morning and exchange kind words can make a difference.

Endo: Having the time doesn't necessarily mean that things will go well, does it? There are some cases where a gulf exists between parent and child even though they spend time together.

Ikeda: Sometimes not having that much time together can keep the relationship fresh and exciting.

Suda: I have also heard some men complaining about being left alone because their wives are always out doing activities.

Saito: I'm sure that husbands who do not practice probably feel that the SGI has taken their family from them. I imagine they would like more attention.

Endo: That's why treasuring those family members who don't practice is important.

RESPECT AND APPRECIATE
ALL FAMILY MEMBERS

Ikeda: Even a little consideration goes a long way. When visiting or calling a member on the phone, we should be courteous and attentive to even the smallest concerns of their family members, particularly if the family is not practicing.

Suda: And it's always important to be pleasant when calling members at home.

Ikeda: Whether practicing or not, people should be respected. We mustn't judge people based on their level of involvement in Soka Gakkai activities or their degree of practice. Such judgments should be completely done away with, and we should use common sense in our encounters with people, treating everyone with sincerity and respect.

Even if someone is the only one in the family practicing, it is because of the other family members that the person can participate in activities. Thanks to the support of a spouse, parents or in-laws, for example, one can participate in activities with peace of mind. We should respect and appreciate those who make it possible for SGI members to practice. Just like the past lifetime of the family of King Wonderful Adornment, SGI activities are often made possible because there are other family members taking care of the family's finances and the home.

Looking at it in this way, one cannot help having respect and appreciation for those people.

Of course, great benefit accrues to family members, as well. Buddhism is vast and encompassing.

Saito: President Ikeda, I recall your having once honored the fathers of youth division members with titles of "honorary chapter leader" and "honorary area leader." At first, I was surprised at this.

But you said to the leaders in charge, "Please present them with the title after clearly explaining the immense responsibilities of a chapter or area leader, and how many people such a leader has to look after."

This left a deep impression on one of the youth division members. I heard him say, "President Ikeda taught me to respect and appreciate my father as a human being, as the man who has raised me."

Ikeda: Family is family. We must not divide people into categories of member and nonmember. Also, it is ridiculous to bring organizational positions into the home. If a public prosecutor went home with the attitude of a public prosecutor, the family would suffocate.

Suda: Once, President Ikeda, you discussed an episode of Britain's Queen Victoria in a speech. On one occasion the queen and her husband had a fight, and her husband shut himself up in his room. Intending to apologize, the queen knocked on the door and said, "This is the Queen. Please open up." But he would not comply. Each time she came to the door, he asked, "Who's there?" To which she replied, "The Queen." And he would not open the door. But when in response to "Who's there," she replied, "Your wife," he opened the door right away. I think that this episode gets at the subtleties of human nature.

Ikeda: When visiting a member at home, I think it's wise to greet the other family members with sincerity and respect. Small things are important.

Earlier we talked about a husband feeling left out. Suppose the wife of this man receives a call from a fellow member while she is preparing dinner. Unless it's something urgent, she could ask the caller if she can call back shortly, and then do so after dinner. I don't think her husband would have a problem with this.

But if she were to drop everything and give priority to the phone call and treat her husband as secondary to her activities, then it would not be unreasonable for him to feel somewhat bitter. If this kind of thing were to happen repeatedly, it would naturally drive them apart. A little consideration actually goes a long way.

Suda: Some people think only of themselves, forgetting about the feelings of their family members who have taken care of things around the house while they were out doing activities.

Some people, on returning home from a meeting, simply say, "I'm tired" or "I still have some calls to make," or they ramble on about their exciting day, without asking about anyone else.

ASSUMING THINGS WILL SOMEHOW WORK OUT IS NOT FAITH

Ikeda: It's really important to take into account people's individual circumstances and living conditions.

For example, Japan is presently in a recession. In many families, the husband has to concentrate solely on his work to make ends meet for his family. Under such circumstances, wives may sometimes need to encourage their husbands to chant daimoku and then focus on doing their best at work. Other times, wives may need to encourage their husbands to exert themselves fully in activities and thereby accumulate good fortune. We need to judge these situations wisely.

Reality is harsh. The worst thing is to be irresponsible. To think things will somehow work out just because we are practicing Buddhism is a misunderstanding of faith. After we pray for something, we need to struggle with all our might to actualize it. This is true faith.

To win in society by showing proof is the way to achieve victory in the family and the path to kosen-rufu. With the attitude to make the impossible possible, we must pray "as earnestly as though to produce fire from damp wood, or to obtain water from parched ground" (WND-1, 444); we must win. This is what is meant by "supernatural ability." Through this kind of effort we will win the trust of society.

At the end of the "King Wonderful Adornment" chapter, the king pledges to the Buddha, "From this day on I will no longer follow the whims of my own mind, nor will I give way to erroneous views or to arrogance, anger, or other evil states of mind" (LSOC, 359). This shows how this person of power has changed.

Although he had not recognized the true teaching because of his own selfishness, egoism, arrogance and feelings of jealousy, through the struggles of his wife and sons he awakens to the true teaching. He is transformed from a person who lives only for himself into a person who lives for the people.

A New Age of Philosophy

Ikeda: The king represents the political arena. In a broader sense, he represents economics and other workings of society. But the "King Wonderful Adornment" chapter teaches that these things alone do not bring happiness; a correct philosophy is necessary.

Politics and economics are means. The end is human happiness. To achieve this end, what is needed most is a philosophy that can answer the questions: "What is life?" and "What is happiness, and how can it be achieved?"

In my opinion, the twenty-first century must become a profound age of life, an age of philosophy, going beyond the exigencies of politics and economics. We are pioneers of this transition. We are changing the "evil king," that is, all the negatives of society, into the positives of good "King Wonderful Adornment." And we are forging this path for the world to follow.

NOTES

1. *Toda Josei zenshu* (Collected Writings of Josei Toda) (Tokyo: Seikyo Shimbunsha, 1982), vol. 2, pp. 300–01.

2. Ibid., 294.

3. Hajime Nakamura, "Genshi Bukkyo no Seikatsu Rinri" (Life Ethics of Early Buddhism), *Nakamura Hajime senshu* (Selected Writings of Hajime Nakamura), vol. 17 (Tokyo: Shunjusha, 1995), p. 254.

4. Private community center: a meeting facility usually adjacent or attached to one's living quarters that serves the local Soka Gakkai membership in smaller-scale activities.

5. *Nakamura Hajime senshu*, p. 197.

6. Ibid., 292.

7. *Words and Phrases of the Lotus Sutra*, T'ien-t'ai, vol. 10.

8. *Toda Josei zenshu,* vol. 2, pp. 283–84.

9. *The Macmillan Book of Proverbs, Maxims, and Famous Phrases*, ed. Burton Stevenson (New York: Macmillan Publishing Company, 1948), p. 757.

PART VI

*"Encouragements of the Bodhisattva
Universal Worthy" Chapter*

7 Treasuring Each Person Is the Conclusion of the Lotus Sutra

Ikeda: I once gave strict advice to a particular leader. In front of everyone, he had berated a member for arriving late to a meeting. I was infuriated when I heard about this and said to him: "What gives you the right to scold that person? It's outrageous. Didn't that member take time out of his busy schedule to come and participate in the world of kosen-rufu? Shouldn't we sincerely praise one another for attending meetings at all and offer each other support?"

That was a long time ago, but the point is even more important today with our struggling economy. Any guidance or encouragement given without an understanding of a person's financial situation or what's going on at home will be empty. We must avoid formalism and never become authoritarian.

In some cases, it might be best to tell someone who has a hard time getting out of work early enough to attend an activity, "I'll go to the meeting and let you know what is discussed, so please concentrate on your work." Such consideration provides encouragement worth a million words.

At other times, a person might gain from hearing something like: "The basis for good fortune is created by giving our all in both work and Soka Gakkai activities. This is your chance to change your karma. Let's do our best together!"

Even strict guidance, as long as it is based on deep prayer and genuine concern for the other person, cannot fail to reach that person's heart. Without compassion, however, it is just not possible to effectively say what truly needs to be said for another's benefit.

The bottom line is that when we really care about someone, boundless wisdom wells forth. This is what the life of Bodhisattva Universal Worthy represents.

Saito: Nichiren Daishonin says in *The Record of the Orally Transmitted Teachings*:

> In the name Fugen, or Universal Worthy, the element *fu*, "universal," refers to the true aspect of all phenomena, the principle of eternal and unchanging truth as embodied in the theoretical teaching [of the Lotus Sutra]. The element *gen*, "worthy" or "wise," expresses the idea of wisdom, the wisdom of the truth that functions in accordance with changing circumstances, as embodied in the essential teaching. (OTT, 189)

Ikeda: The principle of the eternal and unchanging truth indicates a fundamental principle upon which wisdom functions in accordance with changing circumstances. This function of wisdom is to create value. Without fundamental principles, everything becomes arbitrary and falls apart. On the other hand, just brandishing rules amounts to rigid dogmatism. Faith can bring the two together.

Faith means to develop a sense of responsibility to ensure that all people become happy without fail. To have such faith is to embody the spirit of Bodhisattva Universal Worthy, to possess his transcendental powers. This is the driving force behind kosen-rufu. As *The Record of the Orally Transmitted Teachings* states: "It is due to the authority and supernatural powers of Bodhisattva Universal Worthy that this Lotus Sutra is propagated throughout Jambudvipa. Therefore the widespread propagation of this sutra must be under the care and protection of Bodhisattva Universal Worthy" (OTT, 190).

PUTTING ONE'S WHOLE HEART
INTO ENCOURAGING OTHERS

Endo: The late Mr. Hiroshi Hojo, the fourth president of the Soka Gakkai, once shared with me an incident that took place shortly after your inauguration, President Ikeda, when you were giving guidance to someone in your office. The member, who had been practicing for several years, was suffering from lung disease. Since he was showing no signs of improvement, he had come to seek guidance together with his wife.

While you were talking, the phone rang and Mr. Hojo answered it. The call was for him, and so he continued to talk in a low but audible tone. Suddenly, you told him to be quiet. Mr. Hojo, somewhat surprised, put down the phone, and you calmly said to him: "This person is suffering from a lung disease. When I give guidance to anyone, with the Gohonzon in mind, I put my whole life into encouraging that person. Someone who interrupts those interactions is behaving like the thoughtless Wei Yen."

You were referring to the scene in the Chinese classic *Romance of the Three Kingdoms* in which Prime Minister Chuko K'ung-ming is making a final prayer after a long battle with illness. For seven days straight, a flame burned in honor of K'ung-ming. Wei Yen's inconsiderate intrusion snuffed out the flames of both the fire and, consequently, K'ung-ming's life.

Mr. Hojo recounted that your earnestness while encouraging just one person was unforgettable.

Ikeda: I'm sorry for losing my temper with Mr. Hojo! I was so direct with him because I knew he could handle it. If I were to be so direct now, I fear that everyone would disappear! In all seriousness, even though the times may change, we must never forget the strictness of faith.

With whomever I meet, I always put my whole life into each encounter, thinking that I may never have the chance to meet that person again. It has been the same with the struggle to advance kosen-rufu around the globe. In the early days of our movement, no one believed that worldwide kosen-rufu could become a reality. But this is the prophecy of the Lotus Sutra and the decree of Nichiren Daishonin. My thoughts have been: "If I don't take that first step now, a path forward will never open"; "If I travel the world now, planting the seeds of peace of the Mystic Law in each country, someday those seeds will bear fruit"; "If I open the way now, eventually others will proudly follow." I have acted on the firm belief that youth will one day stand up with confidence, encouraged by the extent of my efforts.

From nothing—no funding, no support, no human resources, no time—we have forged a path where none before had existed. And now, true to my conviction, Bodhisattvas of the Earth have appeared in 186 countries around the world.[5]

"Universal worthy" can be taken to mean enabling all people to tap their wisdom and become truly happy. The desire to help everyone we come into contact with is the spirit of Bodhisattva Universal Worthy.

THE CORE TEACHING OF THE LOTUS SUTRA

In this chapter Shakyamuni Buddha revealed the foremost point he wished to convey to us. The Buddha preached the Lotus Sutra over a period of eight years, and eight characters sum up the message that he has left behind for living beings in this later age, the Latter Day of the Law. It is in the passage that reads, "Therefore, Universal Worthy, if you see a person who accepts and upholds this sutra, you should rise and greet him from afar, showing him the same respect you would a Buddha" [LSOC, 365] . . . With this passage the words of Shakyamuni Buddha in the sutra come to an end, thus in effect ending the sutra.

The word "should" shows that these words refer to the future. The words "should rise and greet him from afar" indicate that the sutra passage is saying that one should without fail show the practitioners of the Lotus Sutra the kind of respect one would show to a Buddha. (OTT, 192–93)

Ikeda: Incidentally, I was reminded of the episode of the tardy member I relayed at the outset because Bodhisattva Universal Worthy was, in fact, tardy to Shakyamuni's sermon.

Saito: That's right. He turns up just as the preaching at Eagle Peak is about to end.

Suda: "Encouragements of the Bodhisattva Universal Worthy" is the last chapter of the Lotus Sutra. It abruptly begins with the statement, "At that time Bodhisattva Universal Worthy . . . arrived [at Eagle Peak] from the east" (LSOC, 360).

Endo: When he was in the land of a Buddha named King Above Jeweled Dignity and Virtue and heard that Shakyamuni was expounding the Lotus Sutra in the far-off saha world, Universal Worthy traveled at once to Eagle Peak accompanied by "great bodhisattvas in immeasurable, boundless, indescribable numbers" (LSOC, 360).

Saito: Nichiren Daishonin paints an amusing picture of the scene, saying:

> Probably fearing the Buddha's displeasure at his tardy arrival, he assumed a serious expression and pledged in all earnestness to protect the votaries of the Lotus Sutra in the latter age. The Buddha, no doubt pleased with Universal Worthy's extraordinary sincerity in vowing to spread the Lotus Sutra throughout the continent of Jambudvipa, thereupon praised him— more warmly, in fact, than he had earlier praised the other bodhisattvas of higher rank. (WND-1, 915)

Ikeda: That illustrates the scene very well. The sutra, of course, does not describe its psychological aspect. Based on his thorough understanding of the Lotus Sutra, the Daishonin explains this passage to a follower in terms she can easily understand. How great was the Daishonin's compassion! He always gave himself wholeheartedly to encouraging people.

Suda: Bodhisattva Universal Worthy entreats Shakyamuni to explain how people can "acquire" the Lotus Sutra after the Buddha has passed away (LSOC, 360).

Saito: This is an important question.

From the "Former Affairs of the Bodhisattva Medicine King," the twenty-third chapter, through "The Bodhisattva Wonderful Sound," the twenty-fourth chapter, "The Universal Gateway of the Bodhisattva Perceiver of the World's Sounds," the twenty-fifth chapter, "Dharani," the twenty-sixth, and "Former Affairs of King Wonderful Adornment," the twenty-seventh chapter—the preaching is consistently directed toward the practice of the Lotus Sutra after the Buddha's passing.

The foundation having thus been laid, Shakyamuni relates the main point of the practice of the Lotus Sutra in response to this question from Bodhisattva Universal Worthy.

Ikeda: That is why the Daishonin says of the "Universal Worthy" chapter, "This chapter is a restatement of the Lotus Sutra" (OTT, 241). It is a final review of the entire sutra, so to speak. Shakyamuni essentially summarizes the gist of the sutra as if to say: "This is the point! If you just remember this, you'll be fine."

THE SOKA GAKKAI MEETS ALL
OF THE FOUR CONDITIONS

Endo: Yes. Shakyamuni first explains four conditions. He says: "If good men and good women fulfill four conditions in the time after the Thus Come One has entered extinction, then they will be able to acquire this Lotus Sutra" (LSOC, 361). The four conditions are: "First, they must be protected and kept in mind by the Buddhas. Second, they must plant the roots of virtue. Third, they must enter the stage where they are sure of reaching enlightenment. Fourth, they must conceive a determination to save all living beings" (LSOC, 361).

Ikeda: To sum up the significance of these four conditions, to be "protected and kept in mind by the Buddhas" means to be protected as a result of embracing and upholding the Gohonzon, which is the source of the enlightenment of all Buddhas past, present and future. "Plant the roots of virtue" means to believe in the Gohonzon and chant daimoku for the happiness of oneself and others. Herein lies the source of all goodness. "Enter the stage where they are sure of reaching enlightenment" means joining in solidarity a group of people continually striving to advance and determined never to backslide in faith. Practically speaking, one cannot fulfill these conditions without being part of a harmonious body of practitioners who uphold the correct teaching. In modern terms, I am confident that these conditions are met by living out one's life nobly as a member of the SGI organization.

Josei Toda used to say, "The Soka Gakkai was called forth by Nichiren Daishonin himself." The great flourishing of the True Law began as a result of the Soka Gakkai's appearance at a time when that Law had nearly perished.

President Toda had tremendous confidence. He stated:

> I would like to make a declaration for the sake of the future. Apart from the faith practiced by the Soka Gakkai, there is none that accords with the Daishonin's spirit. Nowhere else can the true benefit of the Gohonzon be found . . .Victory and defeat in Buddhism are very strict. Eventually everything

will become clear. The Daishonin will never forgive those who pit themselves against the Soka Gakkai, whoever they may be. Without this conviction, I could not be president. Anyway, just watch and see what happens.

Why was he able to make such a bold declaration? Only because the SGI meets the Buddha's fourth condition to "conceive a determination to save all living beings." Only the SGI is resolutely carrying out kosen-rufu.

Saito: In other words, the SGI meets all essential points of the practice of the Lotus Sutra that Shakyamuni articulates—the Gohonzon, daimoku, harmonious unity of believers and the advancement of kosen-rufu.

Ikeda: Though you have omitted detailed doctrinal proof—yes, this is the conclusion.

Endo: The Great Teacher T'ien-t'ai of China correlates these four conditions with the concept of "opening, showing, awakening to and inducing people to enter into the Buddha wisdom." This means ultimately giving people access to their Buddha nature.

Suda: These are all encompassed in a life dedicated to working for kosen-rufu together with the SGI. How wonderful!

A Vow To Protect Practitioners of the Lotus Sutra

Universal Worthy, after the Thus Come One has entered extinction, in the last five-hundred-year period, if you see someone who accepts, upholds, reads, and recites the Lotus Sutra, you should think to yourself: Before long this person

*will proceed to the place of enlightenment, conquer the devil
hosts, and attain supreme perfect enlightenment. He will turn
the wheel of the Dharma, beat the Dharma drum, sound
the Dharma conch, and rain down the Dharma rain. He is
worthy to sit in the lion seat of the Dharma, amid the great
assembly of heavenly and human beings.* (LSOC, 364–65)

Ikeda: Nothing is wasted in our struggle for kosen-rufu. All
our efforts turn into great good fortune. Everything works to
our benefit.

As long as we conduct our activities based on the Gohonzon,
we will essentially reach no deadlock nor experience contra-
diction. The Gohonzon is the embodiment of the actual—as
opposed to theoretical—principle of three thousand realms in
a single moment of life. The Gohonzon enables all people of
the Ten Worlds to function as Buddhas, their lives illuminated
by the Mystic Law.

I recall a time when I prayed with my whole being: "May all
the people—though some may be in the world of hell, hunger
or animality—join in the struggle for kosen-rufu! May they
all become our allies!" "Universal worthy" means that all the
people of the Ten Worlds can develop wisdom and dedicate
themselves to creating value.

Also, kosen-rufu is a struggle undertaken while challenging
the malicious and the wicked. I have come this far determined
never to allow a single one of them to lay a finger on our pure
and precious Soka Gakkai. I hope that everyone will share such
resolve. This surely must be the spirit of Bodhisattva Universal
Worthy.

Saito: When he hears the four conditions, Universal Worthy
vows, "In the evil and corrupt age . . . if there is someone who
accepts and upholds this sutra, I will guard and protect him"
(LSOC, 361). He further pledges to "free him from decline and
harm" and to ensure that no one can "take advantage" of him

(LSOC, 361). He also says, "If that person should forget a single phrase or verse of the Lotus Sutra, I will prompt him and join him in reading and reciting so that he will gain understanding" (LSOC, 361); and that "when the lives of these persons come to an end, they will be received into the hands of a thousand Buddhas, who will free them from all fear and keep them from falling into the evil paths of existence" (LSOC, 363). He concludes his vows saying, "after the Thus Come One has entered extinction, I will cause [the Lotus Sutra] to be widely propagated throughout Jambudvipa and will see that it never comes to an end" (LSOC, 363).

Ikeda: That's right. What courage and hope this vow must have given to all present! How it must have lifted their spirits!

Bodhisattva Universal Worthy arrives from afar and calls out: "I will protect you, so do your best! Do not let anything defeat you!" This is the meaning of the word *encouragements* in the chapter's title.

Suda: It means to persuade others to embrace the teachings of Buddhism and to awaken them to faith.

Ikeda: It means to encourage and inspire others.

The components of the Chinese character meaning encouragement could be interpreted to mean the power of ten thousand. Truly, there is no greater force than encouragement. There is significance in the fact that the Lotus Sutra concludes with the encouragement of Bodhisattva Universal Worthy.

The SGI has successfully spread Nichiren Buddhism to the extent it has precisely because it is committed to encouraging each person. People are not robots.

No matter how strong a determination we have made, at times we will be disheartened. That is why I have given my all to offering hope and courage to people using all available means.

The world after the Buddha's passing is an "evil age." This

is a time when good people are scarce while the wicked are many. Because the wicked are so numerous, it is only natural that the few good people will be oppressed. For that reason, unity is crucial, as is mutual support and encouragement.

Endo: I imagine that the concrete forms of encouragement you have given to SGI members over the years in the way of messages, haiku and *waka* poems and calligraphy must number in the hundreds of thousands. Including all the spoken words of encouragement you have offered, the amount is beyond calculation. Encouraging people to take action by saying such things as "Don't give up! Keep going!" you have inspired many.

UTMOST SINCERITY MOVES PEOPLE'S HEARTS

Saito: People tend to view the Soka Gakkai as a tightly organized group. But in fact it is not so much the organization itself that is strong but the bond that exists between you, President Ikeda, and each member. I think our organization cannot be understood correctly if this point is overlooked. Ill-intentioned people, on the other hand, realize this fact and so are concentrating their efforts on destroying this bond.

Ikeda: Putting talk of myself aside, in this day and age, it is absurd to think that people will take part in an organization simply because they've been told to. No organization has the power to coerce people into joining. Furthermore, any group whose members act against their own will cannot produce any lasting strength.

Treasuring each person is the only way to success. Victory is won where people cherish one another. This point cannot be emphasized enough.

There are instances when leaders encourage members, but then don't make an appointment to meet again. Without setting in place another time to meet, however, the member will not have a target. When a leader and member decide together to see each other, say, in two or three months' time, then their determination to produce a result by the designated time will be solidified. This is what is meant by encouragement.

Once we make a promise to someone, we must keep it at all costs, no matter how difficult it may be. Kosen-rufu has advanced because of such consistent efforts based on utmost sincerity.

Suda: I recall how some years ago, President Ikeda, you spent a long time encouraging a particular youth division member during a meeting. Repeatedly saying his name, you urged him to keep going. The person had in fact distanced himself from faith. Through your encouragement, however, his spirits were quickly restored.

But what really struck me was your remark at the end of the meeting when you said: "For that young man to come today, there must have been someone who went to encourage him. Who was that?" Several people raised their hands. Although they were all very busy, they had taken turns going over to see the young man. The way you immediately sense the efforts of those struggling behind the scenes made me reflect on my own behavior.

Saito: I imagine that you can do this because of your own experience working tenaciously in supportive positions, out of the limelight.

Ikeda: I hope all leaders will serve and support the members in my place. Leaders must not be insensitive. In Japan's past, people tended to view nonchalance and inattentiveness to details as a sign of greatness. But this is completely backwards. Buddhism exists solely in the realm of human life. Therefore, practicing Buddhism means helping others lead satisfying and fulfilling lives. Leaders cannot be too perceptive. They should always ask themselves, "What does he need right now?" "Is she tired?" "Is she hungry?" "Is there something he wants to say? Something she needs to talk about?"

FOCUS ON SUBSTANCE, NOT FORMALITY

Ikeda: When it comes to our Buddhist activities, unproductive meetings are only detrimental.

In the 1956 Japanese Upper House elections, we succeeded in electing our Osaka candidate to office but lost the election in Tokyo. At that time, President Toda strictly admonished us to "focus on substance, not formality."

The SGI exists to help those facing hardship. Meetings are a means. It would be utterly pointless if the sole purpose of our organization was to conduct meetings. We need to go out and look for people who are suffering and organizational areas that have become deadlocked. That there are problems around is certain. Once we find them, we should go directly there and offer advice and encouragement.

When I meet someone, I do my best to encourage the person to the very end. Even if that person were to move to the remotest parts of the earth or take a little break from faith, I will do whatever I can to support him or her. And for those considering giving up their faith altogether, I want them to enjoy once again the amazing benefits of practicing the Mystic Law. I want to encourage them as if carrying them on my back or in my arms or pulling them along. I want them to feel deeply just how wonderful is the benefit gained from exerting oneself in faith.

If others can sense our sincerity in wanting them to be truly happy, they will stand up on their own without a lot of pressure or prodding. The important thing is to pray so that our sincerity will reach them.

Also, when holding a meeting, we need to make sure we are prepared. Since those attending are all people with full calendars, we must plan the meeting so that they come with anticipation and leave feeling satisfied. Leaders should give serious thought to the agenda of the meeting, to the order of the speakers and to the content of the presentations so that not one person leaves thinking, "That was boring."

There's no rule saying that meetings have to be long. It's probably preferable if a meeting can end early; the point is that meetings should be worthwhile. We are an organization dedicated to the creation of value, after all. This accords with the spirit to treasure each person. Every meeting is a struggle, and its outcome is either victory or defeat.

Along those lines, requiring members to make unnecessary reports only wears them out and is not concentrating on substance. Just dabbling with numbers produces nothing. Of course, I'm not saying that we should not collect reports and data on matters necessary for the operation of the organization. The point is to create an atmosphere in which everyone enjoys participating and passing on the information. Toward that end we put our hearts into offering encouragement—so that people can happily report on their propagation efforts, saying, "I did it!"

ADORATION FOR THE MYSTIC LAW

Saito: T'ien-t'ai says that the term *encouragements* in the chapter's title means "adoration for the Law."[1] I think this refers to a spirit of such longing and thirst for the wonder of the Mystic Law that one cannot help recommending it to others.

Endo: SGI members who understand the greatness of the Mystic Law and who feel compelled to share it with others are the very essence of such adoration for the Law.

Ikeda: Faith is to genuinely feel, "I love the Gohonzon," "I love to do gongyo," "I love SGI activities." With such faith, we feel joy just for being alive and appreciation for our lives.

Endo: In "Persecution by Sword and Staff," the Daishonin states, "As you crave food when hungry, seek water when thirsty, long to see a lover, beg for medicine when ill, or as a beautiful woman desires powder and rouge, so should you put your faith in the Lotus Sutra. If you do not, you will regret it later" (WND-1, 965).

Ikeda: Faith is a matter of the heart. It's not about formality. Nor is it related to the length of one's practice.

Benefit derives from a spirit to seek the Law. It might be that someone is extremely busy and has a difficult time participating in activities. Nevertheless, if he or she makes an effort to attend meetings for even just thirty minutes or devotes even a few hours a week to activities, that spirit will bring great benefit.

It's also important that the situations of those people are understood and that they are offered support and encouragement. To reject people simply because they are not always present at meetings is the opposite of compassion. Those who always participate in activities, on the other hand, we need not worry so much about. Those who cannot attend regularly are in even more need of our encouragement, and we should think of the best ways to provide it for them. If we can do this, we will see kosen-rufu advance in leaps and bounds.

LIKE THE BOND BETWEEN
PARENT AND CHILD

Endo: Speaking of adoration, the Daishonin says that we should place our trust in the Lotus Sutra "as a woman cherishes her husband, as a man lays down his life for his wife, as parents refuse to abandon their children, or as a child refuses to leave its mother." In this way, he explains that "What is called faith is nothing unusual" (WND-1, 1036). Faith is nothing exceptional or out of the ordinary. Rather, it is the extension of our natural human sentiments.

Ikeda: The phrase about children not wanting to part from their mother brings to mind a story I heard about a child who was born prematurely. One week after birth, the baby's condition suddenly deteriorated, and it would not respond to any stimulus from the nurse. Yet when they brought the mother into the intensive care unit and she called her child's name, the baby's heart rate suddenly increased. Life is truly a mystery.

The Buddha constantly thinks of all living beings with immense compassion, just like that of this mother. Believing this, we should chant daimoku to the Gohonzon with sincere hearts, the way a child naturally runs to its mother's arms. Also, the stronger our adoration toward the Law, the more encouraging we will be to others.

Saito: It is certainly true that sometimes a single word from a pioneer member moves people far more than a thousand words from those of us in the younger generations who have less experience.

Suda: The depth of their conviction and concern for others goes much further.

Ikeda: That concern is itself the spirit of Bodhisattva Universal Worthy. It is a warm and passionate spirit.

In fact, I believe the Sanskrit term for "universal worthy" (*samantabhadra*) was originally an expression of praise for the bodhisattva practice itself.

Suda: Yes. It seems the term can also mean "broadly venerable," "most wonderful" and "praised by all."

A Chinese translation renders it as "more wonderful than any other." A "universally worthy practice" means one that is supreme and altruistic. It is also held that Bodhisattva Universal Worthy personifies the "universally worthy practice" of the Buddha to benefit others.

THE WISDOM OF MANJUSHRI
AND THE PRACTICE OF UNIVERSAL WORTHY

Ikeda: It all comes down to practice. Bodhisattva Universal Worthy symbolizes practice. This corresponds to wisdom, which is symbolized by Bodhisattva Manjushri, who appears in the sutra's "Introduction" chapter. The wisdom of Manjushri is so well known in Japan that there is the saying, "Three heads put together equal the wisdom of Manjushri."

The Lotus Sutra, which begins with a question from the wise Manjushri, concludes with Universal Worthy, who represents practice. This is because it is practice that will spread the Mystic Law expounded in the sutra throughout the world.

Manjushri and Universal Worthy are the two representative bodhisattvas of Mahayana Buddhism. They stand watch over the Lotus Sutra like two guards. In fact, they protect Bodhisattva Superior Practices, who propagates the Mystic Law implicit in the sutra. In a way that anyone can easily understand, this indicates just how noble is the person who spreads the Lotus Sutra in the Latter Day of the Law.

Endo: These two bodhisattvas are indeed heroes of Mahayana Buddhism.

Ikeda: Shakyamuni later explains this when he says, "Universal Worthy, if you see a person who accepts and upholds this sutra, you should rise and greet him from afar, showing him the same respect you would a Buddha" (LSOC, 365).

THE FOREMOST POINT

Saito: Nichiren Daishonin describes this passage as the "foremost point" (OTT, 192). This contains the foremost point of the Buddha's teaching in the "Encouragements of the Bodhisattva Universal Worthy" chapter. Shakyamuni condensed the

Lotus Sutra, which he preached over a period of eight years, into eight characters and left them behind for all living beings in this later age. These eight characters are rendered as: "If you see a person who accepts and upholds this sutra, you should rise and greet him from afar, showing him the same respect you would a Buddha" (LSOC, 365). These words conclude the sutra. "Should" shows that these words refer to the future. "Should rise and greet him from afar" indicates that we should without fail show the practitioners of the Lotus Sutra the kind of respect we would show a Buddha (see GZ, 781).

He is saying that if the entire Lotus Sutra, which was expounded continuously over eight years, were to be summarized in a single statement, it would be that we should revere a practitioner of the Lotus Sutra who will appear in the future as we would the Buddha. To revere that person with "the same respect you would a Buddha" means to revere that person as a Buddha. The true meaning of this statement is that a practitioner of the Lotus Sutra in the Latter Day of the Law is a Buddha.

Ikeda: That point itself is the spirit of the entire Lotus Sutra. That's why the Daishonin calls it the "foremost point." This means that in the Latter Day the Lotus Sutra is meaningless unless one reveres Nichiren Daishonin as the Buddha.

On that premise, the Daishonin instructed that upon seeing disciples with a direct connection in faith to the Daishonin who are dedicated to kosen-rufu, one should "rise and greet them from afar showing them the same respect one would a Buddha."

Suda: The priesthood, in trampling on the Daishonin's declaration of this "foremost point," has completely betrayed him.

Endo: In light of this one point alone, it is perfectly clear that what Nichiren Shoshu calls the "foremost point that [Shakyamuni] wished to convey to us" has absolutely nothing to do with Nichiren Daishonin.

Saito: Nikko Shonin, the second high priest and the one to whom the Daishonin entrusted his teaching, clarifies this in his final "Admonitions." In what represents firm dedication to the spirit of the oneness of mentor and disciple, Nikko says: "As for practitioners who treasure the Law more highly than their own lives, even if they are but humble teachers of the Law, you must hold them in great esteem, revering them as you would the Buddha" (GZ, 1618).

Endo: This is the Soka Gakkai spirit.

Suda: He is saying that those who exert themselves in sharing Buddhism with others are far worthier of respect than any person of high status.

Ikeda: That's right. There may be those, however, who have a difficult time with propagation and whose efforts are not appreciated by other members. But if they truly respect and care for their fellow members, for the SGI and for the Gohonzon and do activities to the best of their ability out of a desire to achieve kosen-rufu, then they are truly noble. They are emissaries of the Buddha.

No matter how they might be slandered or persecuted, in the end they will attain the state of Buddhahood without fail. This is clear when viewed from a long-term perspective. We can definitely see this over five, ten, twenty or thirty years or over the course of a lifetime.

On the other hand, though some may hold high positions in the organization or become famous in society, if they lose their faith and their spirit of concern for fellow members, they cannot attain Buddhahood. And if members, who are the Buddha's children, are made to suffer on account of such people's lack of concern, then those people will naturally suffer retribution.

The First and Last Characters Represent Life and Death

Ikeda: We must not forget that the final Chinese character of the "Universal Worthy" chapter means "departed": "They bowed in obeisance and departed" (LSOC, 366). This signifies death.

Saito: After Bodhisattva Universal Worthy vows to protect practitioners in the Latter Day, Shakyamuni praises him. Shakyamuni then tells Universal Worthy that since he himself will also protect future practitioners, Universal Worthy should revere them all as Buddhas.

Suda: This brings Shakyamuni's preaching in the Lotus Sutra's twenty-eight chapters to a close.

Saito: After that, all those in the great assembly at Eagle Peak rejoiced greatly and, embracing the Buddha's words in their hearts, show reverence to the Buddha and take their leave. This concludes the sutra.

The Daishonin says that the word *departed* that concludes the twenty-eight chapters signifies death. He also explains that the first character in the sutra, often translated as *thus* (in Burton Watson's translation [see "Editor's Note," p. vii], the entire phrase is translated as "This is what I heard"), expresses birth or life.

Suda: I think that Kumarajiva must have done this consciously when he translated the sutra from Sanskrit into Chinese.

Saito: The Daishonin says that this signifies the two principles of birth and death.

Ikeda: It's a wonderful translation.

The verse section of the "Life Span" chapter begins with the word *ji,* or "I," and ends with *shin,* or "body." The Daishonin explains this, saying, "The beginning and end are 'since' and 'body,' that make up *ji-shin* (oneself)" (OTT, 140). One's life itself continues over the eternity of past, present and future. This is the gist of the verse section. These two characters directly express the fundamental intent of the entire section.

In a similar manner, the twenty-eight chapters in their entirety, from the first word *thus* to the last word *departed*, express life and death.

Suda: The translator Kumarajiva was indeed a genius.

THE ENTIRE UNIVERSE IS COMPRESSED INTO ONE'S MIND

Ikeda: Why, then, does *thus* signify life?

Saito: We have a hint in the Daishonin's statement, "When the Dharma-realm is compressed into a single mind, this is the principle of *nyo* [thus]" (OTT, 196). Simply put, it seems that life, which is at one with the universe, is compressed into our individual consciousness. We receive life in this world as an entity of the oneness of the macrocosm and the microcosm.

Suda: "Thus" could be taken to mean "like." In this sense, the Daishonin's statement may indicate that "a single mind is *like* the Dharma realm," that is, the universe. "Thus" also has the meaning "according to."

Endo: In the Judeo-Christian tradition, God created people "in his image, according to his likeness" (Genesis 1:26). If God is viewed as the cosmic life, then there might be some point of commonality with Nichiren Buddhism.

Saito: The Daishonin also states: "When a single mind is opened and pervades the Dharma-realm, this is the principle of *ko* [departed]" (OTT, 196). The microcosm of one's life opens to and dissolves into the macrocosm. At that point, we "depart." This is death.

Of course, macrocosm, here, does not mean only the physical universe but the universe of all life, of which the physical universe is a part. It is the Ten Worlds from hell to Buddhahood.

Ikeda: When persons in the world of hell "depart" this world, their lives will meld into the world of hell pervading the universe. For that life, the entire universe becomes the world of hell. It's not that hell or any of the Ten Worlds exists in a particular location.

EINSTEIN'S INTUITION

Ikeda: With regard to the meaning of the character *nyo*, or *thus*, the Great Teacher Miao-lo of China states: "It is known that one's body is comparable to the universe." He identifies parts of the human body as resembling the sun and moon, mountains and rivers. This is explained in detail in "The Unanimous Declaration by the Buddhas of the Three Existences regarding the Classification of the Teachings and Which Are to Be Abandoned and Which Upheld" (see WND-2, 848–49).

Also, as the Daishonin discusses elsewhere (see GZ, 693), our bodies can be viewed as consisting of the five elements of earth, water, fire, wind and space; with each of these further corresponding to the five planets—Saturn, Mercury, Mars, Venus and Jupiter; and to the five organs—spleen, kidneys, heart, lungs and liver, respectively.

The Daishonin explains that Myoho-renge-kyo is the foundation underlying all of these. In other words, both the macrocosm and the microcosm are entities of the Mystic Law, and so they are one.

We find comparisons between the macrocosm and the microcosm in ancient and medieval Western thought. In the modern age, while coming from a somewhat different angle, it seems that Einstein intuitively believed in the existence of a grand harmonizing principle in the universe. He remarked:

> Everyone who is seriously involved in the pursuit of science becomes convinced that a spirit is manifest in the laws of the Universe—a spirit vastly superior to that of man . . . In this way the pursuit of science leads to a religious feeling of a special sort, which is indeed quite different from the religiosity of someone more naive.[2]

And:

> Everything is determined . . . by forces over which we have no control. It is determined for the insect as well as for the star. Human beings, vegetables, or cosmic dust—we all dance to a mysterious tune, intoned in the distance by an invisible piper.[3]

Saito: He was a man of great intuition.

Ikeda: Einstein believed that the idea of an anthropomorphic God should be abandoned because such a concept pits science and religion against each other.

At any rate, the first and last chapters of the Lotus Sutra express the two aspects of life and death. This is evidence that life and death are the basic theme of the Lotus Sutra. In fact, the same can be said about each of the sutra's twenty-eight chapters. The title of each chapter signifies life and the conclusion of each chapter signifies death. Each chapter reiterates this theme of life and death.

The two phases of life and death are functions of Myoho-renge-kyo. When we uphold the Mystic Law and become one with it, for the first time we attain the state of life in which we enjoy total freedom in both life and death, a state where both life and death are joyful. The Lotus Sutra was expounded to enable us to achieve such a state.

There are many profound teachings concerning the two words *thus* and *departed*, and I would encourage everyone to look further into their meanings.

HUMANKIND'S NEED FOR COMPASSION

Suda: Until now, I had thought of Bodhisattva Universal Worthy as representing merely the power of intellect. But through our study of this chapter, it has become clear that this bodhisattva symbolizes the power of encouragement and the power of action. I have a completely new understanding.

Ikeda: Of course, Universal Worthy also includes intellect. He could perhaps be described as intellect in action. This is not simply knowledge or wit but the light of intelligence to lead people to happiness. That is what makes him a bodhisattva. Concretely speaking, he represents intellect based on faith.

Religion that lacks intelligence becomes self-righteous. Examples of the harm brought on by such religions are too numerous to count. Intelligence alone will not produce happiness.

I am reminded of the unforgettable words of the champion of Korean independence, Kim Ku:

> I want our country to become the most beautiful country in the world. I do not want our country to become the richest and strongest . . . What humankind today lacks is neither force of arms nor economic strength . . . We have already achieved a great deal in the natural sciences, making it fully possible for all people to live happily. The fundamental reason that humankind is miserable at present is the lack of humanity and justice, the lack of a spirit of compassion, the lack of love. If such a spirit could be

developed, it would be possible, with the material resources existing at present, for all two billion people on the planet to lead fulfilled lives.[4]

Kim Ku spoke these words after Korea had achieved independence. Korea had such a great statesman.

It is not intelligence but rather intelligence infused with compassion that humankind lacks. It is true wisdom. Kosen-rufu is a movement to develop such wisdom.

WISDOM ARISES FROM A SENSE OF RESPONSIBILITY

Ikeda: My endeavors to realize kosen-rufu do not derive from a narrow-minded desire to simply spread the religion that I practice. They arise from my conviction that the more people there are in the world who chant and uphold the Mystic Law, the more the world will move in the direction of peace. This will become clear in the long run.

If nuclear war were to break out, the earth would be destroyed. During the Cold War, in particular, no one could guarantee that a third world war would not occur.

This may sound presumptuous, but I have spread the teaching of the treasure tower of life that is the Lotus Sutra throughout the world. While this movement has only just gotten under way, I believe the flow has been established.

President Toda used to say, "I am struggling right now for the sake of people two hundred years in the future." This is exactly how I feel. I ask myself, "How can I guide humankind today, along with our children and grandchildren, in the direction of happiness and peace?" I have taken action with the attitude that I am carrying the world on my shoulders.

When I stood up with such a sense of responsibility, it was as though a gale of wisdom started to blow through my mind. I was able to seize the initiative.

Endo: Your efforts to promote friendship with China and the Soviet Union, your many dialogues with leading figures in various fields, the cultural and educational activities of the Min-On Concert Association, Fuji Art Museum and Soka University— all of these must have been born from that wisdom.

Ikeda: It's not a question of whether one is intelligent. As long as one is earnest, wisdom will well forth without fail. That is why Bodhisattva Universal Worthy pledges that if a practitioner forgets a phrase or verse of the Lotus Sutra, he will appear to instruct the person. If we could not gain wisdom through our practice, then the "Universal Worthy" chapter, the entire Lotus Sutra, would be a lie.

There might be some who say, "I am practicing wholeheartedly, but I'm not gaining wisdom." It is usually in such cases, however, that the person thinks of him- or herself as smart. If we think, on the other hand, "Well, I'm not that bright, but if this is all I can do, then I will be letting everyone down," and then chant with our whole being, it is impossible that the situation will not change.

As long as we have the attitude deep down that "Surely someone else will take care of it" or "This has nothing to do with me," then the "transcendental powers" of Bodhisattva Universal Worthy will not appear in our life. When we stand up in faith, however, determined to do it ourselves, we are able to transcend our ordinary capabilities and take action that accords with supreme wisdom.

"THUS" AND "DEPARTED" INDICATE THE FAITH OF THE ONENESS OF MENTOR AND DISCIPLE

Ikeda: President Toda gave guidance on all kinds of matters during his lifetime. Hearing him speak, many people thought, "You say that, but the reality is different." I, however, listened to him and tried to accept everything he said. And I have put everything into practice exactly as he taught.

He once told me: "Whatever your position, always protect the Soka Gakkai." This was a single comment of my mentor. Even if, against all odds, President Toda were to have forgotten this himself, his having said it was a fact. Therefore, cherishing these words in my heart, I have at all times conducted myself just as he instructed.

Twenty years have passed since I retired from the position of Soka Gakkai president. Because I am now honorary president of the Soka Gakkai, I am technically free of many responsibilities. Organizational positions, however, are only temporary, while faith is a lifetime issue, a matter of one's heart.

"Whatever your position, always protect the Soka Gakkai." I have endeavored to put my whole life into living my mentor's instructions. The oneness of mentor and disciple exists when one practices exactly as the mentor teaches. This is the Lotus Sutra. This is what it means to practice the Buddha's teaching. This is the true meaning of "This is what I heard."

The word *thus* that starts the Lotus Sutra expounds the oneness of mentor and disciple. When we start to take action with the goal of realizing this state of oneness, we can "depart" from the fundamental darkness in our own lives.

We "depart" from the sickness of earthly desires and delusions, and the sun of Buddhahood brilliantly rises within us. This is the significance of the final word of the Lotus Sutra, *departed*.

The twenty-eight chapters of the Lotus Sutra passionately call on us to take action based on the oneness of mentor and disciple.

Notes

1. *Words and Phrases of the Lotus Sutra*, vol. 10.

2. Albert Einstein, *The Quotable Einstein*, ed. Alice Calaprice (New Jersey: Princeton University Press, 1996), p. 152.

3. Ibid., 146.

4. Kim Ku, *Pekupomu Iruji—Kim Gu Jijoden* (Baek Bum Ilji—Autobiography of Kim Ku), trans. Hideki Kajimura (Tokyo: Heibonsha, 1973), p. 331.

5. As of 2012, the Soka Gakkai International (SGI) has more than twelve million members in 192 countries and territories around the world.

8   The Lotus Sutra Is a Teaching
of the Oneness of Mentor and Disciple

Saito: A pioneer member shared the following account with me. President Toda once visited Shimonoseki City in Yamaguchi Prefecture for the completion ceremony of a renovated temple there. After the ceremony, he attended a banquet where people took turns singing songs.

When someone began to sing "Song of the Sons of Japan," a traditional song of the young men's division, President Toda suggested that instead they sing "White Tiger Brigade."[1] As participants energetically sang, President Toda stood listening. Behind his thick glasses, tears welled in his eyes.

Afterward he remarked: "While you are all enjoying yourselves like this, my dear Daisaku is waging a desperate struggle in Osaka. Now that I've heard 'White Tiger Brigade,' I'm going to bed." His voice was choked with emotion as he spoke. Then he took his leave. This completely changed the mood of the evening.

Endo: And that took place when?

Ikeda: I seem to remember it was April 1957. It is my great fortune to have had such a mentor.

Endo: That was when you took leadership of activities in Osaka during the time of the House of Councillors by-election. That struggle led to your arrest on July 3.[2]

Saito: It was a struggle against corrupt power. Ten days later (on April 30), President Toda suddenly fell ill, and one year later he died. Even in his weakened condition, Mr. Toda's concern for you, the person to whom he would entrust the future of kosen-rufu, was tremendous.

Ikeda: He was a mentor of immense compassion. He once told me, "If you should die, I would rush to where you were and lie down with you and join you in death." It was my determination, too, to give my life to protect the Soka Gakkai.

Saito: This will be our last in this series of discussions on the Lotus Sutra. Having come to this point, I deeply feel that the Lotus Sutra is ultimately a teaching of mentor and disciple. That is the core theme running through the entire work.

"Expedient Means," the second chapter, for example, expounds the principle of the true aspect of all phenomena, revealing that all living beings equally possess the Buddha nature. The people of the two vehicles of voice-hearers and cause-awakened ones (learning and realization)—who, it had been taught, could not attain Buddhahood—then receive a prophecy of future enlightenment.

Throughout the sutra's theoretical teaching, or first half, the idea that the Buddha (the mentor) and all living beings (the disciples) are inseparable is elucidated in a variety of ways.

Ikeda: That's right. The sutra also explains in the "Devadatta" chapter that even evil people and women can become Buddhas.

Suda: It proclaims: "All people can become Buddhas!"

Ikeda: A Buddha is one who has awakened to the truth that all people are potentially Buddhas. A Buddha's enlightenment is none other than this. There is therefore no such thing as a

Buddha who is arrogant or who looks down on others. Such behavior would indicate that one is not the genuine article.

A Battle Against Arrogance

Suda: In the description of the three powerful enemies found in the "Encouraging Devotion" chapter, all three are labeled as arrogant. They are called arrogant lay people, arrogant priests and arrogant false sages.

I think arrogance itself is the enemy of the Lotus Sutra. In particular, arrogant false sages are those who, while revered by others as sages, harbor malice in their hearts. The sutra says that they in fact "despise and look down on all humankind" (LSOC, 232).

Endo: The Nichiren Shoshu priesthood is a textbook example. The Lotus Sutra is a struggle between the Buddha's spirit to respect all human beings and that of the devil to look down on them. In my opinion, the battle with the devil king of the sixth heaven is the sutra's ultimate teaching.

Ikeda: Exactly. When we resolutely carry out this struggle in the unity of mentor and disciple, we first experience the world of Buddhahood welling forth from our lives. Then the lotus flower of the Mystic Law begins to blossom.

Myo, or "mystic," corresponds to mentor; and *ho*, or "law," to disciple. They are indivisible. *Renge*, or "lotus flower," symbolizes the simultaneity of cause and effect. *Cause* refers to the nine worlds and thus to the disciple, while *effect* indicates the world of Buddhahood and the mentor. Hence, mentor and disciple are one. The Mystic Law and the lotus flower both express the oneness of mentor and disciple. This is the meaning of Myoho-renge-kyo.

Buddhahood is found in the faith to spread the Mystic Law

far and wide. We should deeply reflect on the Daishonin's words:

> Never seek this Gohonzon outside yourself. The Gohonzon exists only within the mortal flesh of us ordinary people who embrace the Lotus Sutra and chant Nam-myoho-renge-kyo . . . This Gohonzon also is found only in the two characters for faith. (WND-1, 832)

Faith means action. It is struggle. To the very last moment of his life, President Toda burned with passion for kosen-rufu. The same was true of the first Soka Gakkai president, Tsunesaburo Makiguchi. This world-class scholar and person of outstanding character died in prison! Japan's militarist authorities killed him.

The year President Makiguchi was imprisoned (1943), he had declared that it was time to save the nation from crisis, and in the spring of that year, he began lecturing to students on the Daishonin's treatise "On Establishing the Correct Teaching for the Peace of the Land."

He was imprisoned on July 6. Many so-called disciples, who had referred to Mr. Makiguchi as their mentor, suddenly turned around and began denouncing him as a scoundrel and saying he had it coming. The human heart is a fearful thing.

President Toda, on the other hand, was the only one who felt tremendous gratitude toward his mentor. He would later address Mr. Makiguchi in an elegy saying, "In your vast and boundless mercy, you took me with you even to prison."[3] There could be no starker contrast than that between Mr. Toda and the others.

President Makiguchi died in November 1944. He died in prison, where he had poured his life into reading "On Establishing the Correct Teaching for the Peace of the Land."

An Awakening in Prison

Ikeda: Mr. Toda, the disciple who shared Mr. Makiguchi's spirit, read the Lotus Sutra and perceived its essence while in prison at the same time as his mentor.

He realized that "Buddha" is the "great life" that pervades the universe, and that he was a product of that great eternal life—life that from time without beginning has constantly existed and operated in the cosmic world. In other words, he realized that he was a child of the Buddha.

As inquiries about humanity advance, the validity and importance of this profound realization regarding life will no doubt be persuasively demonstrated. We are in fact already entering such a time.

President Toda often said: "This [truth] isn't something I studied and learned. It's something I remembered." As a result of his painful ordeal in prison, President Toda became extremely nearsighted. When reading the Daishonin's writings or some other material, he would take off his glasses and squint his eyes, bringing the object so close that it nearly touched his nose. He would remark: "With my vision the way it is, I don't read the Gosho the way all of you do. Nichiren Buddhism is recalled."

When asked a question about Buddhism, he would give his opinion and say: "I'm sure the Daishonin said the same thing. I know it's written somewhere."

And sure enough, when we would go and look, we would find the Daishonin's same teaching in *The Record of the Orally Transmitted Teachings* or some other writing.

He would also describe how on numerous occasions when pondering a difficult portion of the teachings, the meaning would just come to him as if out of the blue.

President Toda was enlightened to the oneness of mentor and disciple. He "remembered" the truth that he had been exerting himself as a disciple with the same spirit as Nichiren

Daishonin since the remote past. Understanding this, how could he begrudge his life?

With nothing but appreciation, we should advance toward kosen-rufu. There is no enlightenment in the Latter Day of the Law and no world of Buddhahood apart from the faith to move eternally in the direction of kosen-rufu. This is what President Toda taught.

Buddhism of the True Cause Is the Buddhism of Hope

Saito: To continually go forward—this is the Buddhism of the True Cause.

Ikeda: Now is eternity. Right now is the beginning. The past is gone. The future has not yet arrived. The present moment is all that exists.

The present in an instant becomes the past. We may say that it exists; we may also say that it doesn't exist. This is the meaning of non-substantiality. Life continues from moment to moment. Apart from this moment, life has no actuality. One moment we might feel happiness, the next, misery.

To view this moment of life as the direct effect of some cause made in the past is to think in terms of the true effect. To think, in other words, "I did that, so this happened." But that perspective alone will not give rise to hope.

The key is to view one's life at the present moment as the cause for creating future effects. This is the true cause that reaches the very depths of one's being. It is not a superficial cause.

Temporally, our lives are rooted in the life of time without beginning. Spatially, they are the true cause that pervades the entire realm of phenomena. This is Nam-myoho-renge-kyo, the eternal cosmic life, the great principle that moves the entire universe and sparks constant development.

Therefore, when we believe in the Gohonzon as the

embodiment of that Law, chant the Mystic Law and take action, at that moment we are experiencing eternity. It is then that the eternally pure and boundless life force that is "something that was not worked for, that was not improved upon, but that exists just as it always has" (OTT, 141) wells forth. We enjoy complete freedom in both the present and the future. Nichiren Buddhism is the Buddhism of hope.

The Lotus Sutra is precious because in its depths is the Gohonzon. If we forget this one point, all our efforts will amount to nothing.

Saito: So the point is that each moment is time without beginning and everything always starts from now.

Ikeda: This is faith based on the Buddhism of the true cause. Faith means to have boundless hope.

No matter how bad our present circumstances might be, even if it seems we are fighting a losing battle, we must stand up determined not to be defeated and from there show actual proof of the limitless potential of the Mystic Law. Is this not the true purpose of faith?

Without putting our whole lives into creating something from nothing, we cannot know genuine faith. The intense challenge to create value—to change loss into gain, bad into good, and baseness into beauty—this is the spirit of Soka. This is faith.

The Daishonin says, "This passage is saying that, if in a single moment of life we exhaust the pains and trials of millions of kalpas, then instant after instant there will arise in us the three Buddha bodies with which we are eternally endowed" (OTT, 214).

We must not become cowardly and craven people who become disheartened and critical of others and think only about protecting themselves when things get even a little bit tough. Those who can pull together in the direst of circumstances are true comrades. Faith is the spirit to give even our very lives for the sake of kosen-rufu and the happiness of the people, whether we gain from it or not.

In the entire world, the SGI is the only group working to spread the Mystic Law throughout the world. We must steadfastly protect this noble organization. The SGI is the light of hope for humankind.

The Great Mission of the SGI

Suda: In a speech last year (1998) in Okinawa, Kyrgyz writer Chingiz T. Aitmatov said:

> *Humanism* is an extremely important word. Until now there have been systems of thought that served to bring people together in unity within a given ethnic group. But the kind of unity whereby people open their hearts to all others and forge bonds of trust based on friendship is a completely new spirit of unity that has never before been seen.
>
> Such unity cannot be realized without a supreme and sublime philosophy. This philosophy must be spread by an outstanding individual who is a product of the age. Through my long association with President Ikeda, I have come to believe that he is the very person who is promoting just such a philosophy . . .
>
> If I were asked to describe what kind of age the twentieth century has been, I think I would have to say it has been a century of war and frightening brutality. Some might characterize it as the age of the rise and fall of communism. Others might describe it as the age of mass culture born in the West. In other words, a great many would likely describe the twentieth century as having been the age of Westernization.
>
> I would distinguish the Soka Gakkai movement as

an undertaking that has transcended all of that, that has gone beyond the ideologies and politics of the past century. The Soka Gakkai emerged during the twentieth century, and it has advanced and developed while overcoming all manner of ordeals and obstacles. It is because of this continuous effort that we have been able to learn of a fresh perspective on the world. Let us all have great pride in this.

Globalization is proceeding as the overall trend of the times. This is true in economics, as well as in the areas of technology and communications. But it is my belief that unless this is accompanied by a spiritual globalization, humankind will perish.

If the twenty-first century is really an age of globalization, and if globalization is indeed the way for genuine progress, then all of you, the members of the Soka Gakkai, have a truly immense and profound mission as we enter this new time . . .

If youth who are thinking about the future come into contact with the idea of humanism and with people who advocate humanism, then humankind will be able to advance even further. I have hope that the twenty-first century will be one of true progress for humankind.

Last, I would like to share my thoughts on the Soka Gakkai itself. In addition to enjoying utter freedom, the members of the Soka Gakkai believe in and strive to realize the ideals upheld by the organization. Ordinarily, religious doctrine tends to restrict in some way the individual's inner realm. But the Soka Gakkai has no such limitation. While each member is free as a unique individual, all are brought together by a common philosophy. Never before have I seen such a wonderful phenomenon . . .

The planet is a legacy that we must pass on to our

descendants. Human beings must be prevented from creating any more war, conflict, confrontation and other such destructive activity.

Now, as the twentieth century draws to a close and the twenty-first century is at hand, human reason is steadily approaching a universal perspective. We have entered a time when people are taking a more universal approach to life and thinking on a universal level. The sea, the mountains, the plains, the earth, the air—it is the responsibility of human beings to protect these treasures.[4]

DEVOTE ONESELF TO THE PRACTICE OF NEVER DISPARAGING

Endo: Dr. Aitmatov's words are very clear.

At the beginning of this series of discussions, President Ikeda, you explained the idea of cosmic humanism. It seems to me that the times are inevitably moving in that direction.

Ikeda: Viewing the earth from space, it is easy to see just how foolish it is for this beautiful planet to be divided into some two hundred "nations," and for them to be constantly at odds with one another. Before we are Japanese or American or Russian, we are human beings. If we cannot grasp something as natural as this, the twenty-first century will be dark indeed. We run the risk of creating an age where brutish violence runs rampant.

We must build a society in which people work with and help one another in a spirit of humanism; we must pursue a peaceful world in which people can lead happy and fulfilled lives with dignity. The basis for doing so is the spirit of never disparaging found in Nichiren Buddhism and which is the essence of the Lotus Sutra. It is the philosophy of thoroughly treasuring each person. I have said this many times, but of utmost significance is concrete action. Whether young or old, the important thing is to treat others with real love and compassion.

Half-heartedness and irresponsibility don't work in Buddhism. Such behavior only degrades the noble work of an emissary of the Buddha. Faith is not about leaving things up to others or believing that things will just work out somehow. Thinking that way will not bring about real joy; it will only leave one with regret in lifetimes to come. It is the Soka Gakkai's constant and untiring work to help even one person achieve real happiness that makes it truly great.

Suda: The late French art historian René Huyghe once lamented that the world's current obsession with materialism has put humanity in the worst possible state. I also heard that he remarked: "Now is the time when a spiritual civilization must be awakened. Only President Ikeda and SGI members, who uphold a philosophy based on the sanctity of life and are taking action to lead the human spirit onto the correct path, can save the world from crisis."

Ikeda: At any rate, no matter how flashy and decorated the words, if the actual sufferings of the people are ignored, those words are nothing more than a pretense of sincerity. If we were to place ourselves above others while living alone in peace and tranquillity, the spirit of Buddhism would be dead.

The Daishonin, who appeared in this world to teach others the essence of the Lotus Sutra, chose to be born into the lowest station in society. We should carefully reflect on the profound meaning of his declaration that he is the "son of a chandala family" (WND-1, 202). Born among those discriminated against and suffering the most, he waged a struggle for human rights against the discriminators while undergoing great persecution. Such effort itself is the practice of Lotus Sutra.

Suda: Having studied at Mount Hiei [of the Tendai school of Buddhism], one of the main centers of learning in Japan at that time, the Daishonin was qualified for the upper echelons. If he had wanted to live in peace at a temple in his hometown, I don't think it would have been a problem. But he purposely cast aside such an easy life.

HUMAN BEINGS ARE HUMAN BEINGS!

Ikeda: Though on a different level, the idea of deliberately challenging a difficult path in life brings to mind Pearl Buck's work, *The Child Who Never Grew*.[5] In it, she gives a candid account of her hardships while raising her developmentally disabled daughter. She describes her pain and how she would vacillate between feelings of hope and despair.

At one point, she was looking for a school that would be suitable for her only child. The people she met, however, though employed as caregivers for children with disabilities, seemed unaware that those children were human beings, too. She writes:

> The children who never grow are human beings and they suffer as human beings, inarticulately but deeply nevertheless. The human creature is always more than an animal.
>
> That is the one thing we must never forget. He is forever more than a beast. Though the mind has gone away, though he cannot speak or communicate with anyone, the human stuff is there, and he belongs to the human family.[6]

Her words are deeply moving.

"Happiness First and All Else Follows"

Ikeda: Pearl Buck eventually found a school to which she felt comfortable entrusting her daughter. The headmaster of the school had the motto, "Happiness first and all else follows." He explained: "That's not just sentimentality . . . It is the fruit of experience. We've found that we cannot teach a child anything unless his mind and heart are free of unhappiness. The only child who can learn is the happy child."[7]

This is similar to President Makiguchi's philosophy that education exists for the happiness of children.

At any rate, Mrs. Buck also relays in her book that she learned much from her daughter:

> It was my child who taught me to understand so clearly that all people are equal in their humanity and that all have the same human rights. None is to be considered less, as a human being, than any other, and each must be given his place and his safety in the world. I might never have learned this in any other way. I might have gone on in the arrogance of my own intolerance for those less able than myself. My child taught me humility.[8]

"My child taught me humility." How wonderful! The world is becoming a place where people are preoccupied with undermining others. Many go to extraordinary lengths to dig up others' faults and are ready to do whatever it takes to humiliate them even a little. We live in a society plagued by jealousy and envy.

Endo: In addition to being a writer, Pearl Buck is known for her peace activities. A person who respects the dignity of life can't help trying to awaken the same understanding in others.

Ikeda: Exactly. Mrs. Buck knew that a person without humility could not possibly guide others to happiness. She says:

> The attendant must be a person of affectionate and invincibly kind nature, child loving, able to discipline without physical force, in control because the children love him or her. Whether this attendant is well educated is not important. He must understand children, for he has in his care perpetual children.[9]

The same, I believe, applies not only in the realm of education but to leaders in all fields. Only when we truly care for another can we begin to understand that person's heart and thus become able to guide the person.

Saito: This is very inspiring.

The more I think about it, the more I realize just how significant the fact is that the votary of the Lotus Sutra, of the teaching that all people are Buddhas, appeared in this world as "the son of a chandala family" among the lowest class of society.

Ikeda: As practitioners of Nichiren Buddhism, we must always live as ordinary people, together with the people and dedicated to the welfare of the people. If in the future leaders should emerge who, having forgotten this point, think they are special and above everyone else, they must be ousted from our movement.

THE BODHISATTVAS OF THE EARTH ARE PEOPLE OF ETERNAL ACTION

From the Universal Worthy (Fugen) Sutra: *This Mahayana sutra [the Lotus Sutra] is the treasure storehouse of the Buddhas. It is the eye of the Buddhas of the*

*ten directions and the three existences. It is the seed that
gives rise to all Thus Come Ones over the three existences.
Someone who upholds this sutra upholds the Buddha's
body and carries out the works of the Buddha. Know that
this person is the emissary of all Buddhas. This person dons
the cloak of all Buddhas and World-Honored Ones and is
the child of the true Law of all Buddhas and Thus Come
Ones. You should practice the teaching of the Mahayana
and not allow the seeds of the Law to be destroyed.*[10]

Ikeda: At any rate, it is not enough just to say that all people
are Buddhas.

Without efforts to widely spread the Law for the purpose of
enabling all people to become Buddhas, the concept is nothing
more than theory. The essential teaching (second half of the
Lotus Sutra) is about actualization. Actualization equates to
action.

Earlier, we noted that the theoretical teaching explains the
oneness of mentor and disciple. But it is in the essential teaching
that genuine practitioners of this principle actually appear. They
are the Bodhisattvas of the Earth.

Suda: Yes. The essential teaching opens with the emergence
of countless Bodhisattvas of the Earth. These bodhisattvas are
really Buddhas in disguise.

Ikeda: Since their true identity is that of Buddhas, they share
a bond of mentor and disciple with Shakyamuni. Moreover,
though they are Buddhas themselves, they also actively put
the Buddha's teachings into practice as disciples. They are
bodhisattva-Buddhas advancing toward the realization of
kosen-rufu. They are symbols of the Buddhism of the true
cause. It is very significant that the Daishonin describes himself
as a "votary of the Lotus Sutra."

Endo: The Daishonin also refers to Shakyamuni as a "votary of the Lotus Sutra" (see WND-1, 448). *Votary* is a translation of the Japanese *gyoja*, which means a person who puts the teachings into action.

Saito: They are both people of action. They do not stop once they have attained Buddhahood. They are never satisfied with what they have achieved.

Ikeda: Having declared himself to be the votary of the Lotus Sutra, the Daishonin proceeds to rigorously examine whether his assertion is true. And he does so while undergoing incredible opposition.

Suda: That was during the Sado Exile (1271–74).

Endo: He says that at that time "999 out of 1,000 people" gave up their faith (WND-1, 469). His followers harbored doubts, thinking it strange that the Daishonin should be persecuted relentlessly when he had promised that faith in the Lotus Sutra leads to peace and tranquillity in the present existence. They questioned whether he could really be the votary of the Lotus Sutra when he was not receiving protection from the Buddhist gods.

Ikeda: To quell such doubts, as soon as he reached his place of exile on Sado Island, the Daishonin began writing the treatise "The Opening of the Eyes." He begins this work clearly explaining the reasons he has been so violently opposed. What he states directly after this explanation reveals his vast state of life.

Saito: That is in the famous passage: "This I will state. Let the gods forsake me. Let all persecutions assail me. Still I will give my life for the sake of the Law" (WND-1, 280).

The passage continues:

Shariputra practiced the way of the bodhisattva for sixty kalpas, but he abandoned the way because he could not endure the ordeal of the Brahman who begged for his eye. Of those who received the seeds of Buddhahood in the remote past and those who did so from the sons of the Buddha Great Universal Wisdom Excellence, many abandoned the seeds and suffered in hell for the long periods of numberless major world system dust particle kalpas and major world system dust particle kalpas, respectively, because they followed evil companions.

Whether tempted by good or threatened by evil, if one casts aside the Lotus Sutra, one destines oneself for hell. Here I will make a great vow. Though I might be offered the rulership of Japan if I would only abandon the Lotus Sutra, accept the teachings of the Meditation Sutra, and look forward to rebirth in the Pure Land, though I might be told that my father and mother will have their heads cut off if I do not recite the Nembutsu—whatever obstacles I might encounter, so long as persons of wisdom do not prove my teachings to be false, I will never yield! All other troubles are no more to me than dust before the wind.

I will be the pillar of Japan. I will be the eyes of Japan. I will be the great ship of Japan. This is my vow, and I will never forsake it! (WND-I, 280–81)

LIVING THE SPIRIT OF THE LOTUS SUTRA

Ikeda: Though the Daishonin makes various arguments in an effort to resolve the doubts of his followers, in his heart, he cares not in the least whether the Buddhist gods come to his aid. His spirit is to give his life to propagating the Mystic Law. He swears he will never relent, even if enticed with the most powerful position in the land or threatened with the beheading of his parents. He declares he will never break his vow to lead all people to enlightenment.

Regarding the Daishonin's spirit, Nichikan, the twenty-sixth high priest, says: "Each time I read this passage, my tears flow ceaselessly. Disciples in later ages should engrave these words in their hearts."[11]

Saito: Up until this point in the treatise, the Daishonin goes to great lengths to examine whether he is the votary of the Lotus Sutra in light of the sutra's teachings. Once he has done that, he completely transforms his approach.

Ikeda: That's right. He then clearly proclaims his own position as the one living the spirit of the Lotus Sutra, the spirit to achieve kosen-rufu. It's not a question of whether he can prove himself from the standpoint of the sutra. On the contrary, he himself justifies the Lotus Sutra by revealing the sutra's essence. That is, the spirit to enable all people to realize their full potential, come what may.

Endo: The Daishonin goes from evaluating himself based on the standard of the Lotus Sutra to using as his standard his own vow to lead all people to ultimate happiness and then employing the sutra to aid him in fulfilling that vow.

Saito: In my opinion, this passage is the most profound reading of the Lotus Sutra. It mustn't be taken lightly. Furthermore, I don't think these words can be truly grasped without challenging oneself to work for kosen-rufu in the same spirit as Nichiren Daishonin.

THE MYSTIC LAW MOVES LIKE A GREAT WIND

Ikeda: Kosen-rufu is itself the heart of the Lotus Sutra. It is the rhythm of the cosmic life that is Nam-myoho-renge-kyo. It is the endeavor to elevate the life state of all humanity to the world of Buddhahood.

Though we might like it to stand still, time flows ceaselessly. Winter always turns into spring. In the same way, humankind is ever moving in the direction of the wellspring of life that is the Mystic Law, moving toward the world of Buddhahood. As people taking responsibility for advancing this movement, we enjoy the highest honor as human beings.

The Daishonin says, "Now when Nichiren and his followers chant Nam-myoho-renge-kyo, they are like the blowing of a great wind" (OTT, 96). Wind is invisible, but no one can stop it. Wind and water always find their way around any obstruction.

The great wind of Nam-myoho-renge-kyo will not cease no matter who might try to block it. Humankind will without fail awaken to the truth that we are all one with the universe.

On an individual level, those who steadfastly chant daimoku can absolutely steer their lives onto the path of ultimate fulfillment, like a ship catching a powerful tailwind. To have weak faith is to sail on a weak wind. Strong faith brings forth a great wind. It all comes down to determination.

Even from his place of exile on Sado Island, a place from which people were not expected to return alive, the Daishonin stood up with the resolve to guide the people of Japan—the people who had persecuted him—and all humankind to enlightenment.

This immense compassion is Buddhahood. It is the core of the Lotus Sutra. The Gohonzon is infused with the life of Nichiren Daishonin, the life of the Buddha. This incredible mercy and compassion is the pulse of the living expression of the eternal universal life called Nam-myoho-renge-kyo.

RELIGION THAT IS NOT "OPIUM"

Ikeda: Karl Marx argued that "religion is the opium of the people."[12] Certainly there are religions that function as opiates.

Such religions become pawns of the iniquitous nature of authoritarian power, serving to numb the spirit of the people by teaching them to be satisfied with their lot in life and to seek happiness only after death. They function to keep the people in a state of ignorance.

But not all religions are opiates. There are religions that, determined to awaken the people, will not succumb to any power and are devoted to fighting oppression in an effort to enable all people to live freely and with dignity. This is the spirit of the Lotus Sutra. This is the purpose of a religion of the twenty-first century.

Suda: We can surely say that the aim of the Lotus Sutra is to open the eyes of the people—to cause the inherent flower of the Law to bloom in the life of each individual.

Ikeda: That aim is to open the world of Buddhahood; to awaken people to the supreme nobility of their existence. The original meaning of *Buddha* is "to open" or "awaken."

Suda: Yes. It comes from the Sanskrit word *budh*, which suggests the opening of a person's eyes or the blooming of a flower. Buddha literally means a person who is awake, a life in which the lotus flower has blossomed.

Ikeda: The flower of the Law blooms within the human being. It shines through our character. The Lotus Sutra is wholly a teaching for human beings.

The purpose of religion is to help each person become happy. But even a teaching whose original intent was to promote human happiness may start to restrict people. Even the Lotus Sutra could be used incorrectly to justify discrimination.

What is necessary to prevent the danger of such distortion from occurring? It is the mentor–disciple relationship. It is the disciple's inheritance of the resolute spirit and faith of the mentor to lead people to happiness.

Endo: Because the Nichiren Shoshu priesthood has lost the mentor-disciple spirit, they've gone completely astray.

INHERITING THE FAITH OF THE MENTOR

Ikeda: It would be terrible if this spirit were to disappear from the SGI. What is the meaning of the oneness of mentor and disciple in Buddhism? Physically, mentor and disciple are of course two different people. It is the heart, spirit and teaching that each uphold that make them inseparable. Therefore, it is important to seek a mentor who correctly practices the Law and to forge ahead with the aim of becoming one in spirit with that mentor.

A relationship not based on a shared principle or spirit, but where one blindly follows the orders of another in a relationship of boss and underling, or where one claims to be the disciple of the other but only in form, is not the correct way of Buddhism.

Buddhism is about the disciple taking on the spirit of the mentor to aspire eternally for kosen-rufu. Without the mentor-disciple relationship, there can be no advancement. There can only be decline.

Saito: It goes without saying that our faith is grounded on Nichiren Daishonin's teachings. He is the original mentor. Based on that understanding, Nikko Shonin, the Daishonin's successor, emphasized that the mentor-disciple relationship is essential to one's Buddhist practice. He says:

> In this teaching [of the Daishonin], the way to enlightenment is attained through correctly practicing the path of mentor and disciple. If we err in the path of mentor-disciple, then, even though we

might uphold the Lotus Sutra, we will fall into the hell of incessant suffering.

Suda: And as proof that the relationship between mentor and disciple in Buddhism is not just a matter of form, Nikko clearly stated as his last instructions, "Do not follow even the high priest of the time if he goes against the Buddha's teaching and propounds his own views" (GZ, 1618). What matters is whether one is correctly practicing the Buddha's teaching.

FAITH THAT GROWS STRONGER

Good men, this sutra [the Immeasurable Meaning Sutra, which is the preamble to the Lotus Sutra] arouses a spirit of aspiration in bodhisattvas who have not yet aroused a seeking mind; it arouses a spirit of mercy in those who lack a spirit of mercy; it arouses a spirit of compassion in those who are fond of killing; it arouses a spirit of rejoicing in those who are envious; it arouses an inclination to gladly discard attachments in those who have many attachments; it arouses an inclination to make offerings in those who are loath to part with their possessions; it arouses a spirit to uphold the precepts in those who have much arrogance; it arouses a spirit of forbearance in those who have a strong angry nature; it arouses a will to make tenacious effort in those who are lazy; it arouses a spirit of single-minded meditation in those whose minds are disordered and scattered in various directions; it arouses a spirit of wisdom in those who have much ignorance; it arouses a desire to help others in those who are not inclined to help others; it arouses a spirit to perform the ten good acts in those who commit the ten evil acts; it arouses an aspiration for the eternal and everlasting truth in those who yearn for continual flux; it arouses a spirit of never-regressing faith in those who are inclined to regress; it arouses a pure spirit in those who are defiled; it arouses a spirit to extinguish earthly

desires in those with many earthly desires. Good men, such
is the supreme and mystic power of benefit of this sutra.[13]

Ikeda: A disciple is one who carries on the faith of the mentor without any deviation. The important thing is to practice faith that grows ever stronger, without becoming arrogant. In his letters to his followers, the Daishonin repeatedly writes "more than ever" and "still more."

Saito: This is certainly true in his correspondence with the Ikegami brothers.

When they were faced with the hardship of their father Yasu-mitsu disowning the elder brother, the two brothers fought in unity just as the Daishonin instructed and came out completely victorious.

In addition to praising their joint struggle, the Daishonin strictly instructed them, saying: "From now on too, no matter what may happen, you must not slacken in the least. You must raise your voice all the more and admonish [those who slander]" (WND-2, 597).

Ikeda: Yes. We cannot let down our guard for even a moment. This is all the more true with regard to evil. Evil must be challenged with an unrelenting spirit.

Endo: Sure enough, the Daishonin's guidance to Shijo Kingo when the latter came up against a barrage of opposition was the same. He says: "Strengthen your power of faith more than ever" (WND-1, 681); "Strengthen your resolve to seek the way all the more and achieve Buddhahood in this lifetime" (WND-1, 946); and "Spur yourself to muster the power of faith" (WND-1, 1001).

Suda: Nichimyo was a believer who traveled to Sado Island with her daughter, Oto Gozen, to visit the Daishonin. The

Daishonin encourages this person of stalwart faith, saying, "All of you are my lay supporters, so how can you fail to attain Buddhahood?" (WND-1, 615). And he tells her, "Strengthen your resolve more than ever" (WND-1, 615).

Ikeda: He also instructs followers who have practiced for many years that they, too, should strengthen their faith more and more. To the mother of Nanjo Tokimitsu (the wife of the late Lord Ueno), the Daishonin says: "After hearing it, strive even more earnestly in faith. One who, on hearing the teachings of the Lotus Sutra, makes even greater efforts in faith is a true seeker of the way" (WND-1, 457). To make "even greater efforts in faith"—this is faith of the true cause. Where such faith exists, the world of Buddhahood manifests, and great benefit thus arises.

Saito: The Daishonin himself sets an example of faith that grows ever stronger. His life after he moved to Mount Minobu was definitely not one of idle retirement. While lecturing to several scores of his disciples on the Lotus Sutra, T'ien-t'ai's *Great Concentration and Insight* and other works, the Daishonin composed a large number of treatises and letters to each of his followers that provided detailed encouragement.

Endo: The works he produced during the eight years and four months he spent at Minobu are said to number approximately three hundred. This means that, on average, he wrote one piece every ten days. And these include a number of lengthy writings such as "The Selection of the Time" and "On Repaying Debts of Gratitude."

Considering that there are nearly 120 Gohonzon extant today thought to have been inscribed by the Daishonin during this time, these must have been days of intense and awesome struggle.

The Daishonin's Last Lecture on "On Establishing the Correct Teaching for the Peace of the Land"

Ikeda: To the very end, until the last moments of his life, the Daishonin lectured on "On Establishing the Correct Teaching for the Peace of the Land."

Saito: Yes. On the eighth day of the ninth month in 1282, about a month before his death, the Daishonin left Minobu. On the eighteenth, he arrived at the residence of Munenaka, the elder of the Ikegami brothers. Today, this is in Tokyo's Ota Ward.

Suda: The eleven-day journey must have really taken its toll. Although he made the trip on horseback, the Daishonin's age and ill health would surely have left him completely exhausted after his journey.

Endo: Despite his poor condition, however, the Daishonin delivered a final lecture for his followers.

Ikeda: That's right. And doubtless he did so wringing every last ounce of strength from his being. This is what a mentor does. For the sake of the beloved disciples and to forge a path for those to come, the mentor spares no effort. This is a Buddha. A Buddha is someone who fights on to the very end.

Youth Is Constant Growth and Advancement

Ikeda: At the height of the Atsuhara Persecution [in 1279], the Daishonin called on his followers: "Strengthen your faith day by day and month after month. Should you slacken in your resolve even a bit, devils will take advantage" (WND-1, 997). This is the essence of faith.

To the end of his days, President Makiguchi would say: "We are all youth! Youth is not a matter of years according to the calendar. It's about constant growth and advancement." There is no such thing as age in Buddhism. The beneficial power of the Lotus Sutra is "ageless and undying."

Indeed, outside the realm of Buddhism as well, those who are champions of life never stagnate. Johann Wolfgang von Goethe remarked, "For I've been a man for ever / And that means I've had to fight."[14] In *Jean Christophe*, Romain Rolland states that challenging suffering is the backbone of the universe. And Walt Whitman, whose poetry I loved reading as a youth, sings, "Now understand me well—it is provided in the essence of things that from any fruition of success, no matter what, shall come forth something to make a greater struggle necessary."[15]

Kosen-rufu is the same. So is human revolution.

I hope that the youth who will shoulder the twenty-first century will engrave these words in their hearts. Idleness is the cause of decline. Construction takes tenacious and painstaking effort. Destruction takes but an instant.

What kind of philosophy, what kind of movement, will guide people in the twenty-first century? We must keep in mind that the real struggle is now beginning.

Saito: For four-and-a half years we have held these discussions on the Lotus Sutra each month without interruption. During this time, we have delved deeply into the vast and boundless treasures of wisdom contained in the Lotus Sutra.

What really amazes me is how the essential spirit that we have discussed is entirely contained in some impressions that you recorded after listening to President Toda lecture on the Lotus Sutra when you were in your early twenties, President Ikeda. To conclude our discussion, let's introduce those impressions to our readers.

Ikeda: Though we have been studying the Lotus Sutra for

many months now, it would be fair to say that we have barely scratched the surface. Nichiren Buddhism is boundlessly deep.

I therefore hope that in the future an even more thorough study of the Lotus Sutra will be pursued based on our discussion thus far. For it is only we of the SGI, dedicated to spreading the Mystic Law around the globe, who can truly grasp the essence of the sutra's teachings.

IMPRESSIONS OF PRESIDENT TODA'S LECTURES ON THE LOTUS SUTRA
from the Seventh Series of Lectures (September 13, 1948)

How I marvel at the greatness and profundity of
the Lotus Sutra.
Isn't it the path to salvation for all humankind?
The teaching that enlightens one to the origin of
life and the universe,
the fundamental principle revealed to enable all people
to acquire the loftiest character and happiness.

I am twenty-one years old.
Since setting out on my journey of life,
what did I contemplate,
what did I do,
what did I make the wellspring of my happiness?
From this day on, I will advance bravely.
From this day on, I will live resolutely.
I will live within the life of the Great Law, win
over my sufferings.
True sadness inspires one to lead a great life.
I now see the true Great Path and perceive life's
true nature.

Mount Fuji stands solemnly in the evening twilight.
Graceful, multi-hued clouds.

The august moon rising in the east.
And my own existence.
Within my being pulses an activity of life.
And therein exists the zenith of beauty.
I realize my fortune in having encountered the
    fundamental principles of the immensely
    profound and infinite Lotus Sutra.
President Toda will become the mentor of
    humankind.
Lamenting the condition of his native land,
    he has the great confidence to advance, certain
    of imparting supreme happiness to humankind.
And he has the searing passion of justice that can
    burn through anything.

I shed tears of emotion at the vast compassion
    of Nichiren Daishonin, who fought tremendous
    persecution and lit a brilliant light out of the
    desire to enable all people to attain Buddhahood.
Youth must advance—eternally forward.
Youth must advance—for the eternal prosperity
    of the Law.

Followers of the Mystic Law, is there nothing
    shameful in your conduct?
Is your heart free of doubt?
If there is doubt or hesitation, you yourself are
    causing it.

Religious revolution is itself human revolution.
Likewise, it is educational revolution and economic
    revolution,
and will also become true political revolution.
The world is confused and polluted.
Who will purify society and the people?

The Soka Gakkai has a profound and great mission.
Its advance alone will decide everything.

Revolution means dedicating one's life.
We devote our lives to the Mystic Law.
Faithful commitment to a noble cause —
this will be the great cornerstone for the salvation
of the country and the world.

Youth, advance embracing great compassion.
Youth, move onward embracing a great philosophy.
I, at just twenty years of age, know the path
for leading a youth of the highest glory.[16]

NOTES

1. Byakko-tai (White Tiger Brigade): A corps of a few hundred youth organized in March 1868 to oppose the forces of the imperial restoration. Despite its desperate and heroic struggle, the group was decimated. It has come to be a symbol of loyalty, courage and determination.

2. In what has become known as the "Osaka Incident," Daisaku Ikeda was arrested in 1957 on trumped-up charges of violating election law. He was later cleared of any wrongdoing.

3. At Tsunesaburo Makiguchi's third memorial in November 1946. *Toda Josei zenshu* (Collected Writings of Josei Toda) (Tokyo: Seikyo Shimbunsha, 1983), vol. 3, p. 386.

4. From a speech delivered by Chingiz T. Aitmatov at the Seikyo Shimbun Culture Seminar, held at the Okinawa International Peace Center on November 18, 1998.

5. Pearl Buck (1892–1973): Winner of the Nobel Prize for literature in 1938.

6. Pearl Buck, *The Child Who Never Grew* (New York: The John Day Company, 1950), p. 42.

7. Ibid., 45.

8. Ibid., 51–52.

9. Ibid., 56.

10. *Hokekyo narabini kaiketsu* (The Lotus Sutra and Its Opening and Closing Sutras) (Tokyo: Seikyo Shimbunsha, 1974), p. 688.

11. *Commentaries of High Priest Nichikan*, p. 205.

12. *The Macmillan Book of Proverbs, Maxims, and Famous Phrases*, ed. Burton Stevenson (New York: Macmillan Publishing Company, 1948), p. 1948.

13. From the "Ten Benefits" chapter of the Immeasurable Meaning Sutra, *Hokekyo narabini kaiketsu*, pp. 99–101.

14. Johann Wolfgang von Goethe, *West-eastern Divan*, trans. J. Whaley (London: Oswald Wolff Publishers Ltd., 1974), p. 211.

15. Walt Whitman, *Leaves of Grass* (New York: Everymans Library, 1968), p. 134.

16. *See* Daisaku Ikeda, *Kantogen kogishu* (Collection of Editorials and Lectures) (Tokyo: Soka Gakkai, 1966), vol. 4, pp. 153–55.

Glossary

benefit (Skt *guna* or *punya;* Jpn *kudoku*)   Also, merit, virtue or blessing. In Buddhism, (1) meritorious acts or Buddhist practice that produce beneficial reward in this or future existences; and (2) benefit gained as a result of such good deeds or Buddhist practice. The Buddhist view of the law of causality holds that benefits accompany meritorious deeds.

bodhisattva (Skt; Jpn *bosatsu*)   One who aspires to enlightenment, or Buddhahood. *Bodhi* means enlightenment, and *sattva,* a living being. A person who aspires to enlightenment and carries out altruistic practice. The predominant characteristic of a bodhisattva is therefore compassion. Bodhisattvas make four universal vows: (1) to save innumerable living beings, (3) to eradicate countless earthly desires, (2) to master immeasurable Buddhist teachings and (4) to attain the supreme enlightenment.

Bodhisattvas of the Earth (Jpn *jiyu-no-bosatsu*)   An innumerable host of bodhisattvas who emerge from beneath the earth and to whom Shakyamuni Buddha entrusts the propagation of the Mystic Law, or the essence of the Lotus Sutra, in the Latter Day of the Law. They are described in "Emerging from the Earth," the 15th chapter of the Lotus Sutra. They are led by four bodhisattvas—Superior Practices, Boundless Practices, Pure Practices, Firmly Established Practices—and Superior Practices is the leader of them all. In "Supernatural Powers," the 21st chapter of the Lotus Sutra, Shakyamuni transfers the essence of the Lotus Sutra to the Bodhisattvas of the Earth, entrusting them with the mission of propagating it in the Latter Day of the Law.

Buddhahood (Jpn *bukkai*)   The state that a Buddha has attained. The ultimate goal of Buddhist practice and the highest of the Ten Worlds. The word *enlightenment* is often used synonymously with Buddhahood. Buddhahood is regarded as a state of perfect freedom, in which one is awakened to the eternal and ultimate truth that is the reality of all things. This supreme state of life is characterized by boundless wisdom and infinite compassion. The Lotus Sutra reveals that Buddhahood is a potential in the lives of all beings.

casting off the transient and revealing the true   The revealing of a Buddha's true status as a Buddha, and the setting aside of the Buddha's provisional or transient identity.

cause and effect   (1) Buddhism expounds the law of cause and effect that operates in life, ranging over past, present and future existences. This causality underlies the doctrine of karma. From this viewpoint, causes formed in the past are manifested as effects in the present. Causes formed in the present will be manifested as effects in the future. (2) From the viewpoint of Buddhist practice, cause represents the bodhisattva practice for attaining Buddhahood, and effect represents the benefit of Buddhahood. (3) From the viewpoint that, among the Ten Worlds, cause represents the nine worlds and effect represents Buddhahood, Nichiren Daishonin refers to two kinds of teachings: those that view things from the standpoint of "cause to effect" and those that approach things from the standpoint of "effect to cause." The former indicates Shakyamuni's teaching, while the latter indicates Nichiren Daishonin's teaching.

Consciousness–Only school (Skt Vijnanavada; Jpn Yuishiki-gakuha)   Also known as the Yogachara school, one of the two major Mahayana schools in India, the other being the Madhyamika school. This school upholds the concept that all phenomena arise from the *vijnana,* or consciousness, and that the basis of all functions of consciousness is the *alaya*-consciousness.

daimoku (Jpn)   (1) The title of a sutra, in particular the title of the Lotus Sutra of the Wonderful Law (Chin *Miao-fa-lien-hua-ching;* Jpn *Myoho-renge-kyo*). The title of a sutra represents the essence of the sutra. (2) The invocation of Nam-myoho-renge-kyo in Nichiren's teachings. One of his Three Great Secret Laws.

Daishonin (Jpn)   Literally, "great sage." When this honorific title is applied to Nichiren, it shows reverence for him as the Buddha who appeared in the Latter Day of the Law to save all humankind.

dependent origination (Skt *pratitya-samutpada;* Pali *paticcha-samuppada;* Jpn *engi* or *innen*)   Also, dependent causation or conditioned co-arising. A Buddhist doctrine expressing the interdependence of all things. It teaches that no being or phenomenon exists on its own but exists or occurs because of its relationship with other beings or phenomena. Everything in the world comes into existence in response to causes and conditions. In other words, nothing can exist independent of other things or arise in isolation.

devil king of the sixth heaven (Jpn *dairokuten-nomao*) Also, devil king or heavenly devil. The king of devils who dwells in the highest or the sixth heaven of the world of desire. He is also named Freely Enjoying Things Conjured by Others, the king who makes free use of the fruits of others' efforts for his own pleasure. Served by innumerable minions, he obstructs Buddhist practice and delights in sapping the life force of other beings.

dharma (Skt; Pali *dhamma*; Jpn *ho*) A term fundamental to Buddhism that derives from a verbal root *dhri*, which means to preserve, maintain, keep, or uphold. *Dharma* has a wide variety of meanings, such as law, truth, doctrine, the Buddha's teaching, decree, observance, conduct, duty, virtue, morality, religion, justice, nature, quality, character, characteristic, essence, elements of existence and phenomena. Some of the more common usages are: (1) (Often capitalized) The Law, or ultimate truth. For example, Kumarajiva translated *saddharma,* the Sanskrit word that literally means correct Law, as Wonderful Law or Mystic Law, indicating the unfathomable truth or Law that governs all phenomena. (2) The teaching of the Buddha that reveals the Law. The *Dharma* of *abhi-dharma* means the Buddha's doctrine, or the sutras. (3) (Often plural) Manifestations of the Law, i.e., phenomena, things, facts or existences. The word *phenomena* in "the true aspect of all phenomena" is the translation of *dharmas.* (4) The elements of existence, which, according to the Hinayana schools, are the most basic constituents of the individual and his or her reality. (5) Norms of conduct leading to the accumulation of good karma.

Eagle Peak (Skt Gridhrakuta; Pali Gijjhakuta; Jpn Ryoju-sen, Gishakussen, or Ryo-zen) Also known as Vulture Peak, Holy Eagle Peak or Sacred Eagle Peak, and simply Holy Mountain, Sacred Mountain or Holy Peak. A small mountain located northeast of Rajagriha, the capital of Magadha in ancient India. Eagle Peak is known as a place frequented by Shakyamuni, where he is said to have expounded the Lotus Sutra and other teachings. According to *The Treatise on the Great Perfection of Wisdom,* Eagle Peak was so named due to its eagle-shaped summit and many eagles or vultures inhabiting it. "Eagle Peak" also symbolizes the Buddha land or the state of Buddhahood, as in the expression "the pure land of Eagle Peak."

earthly desires (Skt *klesha*; Pali *kilesa*; Jpn *bonno*) Also, illusions, defilements, impurities, earthly passions or simply desires. A generic term for all the workings of life, including desires and illusions in the general sense, that cause one psychological and physical suffering and impede the quest for enlightenment.

earthly desires are enlightenment (Jpn *bonno-sokubodai*) Mahayana principle based on the view that earthly desires cannot exist independently on their own; therefore one can attain enlightenment without eliminating earthly desires. This is in contrast with the Hinayana view that extinguishing earthly desires is a prerequisite for enlightenment. Mahayana teachings reveal that earthly desires are one with and inseparable from enlightenment.

essential teaching (Jpn *hommon*)   Also original teaching. (1) The teaching expounded by Shakyamuni from the perspective of his true identity as the Buddha who attained enlightenment countless *kalpas* ago. It consists of the latter fourteen chapters of the Lotus Sutra, from the "Emerging from the Earth" through the "Universal Worthy" chapters. (2) In his writings, Nichiren Daishonin sometimes uses the term *essential teaching* to indicate the essential teaching of the Latter Day of the Law; that is, the teaching of Nam-myoho-renge-kyo.

expedient means (Skt *upaya;* Jpn *hoben*)   The methods adopted to instruct people and lead them to enlightenment. The concept of expedient means is highly regarded in Mahayana Buddhism, especially in the Lotus Sutra, as represented by its second chapter titled "Expedient Means." This is because expedient means are skillfully devised and employed by Buddhas and bodhisattvas to lead the people to salvation.

five components (Skt *pancha-skandha;* Jpn *go-on* or *goun*)   Also, five components of life, five aggregates or five *skandhas*. The five components are form, perception, conception, volition and consciousness. Buddhism holds that these constituent elements unite temporarily to form an individual living being. Together they also constitute one of the three realms of existence, the other two being the realm of living beings and the realm of the environment. (1) Form means the physical aspect of life and includes the five sense organs—eyes, ears, nose, tongue and body—with which one perceives the external world. (2) Perception is the function of receiving external information through the six sense organs (the five sense organs plus the mind, which integrates the impressions of the five senses). (3) Conception is the function of creating mental images and concepts out of what has been perceived. (4) Volition is the will that acts on the conception and motivates action. (5) Consciousness is the cognitive function of discernment that integrates the components of perception, conception and volition. Form represents the physical aspect of life, while perception, conception, volition and consciousness represent the spiritual aspect. Because the physical and spiritual aspects of life are inseparable, there can be no form without consciousness and no consciousness without form.

four sufferings (Jpn *shi-ku*)   The four universal sufferings: birth, aging, sickness and death. Various sutras describe Shakyamuni's quest for enlightenment as being motivated by a desire to find a solution to these four sufferings.

fundamental darkness (Jpn *gampon-no-mumyo*)   Also, fundamental ignorance or primal ignorance. The most deeply rooted illusion inherent in life, said to give rise to all other illusions. "Darkness" in this sense means inability to see or recognize the truth, particularly, the true nature of one's life. The term *fundamental darkness* is contrasted with the fundamental nature of enlightenment, which is the Buddha nature inherent in life.

Goddess Mother of Demon Children (Jpn Kishimojin)   A demoness said to have hundreds, maybe thousands of children and who took the lives of other children in order to feed her own. Shakyamuni rebuked her for her cruel and evil conduct and made her vow never to kill another child. In the Lotus Sutra, she pledges to safeguard the votaries of the sutra.

Gohonzon (Jpn)   The object of devotion. The word *go* is an honorific prefix, and *honzon* means object of fundamental respect or devotion. In Nichiren Daishonin's teaching, the object of devotion has two aspects: the object of devotion in terms of the Law and the object of devotion in terms of the Person. It takes the form of a mandala inscribed on paper or on wood with characters representing the Mystic Law as well as the Ten Worlds. Nichiren Buddhism holds that all people possess the Buddha nature and can attain Buddhahood through faith in the Gohonzon.

gongyo (Jpn)   Literally, to "exert oneself in practice." Generally speaking, gongyo refers to the practice of reciting Buddhist sutras in front of an object of devotion. The content and method of gongyo differ according to the school of Buddhism. In Nichiren Daishonin's teaching, gongyo means to chant the daimoku of Nam-myoho-renge-kyo and recite the "Expedient Means" chapter and the "Life Span" chapter of the Lotus Sutra with faith in the object of devotion called the Gohonzon. In this practice, chanting the daimoku constitutes the fundamental practice, and therefore it is called the primary practice. Recitation of the "Expedient Means" and "Life Span" chapters helps bring forth the benefits of the primary practice and is hence called the supporting practice.

Gosho (Jpn)   The individual and collected writings of Nichiren Daishonin. Gosho literally means honorable writings; *go* is an honorific prefix, and *sho* means writings. In general the word is used in Japanese as an honorific for certain books and writings, particularly for those of the founders and patriarchs of some Buddhist schools. Nikko Shonin, Nichiren's immediate successor, used the word *gosho* to refer to

Nichiren's works and made efforts to collect, copy and preserve them as sacred texts. As a result, a remarkable number of Nichiren Daishonin's works have been passed down to the present, and many are extant in his own hand.

Hinayana Buddhism (Jpn *shojo-bukkyo*)   One of the two major streams of Buddhism, the other being Mahayana. Teachings that aim at attaining the state of *arhat*. After Shakyamuni Buddha's death, the Buddhist Order experienced several schisms and eventually split into eighteen or twenty schools. Practitioners called themselves bodhisattvas, and their teachings Mahayana (great vehicle), indicating that their teaching was the vehicle to transport a great many people to enlightenment. In contrast, they referred to the earlier schools as Hinayana (lesser vehicle), implying that these teachings could only address a selected few but could not lead to the ultimate goal of enlightenment. This designation "Hinayana" was derogatory, and these schools naturally did not apply the name to themselves. The Sanskrit word *hinayana* is composed of *hina*, meaning lesser, and *yana*, meaning vehicle or teaching.

human revolution   A concept coined by the Soka Gakkai's second president, Josei Toda, to indicate the self-reformation of an individual—the strengthening of life force and the establishment of Buddhahood—that is the goal of Buddhist practice.

inconspicuous benefit (Jpn *myoyaku*)   Benefit deriving from Buddhist practice that accumulates over a period of time and is not immediately recognizable. The term is contrasted with conspicuous benefit, or benefit that appears in clearly recognizable form.

Jambudvipa   One of the four continents situated in the four directions around Mount Sumeru, according to the ancient Indian worldview. Jambudvipa is the southern continent.

Jataka   Also Jataka Tales or "Birth Stories." The stories of the previous lives of Shakyamuni Buddha. One of the traditional twelve divisions of the Buddhist canon. These stories depict the good acts carried out by Shakyamuni in previous lifetimes that enabled him to be reborn as the Buddha in India.

kalpa   An extremely long time. Sutras and treatises differ in their definitions, but kalpas fall into two major categories, those of measurable and immeasurable duration. There are three kinds of measurable kalpas: small, medium and major. One explanation sets the length of a small kalpa at approximately sixteen million years. According to Buddhist cosmology, a world repeatedly undergoes four states: formation, continuance, decline and disintegration. Each of these four stages lasts for twenty small kalpas and is equal to one medium kalpa. Finally, one complete cycle forms a major kalpa.

karma   Potential energies residing in the inner realm of life, which manifest themselves as various results in the future. In Buddhism, karma
is interpreted as meaning mental, verbal and physical action; that is,
thoughts, words and deeds.

kosen-rufu   Literally, to "widely declare and spread [Buddhism]."
Nichiren Daishonin defines Nam-myoho-renge-kyo of the Three
Great Secret Laws as the law to be widely declared and spread during
the Latter Day. There are two aspects of kosen-rufu: the kosen-rufu of
the entity of the Law, or the establishment of the Gohonzon, which
is the basis of the Three Great Secret Laws; and the kosen-rufu of
substantiation, the widespread acceptance of faith in the Gohonzon
among the people.

ku (Jpn)   A fundamental Buddhist concept, variously translated as non-
substantiality, emptiness, void, latency, relativity, etc. The concept that
entities have no fixed or independent nature.

Kumarajiva (344–413 c.e.)   Translator of the Lotus Sutra into Chinese.

Latter Day of the Law   Also, the Latter Day. The last of the three periods following Shakyamuni Buddha's death when Buddhism falls into
confusion and Shakyamuni's teachings lose the power to lead people
to enlightenment. A time when the essence of the Lotus Sutra will be
propagated to save all humankind.

Lotus Sutra   The highest teaching of Shakyamuni Buddha, it reveals that
all people can attain enlightenment and declares that his former teachings should be regarded as preparatory.

Mahayana Buddhism   The teachings that expound the bodhisattva practice as the means toward the enlightenment of both oneself and others,
in contrast to Hinayana Buddhism, or the teaching of the Agon period, which aims only at personal salvation. Mahayana literally means
"greater vehicle."

Many Treasures   Also referred to as Taho Buddha. A Buddha who appears, seated within the treasure tower at the Ceremony in the Air to
bear witness to the truth of Shakyamuni's teachings in the Lotus Sutra.

mentor-and-disciple relationship   *See* oneness of mentor and disciple.

Miao-lo   The sixth patriarch in the lineage of the T'ien-t'ai school in
China, counting from the Great Teacher T'ien-t'ai. Miao-lo reasserted
the supremacy of the Lotus Sutra and wrote commentaries on T'ien-
t'ai's three major works, thus bringing about a revival of interest in
T'ien-t'ai Buddhism. He is revered as the restorer of the school.

Middle Day of the Law   Also, the period of the Counterfeit Law. The
second of the three periods following a Buddha's death. During this

time, the Buddha's teaching gradually becomes formalized, the people's connection to it weakens, and progressively fewer people are able to gain enlightenment through its practice. Some sources define the Middle Day of the Law of Shakyamuni as lasting a thousand years, while others define it as five hundred years.

mutual possession of the Ten Worlds   The principle that each of the Ten Worlds contains all the other nine as potential within itself. This is taken to mean that an individual's state of life can be changed and that all beings of the nine worlds possess the potential for Buddhahood. *See also* Ten Worlds.

Mystic Law   The ultimate Law of life and the universe. The Law of Nam-myoho-renge-kyo.

Nam-myoho-renge-kyo The ultimate Law of the true aspect of life permeating all phenomena in the universe. The invocation established by Nichiren Daishonin on April 28, 1253. Nichiren Daishonin teaches that this phrase encompasses all laws and teachings within itself, and that the benefit of chanting Nam-myoho-renge-kyo includes the benefit of conducting all virtuous practices. *Nam* means "devotion to"; *myoho* means "Mystic Law"; *renge* refers to the lotus flower, which simultaneously blooms and seeds, indicating the simultaneity of cause and effect; *kyo* means "sutra," the teaching of a Buddha.

Nichiren Daishonin   The thirteenth-century Japanese Buddhist teacher and reformer who taught that all people have the potential for enlightenment. He defined the universal Law as Nam-myoho-renge-kyo and established the Gohonzon as the object of devotion for all people to attain Buddhahood. *See also* Daishonin.

ninth consciousness   One of nine kinds of discernment. The ninth consciousness, or *amala*-consciousness, is defined as the basis of all spiritual functions and is identified with the true aspect of life.

nirvana   Enlightenment, the ultimate goal of Buddhist practice.

oneness of life and environment   The principle stating that the self and its environment are two integral phases of the same entity.

oneness of mentor and disciple   This is a philosophical as well as a practical concept. Disciples reach the same state of Buddhahood as their mentor by practicing the teachings of the latter. In Nichiren Buddhism, this is the direct way to enlightenment, that is, to believe in the Gohonzon and practice according to the Daishonin's teachings.

saha world   A world full of suffering, or endurance. It refers to a land in which people must endure suffering and confront the reality of a world filled with earthly desires and illusions. It is in this world that

Shakyamuni chooses to preach the Law, noting that the Buddha land, where the Buddha dwells, is in fact the saha world.

shakubuku   A method of propagating Buddhism by refuting another's attachment to erroneous views and thus leading him to the correct Buddhist teaching.

Shakyamuni   Also, Siddhartha Gautama. Born in India (present-day southern Nepal) about three thousand years ago, he is the first recorded Buddha and founder of Buddhism. For fifty years, he expounded various sutras (teachings), culminating in the Lotus Sutra.

Soka (Jpn)   Literally, "value creation."

Soka Gakkai International   A worldwide Buddhist association that promotes peace and individual happiness based on the teachings of the Nichiren school of Buddhism, with more than twelve million members in 192 countries and territories. Its headquarters is in Tokyo, Japan.

Tatsunokuchi Persecution   An unsuccessful attempt to execute Nichiren Daishonin at Tatsunokuchi on the western outskirts of Kamakura on the night of September 12, 1271.

Ten Worlds   Ten life conditions that a single entity of life manifests. Originally the Ten Worlds were viewed as distinct physical places, each with its own particular inhabitants. In light of the Lotus Sutra, they are interpreted as potential conditions of life inherent in each individual. The ten are: (1) hell, (2) hunger, (3) animality, (4) anger, (5) humanity or tranquillity, (6) rapture, (7) voice-hearers or learning, (8) cause-awakened ones or realization, (9) bodhisattva and (10) Buddhahood.

theoretical teaching   T'ien-t'ai refers to the first fourteen chapters of the Lotus Sutra as the "theoretical teaching" where the historical Shakyamuni, the "provisional Buddha," preaches that he first attained enlightenment during his lifetime in India. The latter fourteen chapters are referred to as the "essential teaching" where Shakyamuni discards his provisional identity and confirms that he has attained enlightenment in the remote past. *See also* essential teaching.

three Buddha bodies   Three kinds of body a Buddha may possess. A concept set forth in Mahayana Buddhism to organize different views of the Buddha appearing in the sutras. The three bodies are as follows: (1) The Dharma body, or body of the Law (Skt *dharma-kaya*). This is the fundamental truth, or Law, to which a Buddha is enlightened. (2) The reward body (*sambhoga-kaya*), obtained as the reward of completing bodhisattva practices and acquiring the Buddha wisdom. Unlike the Dharma body, which is immaterial, the reward body is thought of as an actual body, although one that is transcendent and imperceptible to ordinary people. (3) The manifested body (*nirmanakaya*), or the physical form that a Buddha assumes in this world in order to save the people

time without beginning (Jpn *kuon ganjo*) Literally, *kuon* means the remote past, and *ganjo*, beginning or foundation. This refers to the remote past when Shakyamuni is said to have originally attained enlightenment. For Nichiren Daishonin, it means the eternal Law of Nam-myoho-renge-kyo and the original state of life that embodies Buddhahood, existing in time without beginning or end.

true cause Also, the mystic principle of the true cause. One of the ten mystic principles of the essential teaching (latter half) of the Lotus Sutra formulated by T'ien-t'ai (538–97). It refers to the practice that Shakyamuni carried out countless kalpas in the past in order to attain his original enlightenment. *See also* true effect.

true effect Also, the mystic principle of the true effect. The original enlightenment that Shakyamuni attained countless kalpas before his enlightenment in India. One of the ten mystic principles of the essential teaching (latter half) of the Lotus Sutra formulated by T'ien-t'ai (538–97). *See also* true cause.

votary of the Lotus Sutra A person who practices and propagates the teachings of the Lotus Sutra, staying true to its intent. In particular, Nichiren Daishonin refers to votaries such as T'ien-t'ai in China and Dengyo in Japan in the Middle Day of the Law, and in the Latter Day of the Law, the term applies to Nichiren himself as well as his followers who uphold the spirit through their behavior.

Index

Lotus Sutra and, 74; manifests as, 97, 100; meaning of the, 112–13; non-discriminatory behavior of, 96; oath of the, 129; origins of, 78, 100; reason to be called, 99; represents, 100; revered for, 73–74, 78–79; Shakyamuni says of, 77–78, 99; source of power of the, 75–76, 78–79; spirit of, 123, 145; Virgin Mary in comparison to the, 101–03. *See also* "Perceiver of the World's Sounds" chapter (Lotus Sutra)

Bodhisattva Superior Practices, function of, 227

Bodhisattva Universal Worthy, 11; acquiring the power of, 236; behavior of, 215; question by, 216; represents, 234; Shakyamuni's instruction to, 218–19, 227, 230; spirit of, 212, 214, 219, 226–27; vow of, 219–20, 230, 236. *See also* "Universal Worthy" chapter (Lotus Sutra)

Bodhisattva Wonderful Sound, 11–12, 194; encouragement sound of, 53; function of, 65; origin of the name of, 58; past existences of, 52–53; physical forms of, 62–63; *samadhis* attained by, 60; SGI members and, 63; size of, 42–43; symbolizes, 44–48; T'ien-t'ai and 66. *See also* "Wonderful Sound" chapter (Lotus Sutra)

Bodhisattvas of the Earth, 9–11; Nichiren Daishonin says of, 9; four leaders of the, 9, 199; identity of the, 253; mission of the, 9, 20–21

bodhisattvas of the essential teaching. *See* Bodhisattvas of the Earth

Bodhisattvas in the ten directions, 199

Brahma (deity), 5, 62, 118

Bragt, Jan Van, 104

Buck, Pearl, challenge of, 250–52

Buddha, 240–41, 263; emissaries of the, 229; meaning of, 258; other names of the, 19–20; will of the, 17

Buddhahood, 22; attaining, 88, 241–42, 244; benefit of establishing the world of, 26–27; Nichiren Daishonin says of, 32, 79, 181; effects of manifesting our, 18, 146; manifesting our, 15; Shakyamuni and, 4–5; Toda characterizes, 86; world of, 119

Buddhas, 199; secret language of all, 158–60; source of enlightenment of all, 137–38

Buddhism, 19, 25, 103, 109–10, 123, 136, 165, 204; Nichiren, 184, 244, 265; extinction of, 149; losing the spirit of, 249; encouragement to the followers of Nichiren Daishonin, 252; key to leading others to, 199; music in early, 59–60; Nikko Shonin's last instructions on correctly practicing, 260; prayers answered in, 105; purpose of practicing, 222; stages of practicing, 93–94; teaching of, 24, 34, 63, 259

Buddhist deities, 118, 165, 167; Nichiren Daishonin and, 151–52; protection of the, 165; representations of, 151; Toda and 148. *See also* Buddhist gods

Buddhist gods, Mia-lo and, 82; protection of the, 81–82

budh (Sanskrit), 258

bureaucracy, defeating, 116, 152

Caplan, Gerald, 92

carelessness, 81

caring, 221, 252

for single member of a, 198–99; winning in the, 206

family members, Buddhist, 176

father-daughter, relationship, 171

fathers, 175; concern for our, 172

Faust (Goethe), 101

fife and drum corps, establishment of the, 48–51; Toda's encouragement to the, 49

first-rate individuals, becoming, 51–52

Flores University, 162

Flower Virtue bodhisattva, 52

"Former Affairs of the Bodhisattva Medicine King" chapter (Lotus Sutra) *See* "Medicine King" chapter (Lotus Sutra)

"Former Affairs of King Wonderful Adornment" chapter (Lotus Sutra). *See* "Wonderful Adornment" chapter (Lotus Sutra)

four sufferings, 24, 194; Nichiren Daishonin's view of the, 28–29

Fuji Art Museum, 236

Fuji College, 116

Fukuzawa, Yukichi, 121

Gadgada-svara (stuttering voice), 52, 58

Gandhi, Mahatma, 104

Gandhism, 113

Gijo-bo, Nichiren Daishonin praising, 150

Gladly Seen by All Living Beings Bodhisattva, 12–15, 26; past life of, 15

globalization, Aitmatov's view of, 247

Goddess Mother of Demon Children, 102; Buddhist texts story of, 145; Nichiren Daishonin's interpretation of the name of, 144–46; protection of the, 146; transformation of, 146; two ways of reading the name of, 144–46; vow of, 140

Goethe, Johann Wolfgang von, 102, 264

Gohonzon, 13, 79, 115, 219; benefit of praying to the, 185; Nichiren Daishonin's instruction about the, 242; encountering the, 190; infused with the, 257; misconception of the role of the, 109; practice to the, 108; receiving the protection of the, 152–53; Toda's explanation of the benefits of the, 84–85; words on the upper left-hand corner of the, 141; words on the upper right-hand side of the, 140

gongyo, power of, 65

good fortune, 13; building our, 219; importance of, 129

good friends, 195; choosing, 201

gratitude, benefit of repaying one's debt of, 13; effect of losing our debt of, 13–14; faith of repaying one's debt of, 23–24

Great Bengal Famine, 126–27

Great Concentration and Insight (T'ien-t'ai), 262

Great Kanto Earthquake, 61

grief, benefit of expressing one's, 92; harmful effects of not expressing one's, 92

half-heartedness, 249

happiness, 195, 251; foundation of, 172, 179; individual, 113–14

hard power, 74

Havana University, 58

health, 25; true, 6, 33

heart, 15, 50; understanding a person's, 252

Heart Sutra, 75

heavenly being Freedom, 62

daimoku of the, 138; Nichiren Daishonin and, 66, 225; Nichiren Daishonin as the votary of the, 254–55; essence of the, 256; first word of the, 230–31; in five languages, 40; heart of the, 256–57; Ikeda's gratitude in encountering the, 266; last word of the, 230–31; Latter Day practice of the, 217–18; music and, 54–58; passage of proof illustrating the respect shown to practitioners of the, 214–15; popularity of the, 41; power of the, 3, 5–6; practical significance of the six chapters of the, 11; profundity of the, 265; prophecy of the, 214; purpose of the, 233; Shakyamuni's four conditions to practice the, 217; Shakyamuni's instruction of the, 252–53; significance of the addendum to the, 7–8, 10; spirit of the, 63, 103–04, 258, 264; teaching of the, 25, 103, 139, 189, 240–41, 245, 248–49; theme of the, 233; T'ien-t'ai's interpretation of the four conditions to practice the, 218; Toda's description of the benefit of practicing the, 84–85; understanding the, 21; unifying power of the, 113; words of the, 40–44

"The Lotus Sutra and Its World: Buddhist Manuscripts of the Great Silk Road" (exhibition), 39

Lotus Sutra of the Correct Law (Dharmaraksha), 66

love, real, 198

macrocosm, examples illustrating the oneness of the microcosm and the, 232

Mahakashyapa, 118

Mahayana Buddhism, bodhisattvas of, 227; musical offerings in, 54; provisional, 25

Makiguchi, Tsunesaburo, life of, 242; Mehta's remark about, 113; philosophy of, 252; significance of the death of, 16–17; Toda's address in an elegy for, 242; Toda's support of, 153–56

Many Treasures Buddha, 47, 107

marriages, Nichiren Daishonin with regard to, 193; illusion in, 198; real, 198

Marx, Karl, 257

Mary, Virgin, past images of, 102

"Mary Perceiver of the World's Sounds" (Maria Kannon), 102

Mass in C Major (Beethoven), 50

Matsubagayatsu Persecution, 81

Matsuo Basho, 3

Matsushita, Konosuke, leadership of, 89–90

Maudgalyayana, 118

McClelland, David, 92

"Medicine King" chapter (Lotus Sutra), 7–8, 19, 33; Nichiren Daishonin's view of the, 28; teaching of the, 5–6, 12–15, 34, 216

meetings, Buddhist, 223–24

Mehta, Vrajendra, 113; universe and, 114

members, encouragement to a leader for berating a, 211; scolding, 187

mentor, original spirit of the, 259, 263; seeking a, 259

mentor-disciple relationship, 258–59; Nichiren Shoshu priesthood and, 259; Nikko Shonin's view of the, 259–60; oneness of, 237, 241

Menuhin, Yehudi, 161

193; Nichiren Daishonin's, 199; sharing Buddhism with our, 199–200

patience, 198–99

peace, 112; achieving, 235; culture and, 55–56; inner, 45

people, bridging the gaps between, 65; importance of, 149–50; understanding individual circumstances of, 206, 211; voices of the, 97

"Perceiver of the World's Sounds" chapter (Lotus Sutra), 7–8, 71, 77, 83–85, 88, 95, 105, 216; benefit of revering the, 80, 82–83; having children and, 106; implicit meaning in the, 107; meaning of the, 88; original intent of the, 87; principle in the, 125; spirit of the, 103; teaching of the, 92; thirty-three bodies in the, 120–21; two aspects of blessings in the, 128

"Persecution by Sword and Staff," 225

Petrovsky manuscript, 39

philosophy, need for a correct, 207

pioneer members, encouragement from, 226

Plato, 59

poetry, dharani and, 159; *waka*, 159

poison, symbolizes, 118–19

poison into medicine, principle of changing, 33

politics, 207; Gandhi and, 124; Prince Shotoku and, 124; Fukuzawa's view on Japanese, 124

positions, example illustrating the obsession with organizational, 205; organizational, 167, 237

Potola Palace (Tibet), 87

power, Buddhist monks' enslavement to, 122; religions to avoid becoming a slave to, 123–24

practice, benefit of parents joyful, 201; benefit of a single family member's, 204; broad view of our, 195; conquering families' opposition to the, 180–81; daily, 44; earnest, 45; effect of a joyful, 190–91; purpose of our Buddhist, 24–25; self-centered, 117; Toda's encouragement about families' opposition to the, 173

practitioners, Nichiren Daishonin's view of, 257; instruction to, 265

praise, Nichiren Daishonin's statements of, 150, 152

prayer(s), answering of our, 109–110, 115; confident, 88; Nichiren Daishonin and, 79, 128; doubtful, 88; earnest, 79; example illustrating a mother's diligent, 202; origins of, 105; power of parents, 106; self-centered, 115, 181

"Prayer of the Moon," 31

present moment, 244–45

Prince Shotoku. *See* Shotoku, Prince

problems, world's 177

promise, 222

propagation, benefit of Buddhist, 19; episode illustrating the standard for Buddhist, 118; relation between individual enlightenment and, 117; Shakyamuni describes the benefit of, 19

prosperity, social, 113–14

psychology, Buddhist, 171

public servants, state of Japanese, 125

punishment, doctrine of, 140

Pure Eye (son of King Wonderful Adornment), 174, 178, 181, 192

Pure Flower Constellation King Wisdom Buddha, 44–45

Pure Storehouse (son of King Wonderful Adornment), 174, 178, 181, 192
Pure Virtue (consort of King Wonderful Adornment), 174, 178, 191–92, 194

Radhakrishnan, N., 124
Rana, Seba Singh, 118
reality, 103
Record of the Orally Transmitted Teachings, The 54, 74, 121, 143–44, 158, 187, 243, 212; *dharani* means in the, 158
religion(s), 95, 234; criticism of embracing a, 112; Nichiren Daishonin's view of the role of a, 124; Makiguchi's view on, 64, 111–12, 123; Marx's impression of, 257; opiate, 257–58; origin of, 105; proof of genuineness of a, 176; purpose of, 103–04, 122; purpose for a twenty-first-century, 258; refuting, 110–11; true, 111; world, 104
Religion Today Film Festival (Italy), 64
"Removing Misfortune and Prolonging Life" chapter. *See* "Perceiver of the World's Sounds" chapter (Lotus Sutra)
ren, sound of "r" in, 161
renge, 241
"On Repaying Debts of Gratitude," 107, 150, 262
respect, 123, 204
responsibilities, 97, 116
Rhodin, Auguste, 59
rhythm, universal, 59
Rolland, Romain, 264
Romance of the Three Kingdoms, 213
Russian Academy of Sciences' Institute of Oriental Study, 39

sage, 97
saha world, 103, 147
Saigyo, 159
Sal Tree King Buddha, 191
samadhi, 45
Seifert Jutta, 56
Seikyo Shimbun, 58, 182
"The Selection of the Time," 262
self, blossoming of the, 117; tuning our, 59
self-centeredness, 150
Sen, Amartya, 126
SGI, 118–19; benefit of protecting the, 139, 165; consequences of abandoning the, 136; development of the, 214, 220; effect of inwardly ridiculing the, 201; exists, 223; Huyghe's hopes of the, 249; importance of the, 136; mission of the, 12–13, 218, 246, 265; music and, 60; orbit of the, 117; people who abandon the, 166; spirit of the, 108; strength of the, 73; youth in the, 34
SGI activities, 11, 82
SGI members, Buddhist deities and, 151; concern for, 106, 108; Kychanov's hopes of the, 66; praise for, 118; preciousness of, 152
SGI movement, 62–63
SGI women's division, Ikeda's prayer toward the, 147; praising the, 145
SGI young women's division, Ikeda's prayer toward the, 147; praising the, 145
Shakyamuni Buddha, 6, 12, 15, 44–46, 52, 65, 107, 136–39, 142, 145–46, 153, 194, 216, 218; Nichiren Daishonin's reference to, 254; propagation after the death of, 10; purpose of the advent of, 5

Shakra (deity), 118, 58, 62
Shariputra, 118, 255
Shih K'uang, 81
Shijo Kingo, Nichiren Daishonin's
encouragement to, 261
Shimazaki, Toson, 160
Sho-hokke-kyo (Dharmaraksha),
156–57
Shotoku, Prince, 124
Silk Road, 39
sincerity, 222–23; pretence of, 249
single-parent, families, 195, 197
sleep, power of, 26
society, Buddhism and, 184; means
of detoxifying, 119; music in,
60–61; transforming, 176; winning in, 206
soft power, 74
Soka (value creation), choosing the
name, 153–54; spirit of, 245
Soka Gakkai, Aitmatov's impression of the, 246–47; development of the, 104, 116, 192;
enemies of the, 116; spirit of the,
135, 229, 249; Toda and, 217–18,
236–37; Toda's declaration of
the, 118, 152. *See also* SGI
Soka Gakkai International. *See* SGI
Soka Gakkai movement, 122–23
Soka kyoikugaku taikei (System of
Value-Creating Education)
(Makiguchi), 153; message in
the, 155; mission of the, 266–67;
Toda's help in the compilation
of the publication of, 154–55
Soka University, 236
"Song of the Sons of Japan," 239
sounds, 77; kinds of, 61–62; names
in essential teaching (Lotus
Sutra) that relate to, 76–77
Soviet Union, 235
spousal, problems, 172
struggle(s) 33, 59, 264; Nichiren
Daishonin and, 53

substance, Toda and, 223
suffering(s), ally of the, 63;
cause of, 95; transforming,
86–87
sufferings of birth and death are
nirvana, principle of the, 4–5
Suiko-kai, 135
Suirishiki shido sanjutsu (A De-
ductive Guide to Arithmetic)
(Toda), 154
Sun Moon Pure Bright Virtue
Buddha, 12–14
supernatural ability, 206; example
of, 192. *See also* human revo-
lution
"Supernatural Powers of the
Thus Come One" chapter
(Lotus Sutra). *See* "Supernatural
Powers" chapter (Lotus Sutra)
"Supernatural Powers" chapter
(Lotus Sutra), 7
sutra, reciting the, 44
Symphony no. 6 (Beethoven), 4

Tagore, Rabindranath, 126
Tai-tsung, 91
Takada, Yudo, 116
Tatsunokuchi Persecution, 81
"Teacher of the Law" chapter
(Lotus Sutra), 20, 54
ten demon daughters, appearance
of the, 144; Nichiren Daishonin's interpretation of the, 146;
vow of the, 141–43
theoretical teaching, 253; bodhisattvas of the, 8–12, 18, 21
"This is what I heard," true meaning of, 237
three Buddha bodies, 245.
three powerful enemies, 241
three thousand realms in a single
moment of life, 219
thus, 231, 234; contemporary view
of, 237; Nichiren Daishonin's